Duncan and Neill
on Defamation

Duncan and Neill

on Defamation

Second Edition

Edited by
Sir Brian Neill
One of Her Majesty's Justices
of the Queen's Bench Division
of Corpus Christi College, Oxford
and the Inner Temple

and

Richard Rampton
Barrister,
of The Queen's College, Oxford
and the Inner Temple

Foreword to the First Edition
The Rt Hon Lord Salmon
A Lord of Appeal in Ordinary

London
BUTTERWORTHS
1983

England	Butterworth & Co (Publishers) Ltd, 88 Kingsway, LONDON WC2B 6AB
Australia	Butterworths Pty Ltd, SYDNEY, MELBOURNE, BRISBANE, ADELAIDE and PERTH
Canada	Butterworth & Co (Canada) Ltd, TORONTO Butterworth & Co (Western Canada) Ltd, VANCOUVER
New Zealand	Butterworths of New Zealand Ltd, WELLINGTON
Singapore	Butterworth & Co (Asia) Pte Ltd, SINGAPORE
South Africa	Butterworth Publishers (Pty) Ltd, DURBAN
U.S.A.	Mason Publishing Co, ST PAUL, Minnesota Butterworth Legal Publishers, SEATTLE, Washington; BOSTON, Massachusetts; and AUSTIN, Texas D & S Publishers, CLEARWATER, Florida

© Butterworth & Co (Publishers) Ltd 1983

Duncan, Colin
    Duncan and Neill on defamation.—2nd ed.
    1. Libel and slander—England
    I. Title   II. Neill, *Sir* Brian
    III. Rampton, Richard
    344.2063'4   KD1960
    ISBN 0 406 17830 5

Typeset by Colset Pte Ltd, Singapore
Printed by Billings, Bookplan, Worcester

Foreword to the First Edition by The Rt Hon Lord Salmon

This is a book of outstanding merit which I have read with great interest and admiration. It will be indispensable to all barristers and solicitors who find themselves confronted with any problem relating to the law of defamation. It covers, with outstanding lucidity and thoroughness, every aspect of this branch of the law as it is today. I do not think that any practitioner could have the slightest difficulty in finding, easily and quickly, the correct answer to any problems which may be troubling him.

There are, unfortunately, some aspects of the law of defamation which are still too complex and uncertain. The authors, however, have such a remarkable grasp of underlying legal principle that the solutions they suggest for simplifying and clarifying the law are, in my view, the most likely to be adopted.

Mr Colin Duncan is recognised as the doyen of those counsel who have concentrated most of their attention on the law of defamation and his experience and expertise in this field is unrivalled. His co-author, Mr Brian Neill, is following in his footsteps. It will not be a surprise to anyone that they have written a book of such excellence.

Salmon

HOUSE OF LORDS
NOVEMBER 1977

Preface

Colin Duncan died in July 1979, and the preparation of this new edition has had to proceed without the benefit of his encyclopaedic knowledge of the law and his wide experience. I have been fortunate enough, however, to enlist the help of Richard Rampton as joint editor. As one of the leading practitioners in the field he has a deep understanding of the law of defamation and is well acquainted with recent developments.

In incorporating the various changes in the law since the first edition we have tried to retain the book's straightforward style and approach to what remains a complex area of the law. In particular, Chapter 20 on Criminal Libel has been extensively rewritten to take account of the speeches in the House of Lords in *Gleaves v Deakin*. We have also been assisted by the admirable summary of the law contained in the Law Commission's Working Paper No. 84 on Criminal Libel.

We continue to be troubled by the law of fair comment. It will be seen that the objective test set out in paragraph 12.14 includes a reference to a fair-minded man. We share with Lord Porter an anxiety that the incorporation of the standard of a fair-minded man into the test may lead to the defence of fair comment being restricted to reasonable comments instead of remaining as a protection for the honest comments of those with strong views and prejudices. But the fair-minded man appears in so many judgments in the Court of Appeal that we feel it is wrong any longer to exclude him. We have also drawn the reader's attention to the important decision of the Supreme Court of Canada in *Cherneskey v Armadale Publishers Ltd*, which has cast some doubt on the correctness of the objective test, although the effect of that decision has been modified by subsequent legislation in some of the Canadian provinces.

We hope that this book will continue to be of value to those who are looking for a path through the maze of the law of defamation.

London
September 1983
Brian Neill

Addendum to para. 11.12

In *Williams v Reason and Others,* 10 November 1983, CA (unreported), the plaintiff, a well known Rugby Union player, complained of words which alleged that he had infringed his amateur status by writing a book for reward. The Court of Appeal held that in his Statement of Claim the plaintiff had confined his complaint to that specific allegation, but nevertheless allowed the defendants to amend their defence of justification to plead other alleged infringements by the plaintiff of his amateur status. Stephenson LJ, quoted paragraph 11.12 from the first edition of this book (which was substantially similar to the present paragraph 11.12) and said:

> '. . . on a fair reading of the Statement of Claim the alleged meanings are, in my judgment, all tied to the writing of the book. But, on the authorities cited in *Duncan & Neill* for their submission at the end of the paragraph I have quoted, no plea of a wider meaning by the plaintiff is necessary to enable the defendants to introduce evidence of other infringements of his amateur status, provided that the words which the defendants seek to justify are capable of bearing that wider meaning.'

Stephenson LJ, went on to hold (the other Lords Justices concurring) that the words complained of were reasonably capable of bearing the wider meaning that the plaintiff was a 'shamateur', that is, a professional claiming to be an amateur, and therefore allowed the amendment.

In addition, in ordering a new trial, the Court held that the trial judge had erred in leaving the jury to decide the meaning and effect of the regulations of the International Rugby Football Board, since the interpretation of the regulations was a question of law which the judge should have decided himself. Stephenson LJ, read paragraph 1461 of 12 Halsbury's Laws, 4th edition, and said:

> 'That general principle has been applied by the Court to the interpretation of the rules of such bodies as trade unions alleged to have misunderstood and misapplied them. The judge ought to have applied it to this Board's Rules & Regulations. It is also of course the law that in libel actions the meaning of words alleged to be defamatory is a matter for the jury after the judge has ruled on what they are capable of meaning; but the ordinary rule applies to other documents in an action for defamation; it is for the judge to interpret them, and to tell the jury what they mean.'

It is submitted that this statement merely affirms the well established principle that the judge must decide the meaning and legal effect of documents which require, and are susceptible of, strict construction (such as regulations, rules, contracts and so on), and that it was not intended to alter the practice whereby the ordinary meaning and effect of many documents in defamation actions are left to the jury.

Contents

Table of statutes

References in this Table to *"Statutes"* are to Halsbury's Statutes of England (Third Edition) showing the volume and page at which the annotated text of the Act will be found.

CHAPTER 1

Introduction

1.01 'The defence of reputation on the one hand and the defence of free speech and expression on the other should be beset as little as possible with any complexity.'[1] We have tried to keep this dictum in mind in writing this book and our aim has been to state the law as simply as we can, though it is useless to pretend that the subject is an easy one or that there are not problems which remain unresolved.

1 *Jones v Skelton* [1963] 3 All ER 952 at 960, [1963] 1 WLR 1362 at 1373.

1.02 We have tried to state the law as we believe it to be in June 1983. Where the law is uncertain we have tried to suggest a solution which, in our view, accords with principle. It will be seen that most of the passages cited are from cases decided in the present century: we have chosen modern authorities where possible because we believe that the language used in many of the older cases can so easily be a source of confusion.

1.03 We have also had in mind the dictum of Lord Reid that it is not the function of judges 'to frame definitions or to lay down hard and fast rules. It is their function to enunciate principles and much that they say is intended to be illustrative or explanatory and not to be definitive.'[1] We have therefore often thought it right on important points to refer to more than one authority for the statement of a principle. On the other hand, in an effort to achieve some measure of simplicity and clarity, we have omitted any reference to a large number of cases which, in our view, either do not add anything of value to the cases we have cited or do not represent the law at the present day.

1 *Cassell & Co Ltd v Broome* [1972] AC 1027 at 1085, [1972] 1 All ER 801 at 836.

CHAPTER 2

The distinction between defamation and malicious falsehood

2.01 In order to establish a cause of action in an action for defamation it is necessary to show that the words complained of were defamatory.[1] Even though the
words complained of were not defamatory, however, they may be actionable in an
action for malicious falsehood.[2] In such an action it will be necessary for the plaintiff to prove—

(a) that the words complained of were untrue;
(b) that they were published maliciously; and
(c) that he has thereby been caused special damage or that he is exempted from
     proving special damage by reason of the provisions of section 3 of the
     Defamation Act 1952.[3]

1 As to the meaning of defamatory, see para. 7.01, post.
2 The action is often called an action for injurious falsehood. The Defamation Act 1952, s 3, however, refers to
   'malicious falsehood', and this term was also used in the report of the Faulks Committee (Cmnd 5909,
   Chapter 22).
3 See appendix 1, post.

2.02 In cases where there is doubt as to whether the words complained of are
defamatory, consideration should be given to the question whether an action for
malicious falsehood may lie. This question may often arise where statements are
made by one trade rival about another or where criticisms are made of goods in a
way which reflect on the quality of the goods offered for sale by the plaintiff. The
classic exposition of the distinction between defamation and injurious falsehood
where criticism has been directed at a trader's goods is contained in the judgment
of Lord Esher MR in *South Hetton Coal Co v North-Eastern News Association* where
he said.[1]

> 'Suppose the plaintiff was a merchant who dealt in wine, and it was stated that wine
> which he had for sale of a particular vintage was not good wine; that might be so stated
> as only to import that the wine of the particular year was not good in whosesoever
> hands it was, but not to imply any reflection on his conduct of his business. In that case
> the statement would be with regard to his goods only, and there would be no libel,
> although such a statement, if it were false and were made maliciously, with intention
> to injure him, and it did injure him, might be the subject of an action on the case.[2] On
> the other hand, if the statement was so made as to import that his judgment in the
> selection of wine was bad, it might import a reflection on his conduct of his business,
> and shew that he was an inefficient man of business.[3] If so, it would be a libel. In such a
> case a jury would have to say which sense the libel really bore; if they thought it related
> to the goods only, they ought to find that it was not a libel; but, if they thought it
> related to the man's conduct of business, they ought to find that it was a libel.'

1 [1894] 1 QB 133 at 139. This passage was cited as the best statement of the principle by Lord Pearson in *Drummond-Jackson v British Medical Association* [1970] 1 All ER 1094 at 1103, [1970] 1 WLR 688 at 698.
2 The action for slander of goods is one species of the genus malicious falsehood.
3 An allegation that a man of business is inefficient in the conduct of his business is defamatory: see para 7.03, post.

2.03 The practical distinctions between an action for defamation and an action for malicious falsehood can be summarised as follows—

(a) In an action for defamation it is necessary to prove that the words are defamatory: in an action for malicious falsehood there is no such requirement.

(b) In an action for defamation the falsity of any defamatory words is presumed and the burden of proving that they were true lies on the defendant: in an action for malicious falsehood the plaintiff has to plead and prove as part of the cause of action that the words were false.

(c) In an action for defamation it is not necessary for the plaintiff in order to establish a prima facie case to prove that the defendant was actuated by malice: in an action for malicious falsehood the plaintiff has to prove malice as part of the cause of action.

(d) In an action for libel[1] it is not necessary for the plaintiff to prove that he has suffered damage as damage is presumed: in an action for malicious false-hood the plaintiff has to plead and prove as part of the cause of action that the publication has caused him special damage or that he is exempted from doing so by the provisions of section 3 of the Defamation Act 1952.

(e) A cause of action for defamation does not pass to the personal repre-sentatives of a deceased plaintiff nor does it survive against the estate of a deceased defendant: an action for malicious falsehood survives the death of either party.

(f) In an action for defamation the damages can, and almost certainly will, include damages for injury to the plaintiff's feelings: in an action for mali-cious falsehood the damages are restricted to actual or probable pecuniary loss.[2]

1 In an action for slander it is necessary for the plaintiff to prove special damage unless the slander is actionable per se or the plaintiff is exempted from proving special damage by the provisions of the Defamation Act 1952, s 2: see further para 5.02, post.
2 In *Fielding v Variety Inc* [1967] 2 QB 841 at 850, Lord Denning MR said:
'In the old days in order to make good such a claim a plaintiff had to show that the words were false: he had to show malice: and also had to prove special damage, which might be general loss of business: see *Ratcliffe v Evans* [1892] 2 QB 524. Now by the Defamation Act 1952, s 3(1), it is no longer necessary to allege or prove special damage if the words on which the action is founded are calculated to cause pecuniary damage to the plaintiff and are published in writing or other permanent form. All the necessary elements are here admitted. It is admitted that the words were calculated to cause pecuniary damage. But the question is: what pecuniary damage has been suffered? The plaintiffs on this head of claim can only recover damages for their probable monetary loss, and not for their injured feelings.'

CHAPTER 3

The distinction between libel and slander

INTRODUCTION

Mushens[?]
Hindle +
Pearce's report

3.01 English law provides two separate civil actions in respect of the publication of defamatory matter: the action for libel and the action for slander. In general terms, the action for libel is concerned with the publication of defamatory matter which is in writing or some other permanent form whereas the action for slander is concerned with the publication of defamatory matter by word of mouth or in some other transient form; but the precise dividing line between the two types of action is not finally settled. It is difficult to justify the distinction between libel and slander on any logical grounds.[1] The Faulks Committee have recommended in their report that the distinction between libel and slander in civil proceedings should be abolished and that slander should be assimilated to libel for the purpose of such proceedings.[2]

---

1 For a convenient summary of the history of the distinction between libel and slander, see Report of Faulks Committee (Cmnd 5909) Appendix VI (reprinted in appendix 4, post). See also J.M. Kaye, Libel and Slander—Two Tests or One (1975) 91 LQR 524. It may be noted that in the 1830 edition of Starkie on Laws of Libel and Slander 'slander' was used in its general sense, as comprehending written as well as oral defamation (p 4).
2 Cmnd 5909, para 91. It may be noted that the Porter Committee by a majority favoured the retention of the distinction.

The distinction

3.02 Both an action for libel and an action for slander involve the publication, that is the communication by one person (the publisher) to another person (the publishee), of defamatory matter of and concerning a third person (the person defamed and the potential plaintiff). It has not been finally settled,[1] however, whether *publication in permanent form* is the distinguishing feature of libel or whether libel includes the publication by *any* means of defamatory matter which has been previously reduced to some permanent form. It was held in *Forrester v Tyrrell* that if a man reads out defamatory matter from a written document he publishes a libel; Lord Esher said:[2]

'In *Anon*[3] and *John Lamb's* case[4] it was laid down that if a man reads a libel on another to himself and then reads it out aloud, that makes him a libeller.'

And in *Longdon-Griffiths v Smith*[5] it seems to have been assumed without argument that when one of the trustees of a friendly society read out a written report to a meeting of the general committee he was publishing a libel. On the other hand, in *Osborn v Thomas Boulter & Son*[6] both Scrutton LJ and Slesser LJ expressed the view that the publication of defamatory matter by reading it out from a written document was the publication of a slander rather than of a libel. Furthermore, in *Meldrum v Australian Broadcasting Co Ltd*[7] the Supreme Court of Victoria held that at common law the broadcasting of a defamatory statement, even where the statement is read from a script, is slander and not libel.

1 But in the Report of the Faulks Committee (Cmnd 5909), para 75, it is stated: 'A defamatory statement is libel if it is in permanent form and slander if it consists in significant words or gestures'.
2 (1893) 57 JP 532.
3 (1606) 5 Co Rep 125a.
4 (1610) 9 Co Rep 60.
5 [1951] 1 KB 295, [1950] 2 All ER 662.
6 [1930] 2 KB 226. Greer LJ said at 236 that he was inclined to think that the dictation would be a libel.
7 [1932] VLR 425.

3.03 The wording of the Defamation Act 1952 seems to support the view that the test of libel is whether or not the publication is in permanent form. Thus, for example, section 1 provides as follows:

'**Broadcast statements.**For the purposes of the law of libel and slander, the broadcasting of words by means of wireless telegraphy[1] shall be treated as publication in permanent form.[2]'

It is submitted that the better view, however, is that libel includes publication by *any* means of defamatory matter which already exists in some permanent form.

1 By the Defamation Act 1952, s 16(3), 'broadcasting by means of wireless telegraphy' is defined to mean 'publication for general reception by means of wireless telegraphy within the meaning of the Wireless Telegraphy Act 1949'.
2 The words 'published in permanent form' occur also in the Defamation Act 1952, s 3(1)(a), in relation to malicious falsehood. Furthermore, by the Theatres Act 1968, s 4, 'the publication of words in the course of a performance of a play shall [subject to certain exceptions] be treated as publication in permanent form'.

3.04 The present position can be summarised as follows—

Publications in permanent form

Defamatory matter published in writing or other permanent form is libel. Thus a statue, a caricature, a cartoon, an effigy, chalk marks on a wall or a painting are clearly libels if defamatory. The words 'permanent form' in this context do not mean, however, that the publication has to be in a form which will endure for a long time. The word 'permanent' is to be contrasted with that which is transient such as the spoken word or a gesture.

Oral communications

Defamatory matter published by word of mouth is slander, except, perhaps, where the speaker is reading from a document or reciting words contained in a document or otherwise reproducing by word of mouth that which has been recorded in permanent form.

Conduct, gestures and sounds

Defamatory gestures and defamatory sounds such as hissing are slanders. In addition there may be occasions where the defendant conducts himself in such a way as to convey a defamatory meaning about the plaintiff to third persons and thus provides the foundation for an action for slander. In *Mason v William Hill Organisation Ltd*[1] the plaintiff successfully complained of an incident in which he had been escorted by security officers from the defendant's betting shop. The basis of the claim was that the conduct of the security officers 'conveyed the meaning and impression that the plaintiff was guilty of or was suspected of guilt of a criminal offence justifying arrest to all those present in the betting shop.'

Records, tapes, cassettes, etc

It is submitted that defamatory matter published by mechanical means such as records or tapes (including the sound track of a film) will be treated as a libel.[2]

Cinematograph films, slides, etc

It seems clear that defamatory pictures projected in the course of a film or the showing of slides will be libels.

Broadcasting

Defamatory matter which is broadcast in a radio or television programme for general reception will be treated as a libel.[3] In the case of broadcasts which are not for general reception it seems that defamatory words broadcast from a script or which have been pre-recorded may be treated as libel whereas other defamatory words will be treated as slander. It is submitted that a defamatory television picture broadcast otherwise than for general reception will be a libel.

Theatres

As a general rule the publication of defamatory matter on the stage is treated as publication of a libel. Thus it is provided by the Theatres Act 1968, s 4(1) that for the purposes of the law of libel and slander[4] the publication of words[5] in the course of a performance of a play is to be treated as publication in permanent form. Section 4 of the Theatres Act, however, does not apply—

(a) in relation to a performance of a play given on a domestic occasion in a private dwelling;[6] or
(b) in relation to a performance of a play given solely or primarily for one or more of the following purposes—
(i) rehearsal; or
(ii) to enable a record or cinematograph film to be made from or by means of the performance, or the performance to be broadcast, or the performance to be transmitted to subscribers to a diffusion service.[7]

1 (16 March 1983, unreported) Leonard J and a Jury.
2 In *Grant v Southwestern and County Properties Ltd* [1975] Ch 185, [1974] 2 All ER 465, Walton J held that a tape

on which information was recorded was a document for the purposes of discovery.
3 Defamation Act 1952, s 1.
4 The subsection applies to criminal libel so far as it relates to the publication of defamatory matter, and to malicious falsehood for the purposes of the Defamation Act 1952, s 3.
5 'Words' includes pictures, visual images, gestures and other methods of signifying meaning.
6 Theatres Act 1968, s 7(1).
7 Theatres Act 1968, s 7(2). It may be, however, that irrespective of s 4, a performance which involved reading from a script would be treated as a libel.

The consequences of the distinction between libel and slander

3.05   There are two main consequences of the distinction between libel and slander—

(a) The publication of a libel is a crime as well as a tort, whereas a slander is a tort only. In practice, however, prosecutions for criminal libel are not frequently brought.[1]

(b) In the case of a libel the law presumes that the publication has caused damage to the plaintiff, and it is not necessary for the plaintiff to prove that he has suffered damage in order to establish a cause of action. In the case of a slander, however, the plaintiff has to prove either
(i) that the words are actionable per se at common law or by reason of section 1 of the Slander of Women Act 1891; or
(ii) that he has suffered special damage or that he is exempted from proving special damage by reason of the provisions of section 2 of the Defamation Act 1952.[2]

Accordingly, where the words complained of were published as a slander and not as a libel the plaintiff has to consider not only whether the words were defamatory but also whether in the circumstances the publication is actionable.

1 See further, para 20.02 post.
2 See further, para 5.02, post.

CHAPTER 4

Construction and meanings

INTRODUCTION

4.01 In order to decide whether words are defamatory or refer to the plaintiff it is first necessary to decide what they mean; and this aspect of the law of defamation—the ascertainment of the meaning of words—has been the source of much confusion and difficulty.[1]

1 The Faulks Committee in their report (Cmnd 5909) drew attention to the importance of the meaning of the words in a defamation action (para 92): 'The meaning of the words at issue is probably the most important single factor in a defamation case, since it is of cardinal significance at a great many stages. Upon the meaning depends whether or not the words are defamatory and, therefore, whether or not the plaintiff has a claim at all. If they are defamatory, the nature of any defence which the defendant may plead depends on whether in their correct meaning they are statements of fact or expressions of opinion. If they are statements of fact, the defendant, in order to succeed on justification, must prove that they are true in their meaning; if they consist essentially of expressions of opinions, the defence of fair comment can succeed only if the defendant proves that in their meaning they are fair comment on a matter of public interest. Even if the defence is that the words were published on a privileged occasion, a question may arise with regard to the meaning of the words. Finally, if the plaintiff succeeds at the end of the day, the assessment of damages will depend substantially on the gravity of the defamation, which also hinges on the meaning of the words.'

4.02 Different people may interpret the same words in a number of different ways, and the law of defamation might have developed on the lines that the meaning of the words complained of was to be decided by the evidence of publishees as to their understanding of what they had read or heard. Some publishees might have understood the words in one sense, some in another sense and others in a third sense, and the court in deciding the matter and considering what relief to give would have had to take account of the seriousness of the meanings which the publishees themselves had attached to the words.[1] But the law of defamation has not developed in this way and the court treats the meaning of words as a question of construction and not of evidence. Nevertheless in construing words in a defamation action the court does not use the legal rules of interpretation which are appropriate for the construction of, for example, a contract or a will, but adopts a method of approach which recognises—

(a) that as the law of defamation is concerned with the effect of the words used on ordinary people account must be taken of the fact that 'the layman's capacity for implication is much greater than the lawyer's'.[2]

(b) that in some cases there may be special facts or circumstances known only to a limited number of people which for these people give the words used a special meaning or meanings.

8

The law has therefore developed the concepts of two types of meanings in a defamation action—

(i) natural and ordinary meanings; and

(ii) innuendo meanings.

1 The reaction of publishees may, however, be relevant on the issue of damages: for example, the plaintiff as a result of the publication may have been dismissed from his employment or exposed to abuse. As an example of exposure to abuse: see *Garbett v Hazell, Watson & Viney Ltd* [1943] 2 All ER 359.

2 See *Rubber Improvement Ltd v Daily Telegraph Ltd* [1964] AC 234 at 277, [1963] 2 All ER 151 at 169, per Lord Devlin.

4.03   Both types of meanings are meanings ascribed to the words by the court. They are therefore artificial meanings, as Diplock LJ pointed out in *Slim v Daily Telegraph Ltd*, where he said:[1]

'Libel is concerned with the meaning of words. Everyone outside a court of law recognises that words are imprecise instruments for communicating the thoughts of one man to another. The same words may be understood by one man in a different meaning from that in which they are understood by another and both meanings may be different from that which the author of the words intended to convey. But the notion that the same words should bear different meanings to different men and that more than one meaning should be ''right'' conflicts with the whole training of a lawyer. Words are the tools of his trade. He uses them to define legal rights and duties. They do not achieve that purpose unless there can be attributed to them a single meaning as the ''right'' meaning. And so the argument between lawyers as to the meaning of words starts with the unexpressed major premise that any particular combination of words has one meaning[2] which is not necessarily the same as that intended by him who published them or understood by any of those who read them but is capable of ascertainment as being the ''right'' meaning by the adjudicator to whom the law confides the responsibility of determining it. That is what makes the meaning ascribed to words for the purposes of the tort of libel so artificial.'

These two types of meanings—natural and ordinary meanings and innuendo meanings—require to be considered separately, though most of the principles of construction are common to both.

1 [1968] 2 QB 157 at 171, [1968] 1 All ER 497 at 504.

2 It is submitted that Diplock LJ did not intend to suggest that a combination of words may not have more than one 'right' meaning. Thus some combinations of words may reasonably bear more than one inferential meaning in addition to their literal meaning and they may also convey innuendo meanings to persons who have knowledge of particular facts.

Natural and ordinary meanings

4.04   The natural and ordinary meaning of words is the meaning in which the words would be reasonably understood by ordinary people using their general knowledge and commonsense. This meaning is determined in accordance with the following principles—

(a) The court decides the natural and ordinary meaning as a question of fact by attributing to the words the meaning which the court considers that they would convey to ordinary reasonable persons. It is not limited to the literal meaning of words but includes any inference or implication which would reasonably be drawn.[1]

(b)   The sense in which the words were intended is treated as irrelevant.

(c)   The sense in which the words were *in fact* understood is treated as irrelevant though, it seems, regard will be had to the sort of people to whom the words were or were likely to have been published.

(d)   The words are construed in their context.

(e)   Where a case is tried with a jury the decision as to the natural and ordinary meaning of the words is for the jury, but the judge may first have to rule whether the words are capable in law of bearing one or more of the meanings for which the parties contend.

1   See further, para 4.05, post.

THE NATURAL AND ORDINARY MEANING INCLUDES INFERENCES

4.05   The law recognises that the rules of construction which are used for the interpretation of, for example, a contract or a will are not appropriate for determining the natural and ordinary meaning of words in an action for libel or slander. The correct method of approach to the question of construction was considered at length in the House of Lords in *Rubber Improvement Ltd v Daily Telegraph Ltd*, Lord Reid put the matter as follows:[1]

> 'There is no doubt that in actions for libel the question is what the words would convey to the ordinary man: it is not one of construction in the legal sense. The ordinary man does not live in an ivory tower and he is not inhibited by a knowledge of the rules of construction. So he can and does read between the lines in the light of his general knowledge and experience of worldly affairs[2]. . . . What the ordinary man would infer without special knowledge has generally been called the natural and ordinary meaning of the words. But that expression is rather misleading in that it conceals the fact that there are two elements in it. Sometimes it is not necessary to go beyond the words themselves, as where the plaintiff has been called a thief[3] or a murderer. But more often the sting is not so much in the words themselves as in what the ordinary man will infer from them, and that is also regarded as part of their natural and ordinary meaning.'

1   [1964] AC 234 at 258, [1963] 2 All ER 151 at 154.
2   In the same case Lord Devlin said at 285, 174: 'A man who wants to talk at large about smoke may have to pick his words very carefully if he wants to exclude the suggestion that there is also a fire: but it can be done'.
3   But even the word 'thief' has to be considered in its context: in *Rubber Improvement Ltd v Daily Telegraph Ltd* [1964] AC 234 at 271, [1963] 2 All ER 151 at 165 Lord Hodson said: 'Libels are of infinite variety and the literal meaning of the words, even of such simple phrases as "X is a thief", does not carry one very far, for they may have been spoken in play or other circumstances showing that they could not be taken by reasonable persons as imputing an accusation of theft'.

4.06   To the same effect were the words of Lord Morris of Borth-y-Gest in the Privy Council in *Jones v Skelton*, where he said:[1]

> 'The ordinary and natural meaning of words may be either the literal meaning or it may be an implied or inferred or an indirect meaning: any meaning that does not

require the support of extrinsic facts passing beyond general knowledge but is a meaning which is capable of being detected in the language used can be a part of the ordinary and natural meaning of words. . . . The ordinary and natural meaning may therefore include any implication or inference which a reasonable reader[2] guided not by any special but only by general knowledge and not fettered by any strict legal rules of construction would draw from the words.'

And in *Grubb v Bristol United Press Ltd*, Holroyd Pearce LJ said:[3]

'But in deciding the ordinary and natural meaning of the words the jury must take into account the ordinary reasonable implications of the words. As Cotton LJ said in *Henty's* case in the Court of Appeal:[4] "One must consider, not what the words are, but what conclusion could reasonably be drawn from it, as a man who issues such document is answerable not only for the terms of it but also for the conclusion and meaning which persons will reasonably draw from and put upon the document." If the defendant published of John Smith: "His name is certainly not George Washington", then, however much the defendant may argue that the words were a harmless truism concerned merely with nomenclature, the natural and ordinary implication of the words is that John Smith is untruthful; and presumably the jury would find that to be the ordinary meaning of the words.'[5]

1 [1963] 3 All ER 952 at 958, [1963] 1 WLR 1362 at 1370.
2 It seems plain that in the context '*a* reasonable reader' means reasonable readers generally.
3 [1963] 1 QB 309 at 327, [1962] 2 All ER 380 at 390. This is an important case in which for the first time a clear distinction was drawn between inferential meanings and 'legal' innuendoes which depend on special facts or circumstances known only to a limited number of people.
4 *Capital and Counties Bank v Henty & Sons* (1880) 5 CPD 514 at 536.
5 Holroyd Pearce LJ went on to say that it would be permissible, though probably unnecessary, in the examples he gave to plead an innuendo. It is submitted, however, that in any case where a comparison is made with a historical figure it would be unwise to rely on a jury's assessment of the general knowledge of the ordinary man and that an innuendo should be pleaded, at any rate as an alternative.

THE MEANING INTENDED BY THE PUBLISHER IS IRRELEVANT

4.07   The meaning intended by the publisher is irrelevant for the purpose of construing the words.[1] This important principle in the law of defamation was finally settled by the decision of the House of Lords in *E Hulton & Co v Jones*, where Lord Loreburn LC said:[2]

'A person charged with libel cannot defend himself by shewing that he intended in his own breast not to defame, or that he intended not to defame the plaintiff, if in fact he did both.'

And in *Cassidy v Daily Mirror Newspapers*, Russell LJ put the matter shortly as follows:[3]

'Liability for libel does not depend on the intention of the defamer; but on the fact of defamation.'

More recently in *Slim v Daily Telegraph Ltd*, Diplock LJ emphasised the irrelevance of the intention of the publisher in the following words:[4]

'What is the "natural and ordinary meaning" of words for the purposes of the law of libel? One can start by saying that the meaning intended to be conveyed by the publisher of the words is irrelevant. However evil the imputation upon the plaintiff's character or conduct he intended to communicate, it does not matter if, in the opinion of the adjudicator upon the meaning of the words, they did not bear any defamatory meaning. However innocent an impression of the plaintiff's character or conduct the publisher of the words intended to communicate, it does not matter if, in the opinion of the adjudicator upon the meaning of the words, they did bear a defamatory meaning.'

1 The intention of the publisher will be relevant if a defence of unintentional defamation is raised (see para 15.03, post); and may be relevant on the issues of malice and damages.
2 [1910] AC 20 at 23.
3 [1929] 2 KB 331 at 354.
4 [1968] 2 QB 157 at 172, [1968] 1 All ER 497 at 504.

THE MEANING IN WHICH THE WORDS WERE UNDERSTOOD IS IRRELEVANT

4.08 The meaning in which the words were in fact understood is irrelevant for the purpose of deciding the natural and ordinary meaning of the words. As the law of defamation is concerned with the effect of words on ordinary people it might have been supposed that evidence of the sense in which the words were in fact understood by the publishees would be admissible.[1] It is clear, however, that such evidence is not admitted. This rule, which is of long standing,[2] was stated by Goddard LJ in *Hough v London Express Newspaper Ltd* as follows:[3]

'In the case of words defamatory in their ordinary sense the plaintiff has to prove no more than that they were published; he cannot call witnesses to prove what they understood by the words; . . . the only question is, might reasonable people understand them in a defamatory sense?'

1 Where a legal innuendo is pleaded, however, witnesses can be called to give evidence of the meaning in which they understood the words, though their evidence is not conclusive: see para 4.18, post.
2 See, for example, *Daines and Braddock v Hartley* (1848) 3 Exch 200; *Simmons v Mitchell* (1880) 6 App Cas 156 at 163.
3 [1940] 2 KB 507 at 515, [1940] 3 All ER 31 at 35.

4.09 It follows therefore that a man may be defamed even though the publishee does not believe the imputation against him or even knows it to be false. In *Morgan v Odhams Press Ltd*, Lord Morris of Borth-y-Gest put the matter as follows:[1]

'It was submitted that if defamatory words concerning A are published to B who refuses to believe that the words are true, then A would have no cause of action. I consider that such a contention is completely fallacious. Apart from any question affecting the measure of damages A's rights would be unaffected by the circumstance that B in fact disbelieved the words.'

And in the same case Lord Reid said:[2]

'One of the witnesses thought that the article referred to the appellant but completely disbelieved it: he thought it was rubbish. It was argued that he must be left out of account because no tort is committed by making a defamatory statement about X to a person who utterly disbelieves it. That is plainly wrong. It is true that X's reputation is not diminished but the person defamed suffers annoyance or worse when he learns that a defamatory statement has been published about him. There may be no clear authority that publishing a defamatory statement is a tort whether it is believed or disbelieved.

But very often there is no authority for an obvious proposition: no one has had the hardihood to dispute it.'

1 [1971] 2 All ER 1156 at 1168, [1971] 1 WLR 1239 at 1252. See also *Hough v London Express Newspaper Ltd* [1940] 2 KB 507 at 515, [1940] 3 All ER 31 at 35 per Goddard LJ.
2 [1971] 2 All ER 1156 at 1163, [1971] 1 WLR 1239 at 1246.

4.10 It seems, however, that though the reaction of individual publishees is irrelevant some regard must be paid to the sort of persons to whom the words were published or were likely to have been published. In *Sim v Stretch*, Lord Atkin referred to the difficulty of defining the word 'defamatory' and added:[1]

'The question is complicated by having to consider the person or class of persons whose reaction to the publication is the test of the wrongful character of the words used.'

This aspect of the law has received little attention in the decided cases. In *Drummond-Jackson v British Medical Association* however, (where the Court of Appeal were considering articles in the British Medical Journal dealing with a technique used by the plaintiff, a dental surgeon) Sir Gordon Willmer referred to this passage in Lord Atkin's speech and continued:[2]

'In the present case the plaintiff is an experienced dental surgeon, and the article complained of relates to dentistry; and this circumstance, I think, is sufficient to indicate the class of persons whose reaction to the publication is to be considered.'

And in the same case Lord Denning MR used similar language:[3]

'I propose, therefore, . . . to ask, and try to answer, the important question: are these words reasonably capable of being understood as being defamatory of the Plaintiff? Understood, that is, by the sort of people likely to read them. These are, I take it, the medical men who read the British Medical Journal.'

1 [1936] 2 All ER 1237 at 1240.
2 [1970] 1 All ER 1094 at 1106, [1970] 1 WLR 688 at 700. Cf *Capital and Counties Bank Ltd v George Henty & Sons* (1882) 7 App Cas 741 at 745 per Lord Selbourne.
3 [1970] 1 All ER 1094 at 1099, [1970] 1 WLR 688 at 694.

THE CONTEXT AND THE MODE OF PUBLICATION

4.11 In order to determine the natural and ordinary meaning of the words of which the plaintiff complains it is necessary to take into account the context in which the words were used and the mode of publication. Thus a plaintiff cannot select an isolated passage in an article and complain of that alone if other parts of the article throw a different light on that passage.[1] As Alderson B said in *Chalmers v Payne*:[2]

'[If] in one part of the publication something disreputable to the plaintiff is stated, but that is removed by the conclusion, the bane and the antidote must be taken together'.

Indeed, in some, though rare, cases the defamatory sting of a passage may be removed by that which precedes or follows it. This question was examined by the

Court of Appeal of New South Wales in *Morosi v Broadcasting Station 2GB, Pty Ltd*, where it was argued that the discreditable assertions complained of were made only for the purpose of vigorously refuting them. Samuels JA said this:[3]

> 'I do not doubt that there are occasions when a publication which seeks to refute a calumny which it expressly states may be held incapable of conveying any defamatory meaning. *Bik v Mirror Newspapers Ltd* is an example.[4] But such cases must be comparatively rare. The inquiry upon which the Court must embark differs from that involved in the threshold question which more commonly arises. In each case, the question is whether the material is capable of a defamatory meaning, and in each case guidance is provided by the test formulated by Lord Selborne in *Capital and Counties Bank Ltd v George Henty & Sons*,[5] and its derivatives, for example, the statement by Lord Reid in *Rubber Improvement Ltd v Daily Telegraph Ltd*.[6] The difference, however, is this. In the ordinary case, the material to be examined consists of the words of the publication in their natural and ordinary meaning (I leave aside any question of innuendoes in the true sense) which may or may not support an imputation of a defamatory kind. But in a case such as this the material already contains a defamatory imputation; and the inquiry is as to whether that effect is overcome by contextual matter of an emollient kind so as to eradicate the hurt and render the whole publication harmless. It follows that, in a case such as the present, what is involved is essentially the weighing up and comparison of bane and antidote, to repeat Baron Alderson's evocative formula.[7] It is a question of degree and of competing emphasis. . . . It may be easier to arrive at an answer where the publication contains an express disclaimer, as in *Stubbs Ltd v Russell*,[8] or where the antidote consists in a statement of fact destructive of the ingredients from which the bane has been brewed.'

1   The publication complained of may contain several distinct charges against the plaintiff. In that event the plaintiff may wish to bring proceedings in respect of only one or some of those charges. It will then be for the judge at the trial to rule whether the jury should see or read the whole or only part of the complete publication: see *Plato Films Ltd v Speidel* [1960] 1 AC 1090, [1961] 1 All ER 876. It is submitted that as a general rule the court will allow the jury to see and consider the whole publication because it would be unrealistic to expect the jury to consider the issue of damages (and possibly other issues as well) without being aware of other passages of which the plaintiff does not complain.
2   (1835) 2 Cr MR 156 at 159.
3   (1978) [1980] 2 NSWLR 418n at 419.
4   (1971) [1979] 2 NSWLR 679n.
5   (1882) 7 App Cas 741 at 745.
6   [1964] AC 234 at 258.
7   See *Chalmers v Payne* (1835) 2 Cr M & R 156 at 159.
8   [1913] AC 386.

4.12   The natural and ordinary meaning of words may be affected not only by adjacent passages but also by the mode of publication; for example, by the prominence which is given to the words by their position in a newspaper or magazine, or by the emphasis which is provided by the type and heading employed. This point was explained in *English and Scottish Co-operative Properties Mortgage and Investment Society Ltd v Odhams Press Ltd*, where the plaintiff society complained of a report in a newspaper under the heading 'False profit return charge against society'. Slesser LJ said:[1]

> 'Stopping at that heading, what does the word "false" convey to the ordinary reader? In the dictionary sense the word "false" may mean deceitful, untrue, dishonest or it may have the meaning, and I think the more ordinary meaning, of mistaken or inaccurate or untrue without any moral obliquity. But I do not think this is the type of case . . . where one has to seek for the evil meaning and discard the innocent meaning. I

think the ordinary reader would assume that the word "false" in this context, and stated with this imprint, meant fraudulent. I think one may take into consideration . . . "the manner and the occasion of the publication".[2] This article is published in a popular newspaper. If the words "false profit" in a popular newspaper mean that which is merely untrue in the technical sense that a sum has been attributed to profit which, being the proceeds of sale of freehold land, technically should not have been so called, I do not think that would have found expression in large italicised block type as something worthy of observation by readers of the newspaper.[3] As I pointed out during the argument, we have frequently in this Court, when dealing with revenue cases, to decide the very difficult question whether a particular profit or gain is to be considered income so as to attract tax, or is a capital increment. I have never known the *Daily Herald* or any other daily newspaper, if some person has falsely stated that to be capital which has turned out ultimately to be income, to honour that state of things by a statement in large letters in italics: "False return to the Income Tax Authorities".'

1 [1940] 1 KB 440 at 452, [1940] 1 All ER 1 at 6.
2 See *Capital and Counties Bank Ltd v George Henty & Sons* (1882) 7 App Cas 741 where Lord Selborne approved the words of Wilde CJ in *Sturt v Blagg* (1847) 10 QB 906.
3 Cf the approach of Lord Morris of Borth-y-Gest in his dissenting speech in *Rubber Improvement Ltd v Daily Telegraph Ltd* [1964] AC 234 at 269, [1963] 2 All ER 151 at 163–4.

4.13   In the case of a slander also the meaning of the words may be affected by the mode of publication. For example, the tone of voice used by the speaker or accompanying gestures or facial expressions may materially alter the sense in which the words would be understood.[1] It can be argued that accompanying gestures, for example, should be regarded as extrinsic facts and that they should be pleaded to support a legal innuendo.[2] Moreover in *Grubb v Bristol United Press Ltd* Holroyd Pearce LJ expressed the view that innuendoes 'may be necessary . . . where there are accompanying gestures which may in the words of Dean Swift "convey a libel in a frown and wink a reputation down" '.[3] It is more logical, however, to treat features of the publication such as the tone of voice used and any accompanying gestures as intrinsic elements of the publication so that no legal innuendo is needed. The additional incidents of the publication can be pleaded to show the natural and ordinary meaning of the words used in their context. Thus, for example, the gestures used by a policeman to accompany the words 'Come with me' would be likely to be different from those used by a head waiter. In the former case the gestures and surrounding circumstances might render the words in their context capable of a defamatory meaning.[4]

1 See *Broome v Agar* (1928) 138 LT 698 at 702.
2 This view was taken in the previous edition.
3 [1963] 1 QB 309 at 328, [1962] 2 All ER 380 at 390.
4 Cf *Mason v William Hill Organisation Ltd*, (16 March 1983, unreported) Leonard J and a Jury.

THE FUNCTIONS OF THE JUDGE AND THE JURY

4.14   Where an action for defamation is tried with a jury it is for the jury to decide what meaning or meanings the words in fact bore. They should apply the test: what meaning (or meanings) would the words convey to ordinary reasonable persons? In many cases, however, the defendant will wish to contend that the words are incapable of bearing the meaning or meanings (or some of the meanings) put forward by the plaintiff. This question—whether the words are capable of bearing a particular meaning or meanings—is a question to be decided by the judge.[1]

1 See for example, *Rubber Improvement Ltd v Daily Telegraph* [1964] AC 234 at 286, [1963] 2 All ER 151 at 175 per Lord Devlin.

4.15 Where the issue is raised the judge has to decide the limits of the range of meanings of which the words are capable. In *Rubber Improvement Ltd v Daily Telegraph Ltd* Lord Reid considered how the judge should approach his task of deciding the range of possible meanings and said:[1]

'Ordinary men and women have different temperaments and outlooks. Some are unusually suspicious and some are unusually naive. One must try to envisage people between these two extremes and see what is the most damaging meaning they would put on the words in question.'

The cases before the House of Lords concerned two short reports in *The Daily Telegraph* and the *Daily Mail* under the headings 'Enquiry on firm by City Police' and 'Fraud Squad probe firm'. Lord Reid continued:[2]

'So let me suppose a number of ordinary people discussing one of these paragraphs which they had read in the newspaper. No doubt one of them might say—"Oh, if the fraud squad are after these people you can take it they are guilty." But I would expect the others to turn on him, if he did say that, with such remarks as—"Be fair. This is not a police state. No doubt their affairs are in a mess or the police would not be interested. But that could be because Lewis or the cashier has been very stupid or careless. We really must not jump to conclusions. The police are fair and know their job and we shall know soon enough if there is anything in it. Wait till we see if they charge him. I wouldn't trust him until this is cleared up, but it is another thing to condemn him unheard."

What the ordinary man, not avid for scandal, would read into the words complained of must be a matter of impression. I can only say that I do not think that he would infer guilt of fraud merely because an inquiry is on foot. And, if that is so, then it is the duty of the trial judge to direct the jury that it is for them to determine the meaning of the paragraph but they must not hold it to impute guilt of fraud because as a matter of law[3] the paragraph is not capable of having that meaning.'

1 [1964] AC 234 at 259, [1963] 2 All ER 151 at 155.
2 [1964] AC 234 at 259, [1963] 2 All ER 151 at 155.
3 Lord Reid has said elsewhere that the meaning of words is not a question of law in the true sense, but simply a question which the law reserves for the judge: *Morgan v Odhams Press Ltd* [1971] 2 All ER 1156 at 1160, [1971] 1 WLR 1239 at 1242. And in *Slim v Daily Telegraph Ltd* [1968] 2 QB 157 at 174, [1968] 1 All ER 497 at 505, Diplock LJ said 'The decision as to defamatory meanings which words are capable of bearing is reserved to the judge, and for this reason, and for no other, is called a question of law. The decision as to the particular defamatory meaning within that category which the words do bear is reserved for the jury, and for this reason, and for no other, is called a question of fact.'

4.16 In *Morgan v Odhams Press Ltd* Lord Morris of Borth-y-Gest described the role of the judge as follows:[1]

'The principle is just the same in defamation cases as in any other cases, that the judge in his control of the proceedings will not leave a case to the jury if the jury could not properly find for the plaintiff. So if a plaintiff complains that words which have been published of him are defamatory a judge will withdraw the case if he decides that the words complained of are simply not capable of bearing a defamatory meaning. He will decide whether a reasonable man could (not would) regard the words as defamatory. If they are capable of being so regarded then it will be for the jury to decide whether or not the words did bear a defamatory meaning.'

The judge must therefore withdraw from the jury any meanings put forward on behalf of the plaintiff which in the opinion of the judge a reasonable man could not understand the words to bear. As Lord Morris of Borth-y-Gest said in *Jones v Skelton*:[2]

'In deciding whether words are capable of conveying a defamatory meaning the court will reject those meanings which can only emerge as the product of some strained or forced or utterly unreasonable interpretation.

1 [1971] 2 All ER 1156 at 1168, [1971] 1 WLR 1239 at 1251.
2 [1963] 3 All ER 952 at 958, [1963] 1 WLR 1362 at 1370. The question of the meaning of the words may arise before the trial, for example, on an application to strike out the statement of claim or to strike out a defence of justification or fair comment. It has been said that at that stage the court has to decide whether the meaning put forward is a 'conceivable' meaning which a jury might find the words to bear: see *Waters v Sunday Pictorial Newspapers Ltd* [1961] 2 All ER 758 at 762, [1961] 1 WLR 967 at 972; *S and K Holdings Ltd v Throgmorton Publications Ltd* [1972] 3 All ER 497 at 500, [1972] 1 WLR 1036 at 1040.

Innuendoes

4.17 The law of defamation recognises—

(a) that some words have technical or slang meanings or meanings which depend on some special knowledge possessed not by the general public but by a limited number of persons; and
(b) that ordinary words may on occasions bear some special meaning other than their natural and ordinary meaning because of some extrinsic facts or circumstances.

These special meanings are called innuendoes or, more strictly, legal or true innuendoes to distinguish them from popular or false innuendoes.[1]

1 See, for example, *Rubber Improvement Ltd v Daily Telegraph* [1964] AC 234 at 280, [1963] 2 All ER 151 at 170 per Lord Devlin.

4.18 The principles governing innuendoes may be stated as follows—

(a) The word 'innuendo'—that is a legal innuendo—covers in fact three types of meaning[1]—
(i) a special meaning—additional to the natural and ordinary meaning—which a word (or words) bears because of some extrinsic facts or circumstances;

(ii) a special meaning—additional to the natural and ordinary meaning—which a word (or words) bears because the word has some technical or slang or local meaning or some other meaning which is not known to the ordinary member of the public;

(iii) the meaning which a word (or words) bears, being a word which has *only* some technical or slang or local meaning or some other meaning which is not known to the ordinary member of the public; such a word (or words) has—as far as the law of defamation is concerned—no natural and ordinary meaning.

(b) The court decides an innuendo meaning as a question of fact by attributing to the words the meaning which the court considers they would convey to ordinary reasonable persons who have the necessary knowledge (of, for example, the technical term) or were aware of the extrinsic facts or circumstances which gave the words a special meaning.

(c) A plaintiff who seeks to rely on an innuendo meaning has to plead[2] and prove the facts or circumstances (including, where appropriate, the technical term, etc) which gave the words a special meaning. He has also to prove that the words were published to one or more persons who knew these facts or circumstances or, where appropriate, the meaning of the technical term, etc.

(d) Notwithstanding that an innuendo meaning is a meaning attributed to the words by the court, evidence is admissible where such a meaning is relied upon to show the sense in which an individual publishee understood the words.[3] Such evidence, however, is not conclusive.

(e) The sense in which the words were intended is treated as irrelevant.

(f) The words are considered in their context.

(g) Where the case is tried with a jury the decision as to whether the words bear an innuendo meaning and, if so, what meaning, is for the jury, but the judge may first have to rule whether the words are capable of bearing the innuendo meaning or meanings put forward on behalf of the plaintiff.

(h) Where the words are defamatory in their natural and ordinary meaning any defamatory innuendo constitutes a further and separate cause of action.[4]

---

1 The word 'innuendo' is also used to include 'any implication that leads to identification of the libel with the plaintiff', see *Grubb v Bristol United Press Ltd* [1963] 1 QB 309 at 328, [1962] 2 All ER 380 at 391 per Holroyd Pearce LJ who added: 'It is no doubt strictly correct to refer to the identification as an innuendo.' At 336, 395 Davies LJ took a different view: 'It is of course necessary in every case for the plaintiff to allege and prove that the libel was understood to refer to him. The averment necessary to establish this is frequently referred to as an innuendo. . . . But the more accurate description of such an allegation is that it is an allegation of facts and matters from which it is to be inferred that the words were published of the plaintiff.' In *R v Horne* (1777) 2 Cowp 672 at 684, Lord De Grey CJ explained the function of an innuendo as follows: 'For an innuendo means nothing more than the words "id est", "scilicet", or "meaning", or "aforesaid", as explanatory of a subject-matter sufficiently expressed before; as, such a one, meaning the defendant, or such a subject, meaning the subject in question.'
2 RSC Ord 82 r 3(1) provides: 'Where in an action for libel or slander the plaintiff alleges that the words or matters complained of were used in a defamatory sense other than their ordinary meaning, he must give particulars of the facts and matters on which he relies in support of such sense.'
3 See *Cassidy v Daily Mirror Newspapers* [1929] 2 KB 331; *Hough v London Express Newspaper Ltd* [1940] 2 KB 507, [1940] 3 All ER 31.
4 See *Watkin v Hall* (1868) LR 3 QB 396; *Sim v Stretch* [1936] 2 All ER 1237; *Rubber Improvement Ltd v Daily Telegraph Ltd* [1964] AC 234 at 279, [1963] 2 All ER 151 at 170, per Lord Devlin. The Faulks Committee in their report have recommended that 'a claim in defamation based on a single publication with or without a plea of legal innuendo shall constitute a single cause of action giving rise to one award of damages only'; Cmnd 5909, para 119(b).

INNUENDOES DEPENDING ON EXTRINSIC FACTS OR CIRCUMSTANCES

4.19   The law of defamation recognises that the ordinary man will read between the lines and will draw inferences from what he reads or is told, and the courts realise they 'must accept a certain amount of loose thinking'.[1] These inferences and conclusions which the ordinary man would draw from the words themselves are part of the natural and ordinary meaning of the words. But words may have some other and quite separate meaning in addition to their natural and ordinary meaning because of extrinsic facts or circumstances; or the meaning of words may be uncertain or equivocal and only bear a particular meaning because of extrinsic facts or circumstances. This special meaning which is to be found not in the words themselves nor based on the general knowledge of the ordinary man but which depends on facts or circumstances known only to some persons or some classes of persons is an innuendo, that is, a true or legal innuendo. In *Rubber Improvement Ltd v Daily Telegraph Ltd* Lord Devlin gave a simple illustration:[2]

> 'Thus, to say of a man that he was seen to enter a named house would contain a derogatory implication for anyone who knew that that house was a brothel but not for anyone who did not.'

1 See *Morgan v Odhams Press Ltd* [1971] 2 All ER 1156 at 1163, [1971] 1 WLR 1239 at 1245.
2 [1964] AC 234 at 278, [1963] 2 All ER 151 at 169–170.

4.20   Sometimes the natural and ordinary meaning of the words will be innocent and it will only be the extrinsic facts and circumstances which give the words a sinister and defamatory meaning; on other occasions the words will be defamatory in their natural and ordinary meaning but will bear, or be alleged by the plaintiff to bear, a separate defamatory meaning by way of innuendo.

MEANINGS WHICH DEPEND ON SPECIALISED KNOWLEDGE

4.21   Some words or phrases may be meaningless to the ordinary member of the public and may only be understood by those with knowledge of, for example, a particular dialect, or the terms used in a particular trade or profession, or a particular slang expression,[1] or a particular literary allusion. Other words or phrases, on the other hand, may have a natural and ordinary meaning but also have one or more secondary meanings which depend on the same kind of specialised knowledge. In all these cases when understanding of the meaning of the words is not a matter of general knowledge but needs some specialised knowledge, the meaning is an innuendo meaning.

1 The meaning of particular slang words may vary over a period of time, so old cases may be of little assistance. If a word would be understood by the public generally no innuendo is required and no evidence can be given as to its meaning. In *Barnett v Allen* (1858) 3 H&N 376 at 379, Pollock CB said: 'The word "blackleg" has been used long enough to be understood, not only by experts in slang, but by the public at large, and therefore it was for the judge to expound its meaning. I have always understood the word "blackleg" to mean a person who gets his living by frequenting racecourses and places where games of chance are played; getting the best odds and giving the least he can; but not necessarily cheating.' And see *Allsop v Church of England Newspaper Ltd* [1972] 2 QB 161, [1972] 2 All ER 26 ('pre-occupation with the bent').

4.22 It may sometimes be difficult to decide whether a particular expression would be understood by people generally or whether it needs specialised knowledge. Thus, whereas, it is submitted, an ordinary reasonable person would understand the significance of likening a man to the devil or Judas or Hitler, it is much less certain whether an ordinary reasonable person at the present day would appreciate the significance of a comparison drawn with Casanova[1] or Quisling. Slang expressions provide similar difficulties, and if there is any doubt as to the state of general knowledge a plaintiff who wishes to rely on a slang expression should be prepared to plead and prove it as an innuendo, at any rate in the alternative. If the word or phrase would be understood by ordinary reasonable persons generally—as where, for example, a slang expression has become part of ordinary speech—the meaning of the word or phrase will be regarded as its natural and ordinary meaning; if the word or phrase would not be understood in the suggested sense by ordinary reasonable persons generally but would be by persons with specialised knowledge, that meaning is an innuendo.

1 See *Grubb v Bristol United Press Ltd* [1963] 1 QB 309 at 336, [1962] 2 All ER 380 at 396, where Davies LJ expressed doubt as to whether the pejorative sense of the name 'Casanova' had become part of the English language.

WORDS PUBLISHED IN A FOREIGN LANGUAGE

4.23 It is submitted that words in a foreign language are to be treated in precisely the same way as words published in a local dialect or in, for example, rhyming slang. In both cases it is necessary to plead and prove what the words mean in ordinary English, and it is also necessary to prove that one or more of the publishees understood the words in their original form. Thus no actionable slander would be published by a man who spoke some defamatory words to a group of people none of whom understood the language in which he spoke.[1]

1 See *Price v Jenkings* (1601) Cro Eliz 865; and cf *Anann v Dann* (1860) 8 CBNS 597 at 600 per Williams J.

CHAPTER 5

The ingredients of a prima facie case

5.01 In order to establish a prima facie case in an action for libel or slander it is necessary for the plaintiff to prove

- (a) that the words complained of were published of him;[1]
- (b) that the words were defamatory of him;[2] and
- (c) that the words were published by the defendant or in circumstances in which the defendant is responsible for the publication.[3]

1 See para 6.01, post.
2 See para 7.01, post.
3 See para 8.01, post.

5.02 In an action for libel it is not necessary for the plaintiff to prove that the publication of the words has caused him damage because damage is presumed.[1] In an action for slander, however, where the law does not presume that the publication has caused the plaintiff any damage, the plaintiff has to prove special damage[2] except in the following cases:

- (a) where the words charge the plaintiff with having committed a criminal offence punishable corporally;[3] or
- (b) where they impute that the plaintiff has certain contagious diseases;[4] or
- (c) where they impute unchastity or adultery to any woman or girl;[5] or
- (d) where they are calculated to disparage the plaintiff in any office, profession, calling, trade or business held or carried on by him at the time of the publication.[6]

1 See *Ratcliffe v Evans* [1892] 2 QB 524 at 529 per Bowen LJ.
2 See para 18.10, post.
3 The words must impute conduct which amounts to a criminal offence punishable by death, or by imprisonment with or without the option of a fine. An allegation that the plaintiff has committed an act which is punishable by a fine only is not actionable per se; see *Hellwig v Mitchell* [1910] 1 KB 609 at 614 per Bray J.
4 This exception applies to imputations of venereal disease, leprosy and (probably) the plague. The exception does not apply, however, unless the imputation is to the effect that the plaintiff is suffering from the disease at the time of publication; thus, although an imputation that the plaintiff has had venereal disease may well be defamatory it is not actionable per se. See, generally, *Bloodworth v Gray* (1844) 7 Man & G 334; and for a possible argument that the imputation of *any* contagious disease is actionable per se, see *Watkin v Hall* (1868) LR 3 QB 396 at 399 per Blackburn J.
5 See Slander of Women Act 1891.
6 See Defamation Act 1952, s 2.

CHAPTER 6

Identification

INTRODUCTION

6.01 In every case it is necessary for the plaintiff to prove that the words were published about him. In *Sadgrove v Hole*, A.L. Smith MR put the matter as follows:[1]

> 'The plaintiff to succeed in the action must prove a publication of and concerning him of libellous matter, and if he does not satisfy the onus of proof which is on him in this respect there is no cause of action.'

In many cases the plaintiff's task is a simple one because, for example, the words used include his name and address so that there is no room for confusion or doubt. In other cases, however, the position may be less clear.

1 [1901] 2 KB 1 at 4. See also *Bruce v Odhams Press Ltd* [1936] 1 KB 697 at 708, [[1936] 1 All ER 287 at 291, per Slesser LJ; *Morgan v Odhams Press Ltd* [1971] 2 All ER 1156 at 1165, [1971] 1 WLR 1239 at 1248, per Lord Morris of Borth-y-Gest.

The general test

6.02 In every case where identification is in issue the question is: would reasonable persons reasonably[1] believe that the words referred to the plaintiff? If reasonable persons would so believe, the defendant will not escape liability though he may have tried to disguise his reference to the plaintiff by using initials or asterisks or a fictitious name or some other subterfuge. Nor will he escape liability (unless he can establish a defence of unintentional defamation)[2] even if he had never heard of the plaintiff or intended to refer to someone else. Strictly speaking therefore the intention of the defendant is or should be regarded as irrelevant on the issue of identification in the same way as where the meaning of the words complained of has to be decided. It is necessary to point out, however, that in *Hayward v Thompson* Lord Denning MR took the view that the intention of the defendant is still a relevant circumstance. He said:[3]

> 'If the defendant intended to refer to the plaintiff, he cannot escape liability simply by not giving his name. He may use asterisks or blanks. He may use initials or words with a hidden meaning. He may use any other device. But still, if he intended to refer to the plaintiff, he is liable.[4] He is to be given credit for hitting the person whom he intended to hit. The law goes further. Even if he did not aim at the plaintiff or intend to refer to him, nevertheless if he names the plaintiff in such a way that other persons will read it as intended to refer to the plaintiff, then the plaintiff is liable.'

1 See para 6.03, note 1, post. It is submitted that in all cases the conclusion as to identity must be reasonable.
2 See para 15.01, post.
3 [1982] QB 47 at 60.
4 It is submitted that an intention to refer to the plaintiff is not enough. The question is as stated above: would reasonable persons reasonably believe that the words referred to the plaintiff?

THE TEST WHERE IDENTIFICATION DEPENDS ON EXTRINSIC FACTS

6.03   Where identification is in issue the matter can sometimes be decided by construing the words themselves in their context. More often, however, the plaintiff will be seeking to show that the words would be understood to refer to him because of some facts or circumstances which are extrinsic to the words themselves. In these cases the plaintiff is required to plead and prove the extrinsic facts on which he relies to establish identification and, if these facts are proved, the question becomes: would reasonable persons knowing these facts or some of them reasonably[1] believe the words referred to the plaintiff?

1 In *Morgan v Odhams Press Ltd* [1971] 2 All ER 1156 at 1179, [1971] 1 WLR 1239 at 1264, Lord Donovan said: 'The plaintiff must prove that the words of the article would convey a defamatory meaning concerning himself to a reasonable person possessed of knowledge of the extrinsic facts. This requirement postulates (as the appellant expressly accepted) not merely a reasonable person but also a reasonable conclusion. Mere conjecture is not enough.' Though Lord Donovan's speech was a dissenting one it is submitted that this statement of the law is correct.

THE EXTRINSIC FACTS ARE PART OF THE CAUSE OF ACTION

6.04   Where identification depends on extrinsic facts these extrinsic facts must be pleaded because they form part of the cause of action. In *Bruce v Odhams Press Ltd*[1] the plaintiff complained of an article about the smuggling activities of 'an Englishwoman', but did not state in the statement of claim the facts from which it was to be inferred that she was the Englishwoman referred to. The Court of Appeal held that these facts were a material part of her cause of action and should be pleaded. Greer LJ said:[2]

'. . . it is an essential part of a cause of action of a plaintiff in cases of defamation, whether of slander or libel, that the words are defamatory of the plaintiff. If they are defamatory of some other person, real or imaginary, they do not provide the plaintiff with any cause of action at all. Defamatory statements which are in the air, as it were, and do not appear by their words to refer to the plaintiff, have got to be made referable to the plaintiff by reason of special facts and circumstances which show that the words can be reasonably construed as relating to the plaintiff. It is not sufficient under the existing rules of practice merely to allege in general terms a cause of action. . . . The material facts on which the plaintiff must rely for her claim in the present case seem to me necessarily to include the facts and matters from which it is to be inferred that the words were published of the plaintiff.'[3]

1 [1936] 1 KB 697, [1936] 1 All ER 287.
2 [1936] 1 KB 697 at 705, [1936] 1 All ER 287 at 289.
3 See also paras 8.04, 8.05, post.

THE INTENTION AND KNOWLEDGE OF THE DEFENDANT ARE IRRELEVANT

6.05 For the purpose of deciding whether the words would be understood to refer to the plaintiff, the intention and knowledge of the defendant are irrelevant.[1] This point was finally settled by the House of Lords in *E Hulton & Co v Jones*,[2] where the plaintiff (Mr Artemus Jones, a barrister) recovered damages in respect of an article in the *Sunday Chronicle* describing a motor festival at Dieppe, and in which the following sentence appeared: 'There is Artemus Jones with a woman who is not his wife, who must be, you know—the other thing!'[3] It was argued on behalf of the newspaper that neither the author nor the editor knew of the existence of the plaintiff and that as there was no intention to refer to the plaintiff the defendants were not liable. But Lord Loreburn LC said:[4]

'If the intention of the writer be immaterial in considering whether the matter written is defamatory, I do not see why it need be relevant in considering whether it is defamatory of the plaintiff. The writing, according to the old form, must be malicious, and it must be of and concerning the plaintiff. Just as the defendant could not excuse himself from malice by proving that he wrote it in the most benevolent spirit, so he cannot shew that the libel was not of and concerning the plaintiff by proving that he never heard of the plaintiff. His intention in both respects equally is inferred from what he did.'

And Lord Shaw of Dunfermline, rejecting an argument that the case established any new principle, said:[5]

'Sufficient expression is given to the same principle by Abbott CJ in *Bourke v Warren*[6] . . . in which that learned judge says: ''The question for your consideration is whether you think the libel designates the plaintiff in such a way as to let those who knew him understand that he was the person meant. It is not necessary that all the world should understand the libel; it is sufficient if those who know the plaintiff can make out that he is the person meant.'' I think it is out of the question to suggest that that means ''meant in the mind of the writer'' or of the publisher; it must mean ''meant by the words employed''. The late Lord Chief Justice Coleridge dealt similarly with the point in *Gibson v Evans*,[7] when in the course of the argument he remarked: ''It does not signify what the writer meant; the question is whether the alleged libel was so published by the defendant that the world would apply it to the plaintiff.'' '

To the same effect were the words used by Lord Alverstone CJ in the Court of Appeal in *Jones v E Hulton & Co*, where he said:[8]

'There is abundant authority to shew that it is not necessary for everyone to know to whom the article refers; this would in many cases be an impossibility; but if, in the opinion of a jury, a substantial number of persons who knew the plaintiff, reading the article, would believe that it refers to him, in my opinion an action, assuming the language to be defamatory, can be maintained; and it makes no difference whether the writer of the article inserted the name or description unintentionally, by accident, or believing that no person existed corresponding with the name or answering the description. If upon the evidence the jury are of the opinion that ordinary sensible readers, knowing the plaintiff, would be of opinion that the article referred to him, the plaintiff's case is made out.'

1 But see *Hayward v Thompson* [1982] QB 47 at 60 per Lord Denning MR, and para 6.02, ante.
2 [1910] AC 20.
3 See [1909] 2 KB 444 at 445.

4 [1910] AC 20 at 24.
5 [1910] AC 20 at 26.
6 (1826) 2 C & P 307.
7 (1889) 23 QBD 384 at 386.
8 [1909] 2 KB 444 at 454, CA.

6.06   The decision in *E Hulton & Co v Jones*[1] has not escaped criticism,[2] but the principle seems to be well established and it is now too late for any modification to be made except by statute. Moreover the principle is in accordance with the law in the United States, Australia, New Zealand, Scotland, Ireland and other countries as well. The principle can also be supported on the basis of the reason given by Lord Greene in *Newstead v London Express Newspapers Ltd*:

> 'If there is a risk of coincidence it ought, I think, in reason to be borne not by the inno- cent party to whom the words are held to refer, but by the party who puts them into circulation.'[3]

1 [1910] AC 20.
2 See, for example, Sir William Holdsworth in 57 LQR 74. The decision of the House of Lords was not a reserved decision and it may be that even on the issue of liability some weight was attached to the fact that the plaintiff had been a contributor to the newspaper and that his name was well known in the office. On the question of damages Lord Loreburn LC said ([1910] AC 20 at 24) 'The damages are certainly heavy, but I think your Lordships ought to remember two things. The first is the jury were entitled to think, in the absence of proof satisfactory to them (and they were the judges of it), that some ingredient of recklessness, or more than recklessness, entered into the writing and the publication of this article, especially as Mr. Jones, the plaintiff, had been employed on this very newspaper, and his name was well known in the paper and also well known in the district in which the paper circulated.' See also Salmond on Torts (16th Edn) p 146, note 60.
3 [1940] 1 KB 377 at 388, [1939] 4 All ER 319 at 325, CA.

How the tests are to be applied

6.07   A court in deciding whether a reasonable person would understand the words to refer to the plaintiff does not expect such a person to consider the matter in detail. Thus in *Morgan v Odhams Press Ltd* Lord Pearson said in relation to a report in a Sunday newspaper:[1]

> '. . . I do not think the reasonable man—who can also be described as an ordinary sensible man—should be envisaged as reading this article carefully. Regard should be had to the character of the article: it is vague, sensational and allusive: it is evidently designed for entertainment rather than instruction or accurate information. The ordi- nary, sensible man, if he read the article at all, would be likely to skim through it casually and not give it concentrated attention or a second reading. It is no part of his work to read this article, nor does he have to place any practical decision on what he reads there. The relevant impression is that which would be conveyed to an ordinary sensible man (in this case having knowledge of the relevant circumstances) reading the article casually and not expecting a high degree of accuracy.'

In the same case Lord Reid referred to *Rubber Improvement Ltd v Daily Telegraph Ltd*[2] and said:[3]

> 'If we . . . take the ordinary man as our guide then we must accept a certain amount of loose thinking. The ordinary man does not formulate reasons in his own mind: he gets a general impression and one can expect him to look again before coming to a conclu- sion and acting on it. But formulated reasons are very often an afterthought. The publishers of newspapers must know the habits of mind of their readers and I see no

injustice in holding them liable if readers, behaving as they normally do, honestly reach conclusions which they might be expected to reach. If one were to adopt a stricter standard it would be too easy for purveyors of gossip to disguise their defamatory matter so that the judge would have to say that there is insufficient to entitle the plaintiff to go to trial on the question whether that matter refers to him, but the ordinary reader with perhaps more worldly wisdom would see the connection and identify the plaintiff with consequent damage to his reputation for which the law would have to refuse him reparation.'

1 [1971] 2 All ER 1156 at 1184, [1971] 1 WLR 1239 at 1269. See also the speech of Lord Morris of Borth-y-Gest where he said at pages 1170, 1254: 'What must be contemplated is a reading of a newspaper in what a jury would consider to be the ordinary way in which a newspaper article would be read. The average reader does not read a sensational article with cautious and critical analytical care. A plaintiff who successfully complained of an article which described someone as a churchwarden at Peckham was neither a churchwarden nor did he reside at Peckham.'
2 [1964] AC 234, [1963] 2 All ER 151.
3 [1971] 2 All ER 1156 at 1162–3, [1971] 1 WLR 1239 at 1245.

EVIDENCE AS TO IDENTIFICATION

6.08 The issue as to identification is to be decided by an objective test—would reasonable persons reasonably understand the words to refer to the plaintiff—but the plaintiff is entitled to call witnesses to prove that they in fact understood the words so to refer. In *Morgan v Odhams Press Ltd*[1] the plaintiff was allowed to call witnesses to show that they had understood the article complained of to refer to him. Furthermore, the evidence which is admissible is not limited to that of the witnesses who made the identification but can include evidence (including that of the plaintiff) as to the reaction of third parties who heard or read the words. Thus in *Cook v Ward*[2] a witness was called to prove that, following the publication of the article complained of, the plaintiff had been laughed at. Tindal CJ said that this evidence had been properly admitted 'as identifying the plaintiff with the subject of the libel'.[3] And in *Jozwiak v Sadek*[4] the plaintiff was allowed to tender evidence of (a) statements made at public meetings after the article complained of had been published and (b) anonymous telephone calls received by the plaintiff, to show that third parties had understood the article to refer to him.[5]

1 [1971] 2 All ER 1156, [1971] 1 WLR 1239; and see *Hough v London Express Newspapers Ltd* [1940] 2 KB 507, [1940] 3 All ER 31.
2 (1830) 4 Moo & P 99.
3 (1830) 4 Moo & P 99 at 111.
4 [1954] 1 All ER 3, [1954] 1 WLR 275.
5 See [1954] 1 All ER 3 at 4, [1954] 1 WLR 275 at 277, per Ormerod J who added: 'It may be that such evidence is of no very great value, and quite clearly the jury will have to be warned to treat evidence of that kind with the caution which is necessary.'

DEFAMATION OF A CLASS

6.09 Difficult questions may arise where the words complained of contain defamatory allegations against a group of people. In such cases the test to be applied is that laid down by Lord Simon LC in *Knupffer v London Express Newspaper Ltd* where he said:[1]

'Where the plaintiff is not named, the test which decides whether the words used refer to him is the question whether the words are such as would reasonably lead persons acquainted with the plaintiff to believe that he was the person referred to. There are cases in which the language used in reference to a limited class may be reasonably understood to refer to every member of the class, in which case every member may have a cause of action. A good example is *Browne v Thomson & Co*,[2] where a newspaper article stated in Queenstown "instructions were issued by the Roman Catholic religious authorities that all Protestant shop assistants were to be discharged", and where seven pursuers who averred that they were the sole persons who exercised religious authority in the name and on behalf of the Roman Catholic church in Queenstown were held entitled to sue for libel as being individually defamed. Lord President Dunedin in that case said:[3] "I think it is quite evident that if a certain set of people are accused of having done something, and if such accusation is libellous, it is possible for the individuals in that set of people to show that they have been damnified, and it is right that they should have an opportunity of recovering damages as individuals." '

1 [1944] AC 116 at 119, [1944] 1 All ER 495 at 496.
2 [1912] SC 359.
3 [1912] SC 359 at 363.

6.10 In the same case Lord Atkin said:[1]

'The only relevant rule is that in order to be actionable the defamatory words must be understood to be published of and concerning the plaintiff. It is irrelevant that the words are published of two or more persons if they are proved to be published of him, and it is irrelevant that the two or more persons are called by some generic or class name. There can be no law that a defamatory statement made of a firm, or trustees, or the tenants of a particular building is not actionable, if the words would reasonably be understood as published of each member of the firm or each trustee or each tenant. The reason why a libel published of a large or indeterminate number of persons described by some general name generally fails to be actionable is the difficulty of establishing that the plaintiff was, in fact, included in the defamatory statement, for the habit of making unfounded generalizations is ingrained in ill-educated or vulgar minds, or the words are occasionally intended to be a facetious exaggeration. . . . It will be as well for the future for lawyers to concentrate on the question whether the words were published of the plaintiff rather than on the question whether they were spoken of a class.'

1 [1944] AC 116 at 121, [1944] 1 All ER 495 at 497.

6.11 An important factor to consider in deciding whether the words complained of refer to the plaintiff is the size of the class of which he is a member. Thus if the class is a very large one such as, for example, 'all lawyers' or 'all grocers' it may be difficult, if not impossible, for the individual to prove that the words complained of refer to him as an individual. But as Lord Porter pointed out in *Knupffer v London Express Newspaper Ltd*, a member of even a large class may have a cause of action in appropriate circumstances:[1]

'The question whether the words refer in fact to the plaintiff or plaintiffs is a matter for the jury or for a judge sitting as a judge of fact, but as a prior question it has always to be ascertained whether there is any evidence on which a conclusion that they do so refer could reasonably be reached. In deciding this question the size of the class, the generality of the charge and the extravagance of the accusation may all be elements to be taken into consideration, but none of them is conclusive. Each case must be considered according to its own circumstances. I can imagine it being said that each member of a body, however large, was defamed where the libel consisted in the assertion that no one of the members of a community was elected as a member unless he had committed a murder.'

1 [1944] AC 116 at 124, [1944] 1 All ER 495 at 499.

6.12   Another source of difficulty is where the words complained of indicate that one or more but not all of the members of the class are being referred to. In the old cases a very strict view was taken, and this strict view was followed by Madden CJ in *Chomley v Watson*, where the words complained of were 'either Mr Dick or Mr Chomley must have suppressed or delayed the letter'. The judge said:[1]

'I think that the law, as it stands, is . . . that where defamatory words are spoken impartially in relation to either of two persons, the publication of the words affords no right of action to either of them.'

1 [1907] VLR 502. And in *Sir John Bourne's case*, cited Cro Eliz 497, it was held that no action lay where the defendant said: 'One of you three is perjured.'

6.13   It is submitted, though there is no satisfactory modern English authority on the matter, that the right approach is that even a general derogatory reference to a group may affect the reputation of every member, and that the court would adopt as its test the intensity of the suspicion cast upon the plaintiff.

Where therefore allegations are made against members of a class the question for consideration is whether, having regard to the size of the class,[1] the nature and gravity of the imputation, the number of members of the class against whom the allegation is made and any other relevant circumstance, reasonable persons would understand that the plaintiff himself had actually done the act alleged or (as the case may be) was reasonably to be suspected of having done it. Furthermore, there may be cases where the allegation in the words complained of implicates directly only some of the members of a class but the words may nevertheless bear a further inferential meaning (which would involve all the members of the class) that the remainder were, for example, associates of criminals, or were persons who had not made sufficient inquiry as to the character of their business associates. Indeed the problems presented by class libels underline the importance in every case of deciding what the words in their context would be reasonably understood to mean.

1 In *Abraham v Advocate Co Ltd* [1946] 2 WWR 181, Lord Goddard, giving the opinion of the Privy Council, referred to the decision in *Knupffer v London Express Newspaper Ltd* [1944] AC 116, [1944] 1 All ER 495, and said at page 185: 'It is enough to say that if on a fair construction the words are spoken of a class or body of persons an individual member of a class or body cannot sue in respect of them unless there are circumstances that show that they may be aimed at him. . . . Among such circumstances may be the smallness of the class referred to, so that it could fairly be said that all its members are aimed at.' But see also para 6.11, ante.

CHAPTER 7

The meaning of defamatory

INTRODUCTION

7.01   In addition to proving that the words complained of refer to him the plaintiff has to prove that the words were defamatory. There is no wholly satisfactory and comprehensive definition of the word 'defamatory' in the cases. The classic definition is that of Parke B in *Parmiter v Coupland*, where he said:[1]

> 'A publication . . . which is calculated to injure the reputation of another by exposing him to hatred, contempt or ridicule.'

But this definition is not adequate to cover all cases. In *Tournier v National Provincial and Union Bank of England*, Scrutton LJ said:[2]

> 'I do not myself think this ancient formula is sufficient in all cases, for words may damage the reputation of a man as a business man, which no one would connect with hatred, ridicule, or contempt.'

And in the same case Atkin LJ said:[3]

> 'I do not think that it is a sufficient direction to a jury on what it meant by "defamatory" to say, without more, that it means: Were the words calculated to expose the plaintiff to hatred, ridicule, or contempt, in the mind of a reasonable man? The formula is well known to lawyers, but it is obvious that suggestions might be made very injurious to a man's character in business which would not, in the ordinary sense, excite either hate, ridicule, or contempt—for example, an imputation of a clever fraud which, however much to be condemned morally and legally, might yet not excite what a member of a jury might understand as hatred, or contempt.'

1 (1840) 6 M & W 105 at 108.
2 [1924] 1 KB 461 at 477.
3 [1924] 1 KB 461 at 486.

7.02   In *Youssoupoff v MGM Pictures Ltd*, Scrutton LJ said[1] that he thought it was difficult to improve upon the language of Cave J in *Scott v Sampson*:[2]

> 'The law recognises in every man a right to have the estimation in which he stands in the opinion of others unaffected by false statements to his discredit.'

But it has been pointed out that the word 'discredit' is equally incapable of precise explication and that in this respect this definition ceases to define.[3] In *Sim v Stretch*, Lord Atkin again expressed the view that the definition of Parke B seemed to be too narrow:[4]

29

'Judges and text book writers alike have found difficulty in defining with precision the word "defamatory". The conventional phrase exposing the plaintiff to hatred, ridicule or contempt is probably too narrow. The question is complicated by having to consider the person or class of persons whose reaction to the publication is the test of the wrongful character of the words used. I do not intend to ask your Lordships to lay down a formal definition, but after collating the opinions of many authorities I propose in the present case the test: would the words tend to lower the plaintiff in the estimation of right-thinking members of society generally?'[5]

1 (1934) 50 TLR 581 at 587.
2 (1882) 8 QBD 491 at 503.
3 See Fraser on Libel and Slander (7th Edn), p 3. The Faulks Committee in their report took the same view (Cmnd 5909, para 62).
4 [1936] 2 All ER 1237 at 1240.
5 See para 7.05, note 1, post.

7.03 It is clear that allegations of dishonesty or immorality or other dishonourable conduct[1] (or that the plaintiff is suspected of such conduct), or allegations which impute some serious defect of character, would be held to be defamatory. But the word 'defamatory' covers many cases where there is no imputation of moral faults. Thus allegations against the competence of a trader or a business or professional man may be defamatory though no imputation is made against his moral character. In *Drummond-Jackson v British Medical Association*, the Court of Appeal were concerned (on an interlocutory application to strike out the statement of claim) with an article in a medical journal which, the plaintiff suggested, impugned his reputation as a dentist. Lord Pearson said:[2]

'. . . words may be defamatory of a trader or business man or professional man, though they do not impute any moral fault or defect of personal character. They can be defamatory of him if they impute lack of qualification, knowledge, skill, capacity, judgment or efficiency in the conduct of his trade or business or professional activity.'

Lord Pearson then referred[3] to the American case of *Hoepner v Dunkirk Printing Co*, where it was said:[4]

'While the articles complained of fail to charge the plaintiff [who was a football coach] with the commission of any crime, or to attack his moral character, the fair inference to be drawn from the language used is that the plaintiff is an inefficient coach, and has failed to properly instruct the team in modern play and in the technique of the game, so that they could successfully meet and compete with other teams in their class.'

1 In *Angel v H H Bushell & Co Ltd* [1968] 1 QB 813 at 825, [1967] 1 All ER 1018 at 1023, Milmo J (who tried the case without a jury) said: 'I think it is a serious imputation to say of a businessman that he is not conversant with business ethics. . . . Ethics involve a moral standard, and in my judgment, a breach of ethics connotes at a minimum dishonourable behaviour.'
2 [1970] 1 All ER 1094 at 1104, [1970] 1 WLR 688 at 698.
3 [1970] 1 All ER 1094 at 1104, [1970] 1 WLR 688 at 699.
4 [1929] 237 NYS 123 at 127.

7.04 It will be seen, therefore, that in many cases the question whether the words are defamatory cannot be decided by reference to a wholly objective standard but will depend to some extent on the occupation of the plaintiff. Thus, though it would be defamatory of a professional musician to say that he had no aptitude for music or of an accountant that he had no understanding of accounts, such allegations would not be defamatory if made of persons whose profession or business did not require such skills or talents.

The question whether or not words are defamatory has also to be judged in the light of contemporary opinion. Thus, for example, at certain periods it would have been defamatory to refer to a person as a Papist or a Francophile.

THE STANDARD OF RIGHT-THINKING MEMBERS OF SOCIETY GENERALLY

7.05   It is clear that the standard to be applied is that of right-thinking members of society. Accordingly, the law will not treat as defamatory words which impute, for example, that the plaintiff has given information to the police in order to assist the suppression of crime even though many of his colleagues might regard the plaintiff's action with disfavour. Thus in *Byrne v Deane*, Slesser LJ said:[1]

'. . . in my view, to say or to allege of a man . . . that he has reported certain acts, wrongful in law, to the police, cannot possibly be said to be defamatory of him in the minds of the general public. We have to consider in this connection the arbitrium boni, the view which would be taken by the ordinary good and worthy subject of the King, and I have assigned to myself no other criterion than what a good and worthy subject of the King would think of some person of whom it had been said that he had put the law into motion against wrongdoers, in considering that such a good and worthy subject would not consider such an allegation in itself to be defamatory.'

1 [1937] 1 KB 818 at 832, [1937] 2 All ER 204 at 209. In that case the plaintiff had given information to the police that there were gaming machines on the premises of the golf club of which he was a member and he brought an action in respect of a notice on the club notice board which referred to his action. See also at 839–40, 214, per Greene LJ and *Myroft v Sleight* (1921) 90 LJ KB 883. In *Berry v Irish Times Ltd* [1973] IR 368 the plaintiff, a civil servant in the Department of Justice in Eire, sued in respect of a placard alleging that he had assisted in helping to jail Republicans in England. It was held that such an allegation did not constitute defamation.

WORDS WHICH CAUSE A PERSON TO BE SHUNNED OR AVOIDED

7.06   There may be cases where the words complained of, though not involving any suggestion of moral blame, will tend to make other people shun or avoid the plaintiff. In *Youssoupoff v MGM Pictures Ltd* Slesser LJ stated the matter as follows:[1]

'I, for myself, cannot see that from the plaintiff's point of view it matters in the least whether this libel suggests that she has been seduced or ravished. The question whether she is or is not the more or the less moral seems to me immaterial in considering this question whether she has been defamed, and for this reason, that, as has been frequently pointed out in libel, not only is the matter defamatory if it brings the plaintiff into hatred, ridicule, or contempt by reason of some moral discredit on her part, but also if it tends to make the plaintiff be shunned and avoided and that without any moral discredit on her part. It is for that reason that persons who have been alleged to have been insane, or to be suffering from certain diseases, and other cases where no direct moral responsibility could be placed upon them, have been held to be entitled to bring an action to protect their reputation and their honour. One may, I think, take judicial notice of the fact that a lady of whom it has been said that she has been ravished, albeit against her will, has suffered in social reputation and in opportunities of receiving respectable consideration from the world.'

It is submitted, however, that words should not be regarded as defamatory unless they involve some lowering of the plaintiff's reputation or of the respect with which he is regarded, and that it would not be defamatory to state, for example, that the plaintiff or his business premises was liable to be attacked by terrorists, even though the effect of such a statement would be to cause members of the public to 'shun or avoid' the plaintiff.[2] Thus cases where the defamatory nature of the words consists of their tendency to cause the plaintiff to be shunned or avoided themselves represent some extension of the general rule. This point was recognised in *Boyd v Mirror Newspapers Ltd*, where Hunt J said:[3]

> 'At common law, in general, an imputation, to be defamatory of the plaintiff, must be disparaging of him. . . . I say that this is "in general" the position, as the common law also recognises as defamatory an imputation which, although not disparaging, tends to make other persons "shun or avoid" the plaintiff, for example by attributing to him that he is insane: *Morgan v Lingen*;[4] or by attributing to her that she has been raped, as well as an imputation that displays the plaintiff in a ridiculous light, notwithstanding the absence of any moral blame on his part.'

1 (1934) 50 TLR 581 at 587.
2 In *Middle East Airlines Airliban SAL v Sungravure Pty Ltd* [1974] 1 NSWLR 323 at 341 (where the Court of Appeal was concerned with the statutory definition of defamation in section 5 of the Defamation Act in New South Wales), Glass JA expressed the view that it was defamatory of the plaintiffs at common law to allege that travellers on their airline would be faced with a serious risk of hijacking. It is submitted, with respect, that this view does not represent the law in England.
3 [1980] 2 NSWLR 449 at 453.
4 (1863) 8 LT 800.

THE REPORT OF THE FAULKS COMMITTEE

7.07   The Faulks Committee in their report have recommended that for the purpose of civil cases the following definition of defamation should be adopted:[1]

> 'Defamation shall consist of the publication to a third party of matter which in all the circumstances would be likely to affect a person adversely in the estimation of reasonable people generally.'

This definition has much to commend it, but it is submitted that on balance it will be better to avoid a statutory definition which might introduce into the law of defamation further complications of interpretation. Indeed it is doubtful whether a single definition is adequate to cover every kind of case which may be encountered in practice, and it is therefore submitted that the most satisfactory solution would be to leave it to the judge to select from the existing judicial definitions the form of words which seems most appropriate to the particular case.

1 Cmnd 5909 para 65.

CHAPTER 8

Publication

INTRODUCTION

8.01 No action can be maintained for libel or slander unless there be a publication, that is, a communication of the words complained of to some person other than the plaintiff. Thus there is no publication, and therefore no action can lie,[1] if the defamatory matter be communicated only to the plaintiff himself. In *Pullman v Hill & Co* Lord Esher MR said (in relation to the publication of a letter):[2]

> 'What is the meaning of "publication"? The making known the defamatory matter after it has been written to some person other than the person of whom it is written. If the statement is sent straight to the person of whom it is written, there is no publication of it; for you cannot publish a libel of a man to himself.'

Moreover in order to bring an action against a particular defendant it is necessary to prove that the defendant published the words or, though the defendant was not himself the publisher, that in the circumstances he was responsible for the publication.

1 The rule is different in the case of criminal libel.
2 [1891] 1 QB 524 at 527.

Proof of publication

8.02 The burden of proving that the words were published to a third party rests on the plaintiff. In some circumstances, however, such publication is presumed and it is unnecessary for the plaintiff to plead or prove that the words were published to any specific person or persons. Thus where the publication takes place in a book or newspaper or in the course of a broadcast transmitted to the general public a publication of the words is presumed.[1]

1 It is to be noted, however, that where a legal innuendo is relied on, proof of publication to a person or persons with knowledge of the extrinsic facts will usually be necessary even though the publication was, for example, in a newspaper: see *Fullam v Newcastle Chronicle and Journal Ltd* [1977] 3 AU ER 32 at 37, 39 [1977] 1 WLR 651 at 656, 659.

TELEGRAMS, POST-CARDS AND ENVELOPES

8.03 Where defamatory words are included in a telegram or written on a post-card or envelope there is a presumption of fact[1] that the words are published in the course of transmission.[2] But in the case of a post-card or envelope the presumption will be rebutted if the defendant proves that in fact the words were never read by any person other than the plaintiff.[3] Moreover it is always to be remembered that it is for the plaintiff to establish that the words complained of were defamatory of him; accordingly if he is not mentioned by name or if the words are in cipher or otherwise not ex facie defamatory the plaintiff will have to plead and prove sufficient facts to establish that the words would have been understood as defamatory of him.

1 'A presumption of fact is one which arises from the high degree of probability of the existence of the fact': per Bray J In *Huth v Huth* [1915] 3 KB 32 at 46.
2 '. . . A communication . . . if sent through the telegraph office . . . is necessarily communicated to all the clerks through whose hands it passes. It is like the case of a libel contained on the back of a post-card': per Brett J in *Williamson v Freer* (1874) LR 9 CP 393 at 395. See also *Sadgrove v Hole* [1901] 2 KB 1 at 4 per A.L. Smith MR; *Huth v Huth* [1915] 3 KB 32 at 39 per Lord Reading CJ and at 44 per Swinfen Eady LJ.
3 See *Huth v Huth* [1915] 3 KB 32 at 39 per Lord Reading CJ.

PROOF OF PUBLICATION WHERE THE PLAINTIFF RELIES ON AN INNUENDO MEANING

8.04 Where the plaintiff relies on a true innuendo meaning[1] the general rule is that it is necessary for the plaintiff to plead and prove:

(a) that the words were published to a specific publishee or to specific publishees; and

(b) that the publishee or publishees knew of specific facts which would enable them to understand the words in the innuendo meaning or to understand the words to refer to the plaintiff.

In *Hough v London Express Newspapers Ltd* Slesser LJ said:[2]

'The burden on the plaintiff is to give evidence of special circumstances which would lead reasonable persons to infer that the words were understood in a defamatory meaning provided such circumstances were known to those persons to whom the words were published.'

And in *Consolidated Trust Co v Browne* Jordan CJ put the matter as follows:[3]

'If the matter complained of is ex facie defamatory and refers by name to the person defamed, it is necessary to prove only that it was published, and publication to one person is enough. . . . If, however, the matter is not ex facie defamatory, or does not refer by name to a person alleged to be defamed, and the defamatory character which is attributed to the matter, or the identity of the person defamed, would be apparent only to persons who had knowledge of special circumstances, it is necessary, in order to prove publication,[4] to prove that it was published to a person or persons who had knowledge of those cirumstances.'

1 See para 4.17, ante.
2 [1940] 2 KB 507 at 513, [1940] 3 All ER 31 at 34.
3 [1948] 49 SR (NSW) 86 at 89.
4 In all cases where publication of the words in an innuendo meaning to specific publishees has to be proved the jury should be warned that in assessing damages account must be taken of the fact that publication in that meaning is limited to those persons.

8.05   Where the plaintiff seeks to rely on an innuendo meaning in respect of matter contained in a newspaper, magazine or book or in a television or radio broadcast he cannot rely on any general presumption of fact that the matter was understood in that meaning.[1] In many, and perhaps most, cases the plaintiff will have to plead and prove that there were one or more publishees of the article, book or broadcast who knew the relevant facts which gave the words their special innuendo meaning. But there will be cases involving newspapers and similar media where the relevant facts, though not generally known, are known sufficiently widely to enable the plaintiff to rely in the circumstances on a presumption or inference that some persons who read the words knew those facts.[2] It is submitted that in such cases the plaintiff will be able to discharge the burden of proving publication by establishing:

(a) that the newspaper containing the article (or as the case may be) circulated among a substantial number of people; and

(b) that the special facts were widely known among persons who were likely to read the article.

The extrinsic facts must have existed and have been known to the publishees at the date of publication.[3]

1 *Fullam v Newscastle Chronicle and Journal Ltd* [1977] 3 All ER 32, [1977] 1 WLR 651.
2 See *Fullam v Newscastle Chronical and Journal Ltd* [1977] 3 All ER 32 at 39 [1977] 1 WLR 651 at 659, per Scarman LJ.
3 *Grappelli v Derek Block (Holdings) Ltd* [1981] 2 All ER 272, [1981] 1 WLR 822.

Each communication is a separate publication

8.06   Each communication of defamatory matter to a publishee is in law a separate publication. This means, for example, that in the case of a letter which is read by a number of different people in turn a series of publications takes place. And if the libel is contained in a book or newspaper each publication to each publishee of each copy of the book or newspaper is a separate publication.[1] In practice, however, a plaintiff does not in the ordinary way bring an action in respect of the publication of an individual copy of a book or newspaper or circular letter;[2] he sues in respect of all the copies as though they constituted a single publication and the number of copies is treated as relevant only to the issue of damages.[3]

1 Similarly in the case of a slander the publication to each hearer of the defamatory words is a separate publication.
2 It is submitted that except in special circumstances it would be an abuse of the process of the court to bring a series of actions in respect of different copies of a book, newspaper or similar material: see *Jones v Pritchard* (1849) 6 Dow & L 529 (the plaintiff brought separate actions against the defendant in respect of the publication of the same libel to seven different persons; Erle J ordered the proceedings to be stayed in all actions, except one, until that one had been tried). See also *MacDougall v Knight* (1890) 25 QBD 1; *Goldsmith v Sperrings Ltd* [1977] 2 All ER 566 at 574, [1977] 1 WLR 478 at 489 per Lord Denning MR. On the other hand where there is a claim for aggravated or exemplary damages and more than one person is responsible for the publication of the libel it may be wise to bring separate actions against the different defendants: see *Cassell & Co Ltd v Broome* [1972] AC 1027 at 1063, [1972] 1 All ER 801 at 817 per Lord Hailsham of St Marylebone LC.
3 It may often happen in the case of a libel in a newspaper that the words complained of will be repeated, though in slightly differing forms, in a number of successive editions of the same issue. In such an event the plaintiff may wish to rely on one or more of these editions as separate publications.

8.07 There are cases, however, where it is necessary to consider separately the publication of an individual copy (or group of copies) of a multiple-copy libel, or, where successive publications of the same libel have taken place, the publication of the libel to one or some only of the publishees. For example, in the case of a circular letter the meaning to be attached to the letter may vary according to the knowledge of individual publishees. Moreover the circumstances of publication may vary so that whereas publication of such a letter to one publishee or to a particular group of publishees is protected by qualified privilege the publication to others is not. The fact that each communication of a libel is a separate publication may also be relevant in the calculation of the period of limitation.[1]

1 See *Duke of Brunswick v Harmer* (1849) 14 QB 185 (The plaintiff recovered damages in respect of the publication to the plaintiff's agent of a copy of an 1830 newspaper which the agent bought at the defendant's office in 1848).

Place of publication

8.08 Publication takes place at the point where the words complained of are heard or read by the publishee. Thus a letter is published at the place where it is read by the recipient,[1] and words spoken in the course of a telephone conversation are published at the place where they are heard by the person at the other end of the line.[2] Moreover it seems clear that in the case of television and radio broadcasts the words and pictures transmitted are published at each point at which the broadcasts are received.[3]

1 *Bata v Bata* [1948] WN 366 (copies of a circular letter sent from Zurich to London: publication in London). There may of course be other separate publications of the letter before it is sent, for example, to staff employed by the writer.
2 The words may be published also to persons who are with the speaker at his end of the line.
3 It is submitted that in an appropriate case an English court would follow *Jenner v Sun Oil Co* [1952] 2 DLR 526 (an Ontario court gave the plaintiff leave to serve proceedings outside the jurisdiction in respect of a radio broadcast transmitted from New York but heard by many listeners in Ontario). See also *Gorton v Australian Broadcasting Commission* (1973) 22 FLR 181.

PUBLICATIONS OUTSIDE THE JURISDICTION OR BY PERSONS OUTSIDE THE JURISDICTION

8.09 Where the publication of the defamatory matter took place outside the jurisdiction or where the person who published the defamatory matter is outside the jurisdiction it is necessary to consider:

(a) whether proceedings can be brought in an English court in respect of the publication; and
(b) whether the proceedings can be served on the defendant.

8.10 Where a publication takes place outside the jurisdiction an action will lie in England in respect of that publication if the publication is actionable according to English law and is also actionable according to the law of the place of publication (the *lex loci delicti*). The general rule was formulated by Lord Wilberforce in *Chaplin v Boys* as follows:[1]

> 'The broad principle should surely be that a person should not be permitted to claim in England in respect of a matter for which civil liability does not exist, or is excluded, under the law of the place where the wrong was committed. This non-existence or exclusion may be for a variety of reasons and it would be unwise to attempt a generalisation relevant to the variety of possible wrongs. . . . I would, therefore re-state the basic rule of English law with regard to foreign torts as requiring actionability as a tort according to English law, subject to the condition that civil liability in respect of the relevant claim exists as between the actual parties under the law of the foreign country where the act was done.'

1 [1971] AC 356 at 389, [1969] 2 All ER 1085 at 1102.

8.11 It may be arguable, however, that in a case where the parties are resident within the jurisdiction and the plaintiff has a reputation in England to protect an action will lie even though the publication would not be actionable according to the lex loci delicti. Thus in *Scott v Lord Seymour* Wightman J said (in relation to a claim for damages for assault):[1]

> '. . . Whatever might be the case between two Neapolitan subjects or between a Neapolitan and an Englishman, I find no authority for holding that, even if the Neapolitan law gives no remedy for assault and battery, however violent and unprovoked, by recovery of damages, that therefore a British subject is deprived of his right to damages given by the English law against another British subject.'

And in *Church of Scientology v Metropolitan Police Commissioner*[2] (where a report about the plaintiffs had been sent to the West German police) the Court of Appeal declined to strike out the statement of claim on the ground (inter alia) that, even if the defendant could not be sued in Germany (because according to German law he would not be liable vicariously for the publication)[3] the case might fall outside the general rule in *Chaplin v Boys*[4] as the parties were resident in England and the plaintiffs had a reputation in England to protect. It is submitted, however, that there is an important distinction between an action in respect of a physical injury suffered abroad where the effect on the plaintiff may continue after he returns to England and an action for defamation where, in the absence of a re-publication, the 'injury' and the consequences take place wholly in the country of the lex loci delicti. In defamation actions therefore there is a strong argument in favour of preserving the rule of double actionability intact.

1 (1862) 1 H & C 219 at 235. Willis J said at 236: 'I am far from saying that I differ from any part of the judgment of my brother Wightman.' This passage from the judgment of Wightman J was cited by Lord Hodson in *Chaplin v Boys* [1971] AC 356 at 377, [1969] 2 All ER 1085 at 1091 as an indication that the general rule of double actionability should not be regarded as an invariable rule.
2 (1976) 120 Sol Jo 690, [1976] BLT No 335.
3 Under English law a chief officer of police is 'liable in respect of torts committed by constables under his direction and control in the performance or purported performance of their functions in like manner as a master is liable in respect of torts committed by his servants in the course of their employment, and accordingly shall in respect of any such tort be treated for all purposes as a joint tortfeasor'; Police Act 1964, s 48(1).
4 [1971] AC 356, [1969] 2 All ER 1085.

Responsibility for publication

8.12 Every person who takes part in the publication of defamatory matter is prima facie liable in respect of that publication. Thus, for example, in the case of a libel in a newspaper the writer of the article and the proprietors,[1] the editor and the printers of the newspapers are liable and so too, subject to the defence of innocent dissemination, are persons such as newsagents who sell the newspaper to the public.[2]

---

1 The proprietors of the newspaper will be liable as participants in the publication and are likely also to be liable vicariously as the employers of the editor and the journalist concerned.
2 See para 16.02, post.

8.13 A person may be liable not only in respect of the publication of a libel to the person or persons to whom the libel was sent but also in respect of publications to other people which, though not intended by the publisher, occurred in the course of transmission. Thus, for example, if a defamatory letter or other document is sent in circumstances in which it is likely to be read by someone other than the addressee the writer may be liable in respect of the publication to that other person.[1] Similarly the publisher of a slander will be liable for the publication of his words to persons whom he ought to have anticipated were likely to hear them.

---

1 See, for example, *Pullman v Hill & Co* [1891] 1 QB 524 (letter addressed to a firm and opened in the course of business by a clerk); *Theaker v Richardson* [1962] 1 All ER 229, [1962] 1 WLR 151 (letter opened by the plaintiff's husband; Court of Appeal upheld the jury's verdict in favour of the plaintiff in the particular circumstances of the case). There is a presumption of fact that words on an envelope or post-card or in a telegram which are ex facie defamatory of the plaintiff are published in the course of transmission: see para. 8.03, ante. But the writer will not be liable if it is a mere possibility that the words will be read by someone other than the addressee: see *Huth v Huth* [1915] 3 KB 32 at 47 per Bray J (envelope opened by butler out of curiosity; Court of Appeal held there was no publication of defamatory letter).

RESPONSIBILITY FOR REPUBLICATION

8.14 In certain circumstances the publisher of defamatory matter may be liable not only in respect of the original publication but also in respect of the re-publication of such matter by someone else. These circumstances can be considered under the following headings:[1]

(a) Where the defendant authorised or secured the repetition;
(b) where there was an obligation[2] on the other person to repeat the words;
(c) where the repetition was the natural consequence of the publication by the original publisher.

Furthermore it is necessary to recognise that there may be a distinction to be drawn between cases where the cause of action relied on is the republication and the original publisher is sued as being liable therefor, and cases where the cause of action relied on is the original publication but damages are claimed to include injury suffered as a result of a republication or republications by others.

1 The headings are based on the judgment of Lopes LJ in *Speight v Gosnay* (1891) 60 LJQB 231 at 232 (which was decided shortly before the Slander of Women Act 1891 came into force). In that case the plaintiff alleged that her engagement had been broken by her fiancé because she had repeated to him a suggestion made by the defendant to the plaintiff's mother about the plaintiff's chastity. The Court of Appeal held that the plaintiff's repetition of the words was not the natural consequence of the publication by the defendant and that therefore the breaking of the engagement did not constitute special damage.

2 Lopes LJ referred in his judgment to 'a moral obligation'. It is submitted, however, that the position is the same where the obligation is legal; for example, an obligation imposed on the publishee by contract.

WHERE THE DEFENDANT AUTHORISED OR SECURED THE REPETITION

8.15   If the defendant authorised the republication of the defamatory words by someone else, he will be liable not only in respect of the original publication but also in respect of the republication.[1] For example, if the defendant makes a defamatory statement to a newspaper reporter intending that his words should be published in the newspaper or if he sends a defamatory letter to a newspaper for publication he will be liable for causing the publication in the newspaper as well as for the publication of the slander or libel (as the case may be) to the reporter or editor.[2]

1 There are likely to be two separate causes of action, one in respect of the original publication and the other in respect of the repetition. It seems that if the plaintiff sues in respect of the first publication alone he can recover damages in respect of both publications: see *Cutler v McPhail* [1962] 2 QB 292 at 299, [1962] 2 All ER 474 at 476, where Salmon J said: 'It matters not whether the damages caused by the repetition of the libel are sued for as part of the damage flowing from the original publication to the editor, or separately as the damages flowing from the publication in the newspaper. In newspaper cases the usual practice is to sue in respect of the publication in the press and not to bother about publication to the editor.'

2 The original publisher may not be liable in respect of the repetition if his words are so distorted that the meaning of the original publication is substantially changed.

WHERE THERE WAS AN OBLIGATION ON THE OTHER PERSON TO REPEAT THE WORDS

8.16   In some circumstances the person to whom the original publication was made will be under a legal or moral duty to repeat the words to a third person. In such an event the original publisher will be liable in respect of the republication if he was aware at the time he published the words of the circumstances giving rise to this duty. In an appropriate case therefore the original publisher will be liable in respect of a subsequent publication even where the original publication was to the plaintiff himself, and therefore not actionable, and republication to a third person was by the plaintiff.[1]

1 See, for example, *Collerton v MacLean* [1962] NZLR 1045. A similar situation would have arisen in *Speight v Gosnay* (1891) 60 LJQB 231 if the court had taken the view that the allegation was one which the plaintiff was under a moral duty to repeat to her fiancé.

WHERE THE REPUBLICATION WAS THE NATURAL CONSEQUENCE OF THE PUBLICATION BY THE ORIGINAL PUBLISHER

8.17   There are dicta which suggest that the original publisher may be liable even though he did not authorise or intend the republication and even though there were no cirumstances imposing a duty on the original publishee to repeat the slander or libel, provided the repetition was the natural consequence of the original publication. Thus in *Ratcliffe v Evans* Bowen LJ said:[1]

'Verbal defamatory statements may, indeed, be intended to be repeated, or may be uttered under such circumstances that their repetition flows in the ordinary course of things from their original utterance. Except in such cases, the law does not allow the plaintiff to recover damages which flow not from the original slander but from its unauthorised repetition.'

And in *Speight v Gosnay* Lopes LJ said:[2]

'. . . If the repetition of these words had been the natural consequence of the defendant's uttering them, that would have been sufficient.'

1 [1892] 2 QB 524 at 530.
2 (1891) 60 LJQB 231 at 232. It is also to be noted that in *Cellactite and British Uralite v Robertson Inc* (1957) Times, 23 July, p 12, (a case of malicious falsehood), Hodson LJ said that he considered that the republication of the defendants' pamphlet, though expressly prohibited, was the natural consequence of its publication by the defendants and fell within the second rule formulated by Lopes LJ. It is plain, however, that the defendants intended their agents to use the information contained in the pamphlet and it is submitted that the case can be explained by the words used by the trial judge and approved by Hodson LJ: 'the material in this document was like a poisonous brew which the agents were expected to dish out in small portions, keeping the main jug containing the brew in their own possession'.

8.18   It is submitted, however, that the original publisher will not be liable in respect of a subsequent republication *merely* because such re-publication was a natural or probable consequence of the original publication and that it is important to bear in mind the words of Tindal CJ in *Ward v Weeks:*[1]

'It was the repetition of (the words) . . . which was the voluntary act of a free agent, over whom the defendant had no control, and for whose acts he is not answerable, that was the immediate cause of the plaintiff's damage.'

It follows therefore that as a general rule the publishers of a newspaper will not be liable for the republication of their story in another newspaper.

1 (1830) 7 Bing 211 at 215. And see *Weld-Blundell v Stephens* [1920] AC 956 at 999 per Lord Wrenbury; *Macy v New York World–Telegram Corpn* (1957) 161 NYS (2d) 54 at 60 per Desmond J.

8.19   The question of the liability of the original publisher is often relevant where a newspaper publishes a report of a speech made by the defendant in circumstances where the defendant knew that a reporter would be present. It is submitted that the speaker will not be liable in respect of the report unless it can be shown that he authorised or in some way secured its publication, and that Hallett J adopted the correct approach in *McWhirter v Manning* where he said:[1]

'It was argued that because Mr Manning knew that there were reporters at the meeting and that a report of what he said might and probably would appear in the printed report he must be taken as having caused the publication of the defamatory words in the report. . . . It was plain that once the words had flown out of Mr Manning's mouth he did nothing further whatever to procure publication of those words, or some or any of them, in a printed form. From then onwards it was other people who got them into print'.

1 (1954) Times, 30 October, p 3. The case did not involve a newspaper report, but it is submitted that the same principle applies to such a report. *Cf J Lyons & Co Ltd v Prescot-Decie* (1923) Times, 16 July, p 3.

Husband and wife

8.20   The communication of defamatory matter by one spouse to another does not constitute a publication in law because for this purpose a husband and wife are treated as one person.[1] But a communication to one spouse of matter defamatory of the other spouse does constitute a publication sufficient to found an action for libel or slander.[2] One spouse can sue the other for defamation,[3] but the court has power to stay the action 'if it appears that no substantial benefit would accrue to either party from the continuation of the proceedings'.[4]

1 *Wennhak v Morgan* (1888) 20 QBD 635. The rule is of long standing and would not seem to have been affected by the decision in *Rumping v Director of Public Prosecutions* [1964] AC 814, [1962] 3 All ER 256, that apart from statutory provisions there was neither a rule of law nor a requirement of public policy which precluded the reception in evidence of communications between spouses. See also *Duchess of Argyll v Duke of Argyll* [1967] Ch 302, [1965] 1 All ER 611 (communications between husband and wife are confidential).
2 *Watt v Longsdon* [1930] 1 KB 130; *Theaker v Richardson* [1962] 1 All ER 229, [1962] 1 WLR 151.
3 The Law Reform (Husband and Wife) Act 1962 provides: 'Subject to the provisions of this section each of the parties to a marriage shall have the like right of action in tort against the other as if they were not married.'
4 The Law Reform (Husband and Wife) Act 1962, s 1(2)(a). See also RSC Ord 89, r 2.

CHAPTER 9

Parties

INTRODUCTION

9.01 The general rule is that any person may bring an action in respect of a libel or slander published of and concerning himself against any other person who was the publisher of the defamatory matter or responsible for its publication. The rights and liabilities of the following categories of persons and groups of persons, however, require individual attention—

(a) trading corporations and companies;
(b) non-trading corporations and companies;
(c) partnerships;
(d) trade unions and employers' associations;
(e) unincorporated associations (other than partnerships, trade unions and employers' associations);
(f) bankrupts.

Trading corporations and companies

9.02 A trading corporation or company may bring an action for defamation in respect of the publication of defamatory matter which affects its business or trading reputation. Thus, for example, any allegation which impugns the honesty or fairness of the business methods employed by the corporation or company will be actionable,[1] as will allegations which reflect adversely on the financial position[2] or the efficiency of the company.[3]

1 See, for example, *London Computer Operators Training Ltd v BBC* [1973] 2 All ER 170, [1973] 1 WLR 424; *DDSA Pharmaceuticals Ltd v Times Newspapers Ltd* [1973] 1 QB 21, [1972] 2 All ER 417.
2 See *South Hetton Coal Co v North-Eastern News Association* [1894] 1 QB 133 at 141 per Lopes LJ; and *Jones v Jones* [1916] 2 AC 481 at 491, 495–6, 498, 502–3, 508–9.
3 See *South Hetton Coal v North-Eastern News Association* [1894] 1 QB 133 at 139 where Lord Esher MR said: 'With regard to a firm or a company, it is impossible to lay down an exhaustive rule as to what would be a libel on them. But the same rule is applicable to a statement made with regard to them. Statements may be made with regard to their mode of carrying on business, such as to lead people of ordinary sense to the opinion that they conduct their business badly and inefficiently. If so, the law will be the same in their case as in that of an individual, and the statement will be libellous.'

9.03 On the other hand a corporation or company 'cannot be injured in its feelings'[1] so that some allegations which would be actionable at the suit of an individual person would not be defamatory of a corporation or company. For example, it has been said that a company cannot sue in respect of an allegation of ill-manners 'because a firm or company as such cannot have indecent or vulgar manners'.[2] Nevertheless it is submitted that an allegation against a company of inconsiderate or high-handed behaviour would be actionable as being likely to damage its goodwill[3] and its trading reputation.[4]

1 See *Rubber Improvement Ltd v Daily Telegraph Ltd* [1964] AC 234 at 262, [1963] 2 All ER 151 at 156, per Lord Reid.
2 See *South Hetton Coal Co v North-Eastern News Association* [1894] 1 QB 133 at 138 per Lord Esher MR. See also Faulks Report (Cmnd 5909, para 329).
3 See *Rubber Improvement Ltd v Daily Telegraph Ltd* [1964] AC 234 at 262, [1963] 2 All ER 151 at 156, where Lord Reid said: 'A company cannot be injured in its feelings, it can only be injured in its pocket. Its reputation can be injured by a libel but that injury must sound in money. The injury need not necessarily be confined to loss of income. Its goodwill may be injured.'
4 The Faulks Committee have recommended that no action should lie at the suit of any trading corporation unless such corporation can establish either that it has suffered special damage or that the words were likely to cause it pecuniary damage (Cmnd 5909, paras 336, 342). It is submitted, however, that it would be better not to introduce a further complication into the law, particularly as in many cases the directors of the company are likely to join with the company as plaintiffs. See also para 9.08, post.

9.04   A trading corporation or company will be liable for the publication of any defamatory matter by its servant or agent where such publication has been authorised or where such libel or slander has been published in the course of the employment of such servant or agent.[1]

1 See *Citizens Life Assurance Co v Brown* [1904] AC 423 at 428. As a general rule the corporation or company will be liable for the malice of its servant or agent: see further para 17.20, post.

Non-trading corporations and companies

9.05   The law as to non-trading corporations and companies is less clear. It was held in *Manchester Corpn v Williams* that a municipal corporation could not sue in respect of an allegation that bribery and corruption prevailed in some of its departments. Day J said:[1] 'A corporation may sue for libel affecting property, not for one merely affecting personal reputation.' This decision has been questioned[2] but, being a decision of the Divisional Court, is still technically binding on a court of first instance.

1 [1891] 1 QB 94 at 96. Lawrance J concurred. Day J based himself upon the judgment of Pollock CB in *Metropolitan Saloon Omnibus Co v Hawkins* (1859) 4 H & N 87 at 90. The decision in the *Manchester Corpn* case is more fully reported in 63 LT 605.
2 See, for example, Fraser on Libel and Slander (7th Edn) p 90; *Willis v Brooks* [1947] 1 All ER 191 at 192 per Oliver J.

9.06   In *Bognor Regis UDC v Campion*,[1] however, Browne J distinguished *Manchester Corpn v Williams*[2] and held that an urban district council could sue in respect of a libel affecting its governing reputation:[3]

'Just as a trading company has a trading reputation which it is entitled to protect by bringing an action for defamation, so in my view the plaintiffs as a local government corporation have a ''governing'' reputation which they are equally entitled to protect in the same way—of course, bearing in mind the vital distinction between defamation of the corporation as such and defamation of its individual officers or members.'

It is submitted that this decision is correct and that there is no distinction in principle between the rights of a trading corporation and the rights of a non-trading corporation.[4]

1 [1972] 2 QB 169, [1972] 2 All ER 61. At 178, 69, Browne J said: 'The actual decision in the *Manchester Corpn* case can perhaps be supported . . . on the argument that the libel there was not capable of referring to a corporation consisting (as the plaintiffs did) of the Mayor, Aldermen and Citizens, and not, as here, of the Chairman and Councillors. I think that that case is distinguishable from this on that ground, and also on the ground that in my view none of the statements in the leaflet in this case actually impute corruption. But I hope that the Court of Appeal will soon have occasion to consider the *Manchester Corp* case.'
2 [1891] 1 QB 94.
3 [1972] 2 QB 169 at 175, [1972] 2 All ER 61 at 66.
4 The decision has been strongly criticised by J.A. Weir in an article in (1972) 30 Camb LJ 238. The Faulks Committee have recommended that no action should lie at the suit of any non-trading corporation (including government bodies and local authorities) unless such corporation can establish either that it has suffered special damage or that the words were likely to cause it pecuniary damage. It is submitted, however, that it would be better not to introduce a further complication into the law. Actions by non-trading corporations and organs of central or local government are likely to be rare, but there may be cases; for example, allegations about the housing policy of a local authority where an action for libel might be appropriate.

9.07   A non-trading corporation will be liable for the publication of any defamatory matter by its servants or agents where such publication has been authorised or where such libel or slander has been published in the course of the employment of such servant or agent.[1]

1 As a general rule the corporation will be liable for the malice of its servant or agent.

ALLEGATIONS AGAINST THE OFFICERS OR EMPLOYEES OF A CORPORATION OR COMPANY

9.08   A corporation or company cannot bring an action in respect of allegations which reflect solely upon individual officers or employees and not upon itself.[1] But allegations about the officers of a corporation or company, or even about an individual employee if they relate to his work in his employment, will often reflect on the corporation or company itself, either because the act of the individual or individuals will be identified in the mind of the publishee with the employer, or because the allegations involve some imputation against the methods of selection of staff or their supervision. Similarly, allegations against a corporation or company will often involve by necessary inference imputations against those who are responsible for its direction and control.[2] In many recent cases actions have been brought both by the company concerned and by one or more of its directors.[3]

1 See for example, *Bognor Regis UDC v Campion* [1972] 2 QB 169 at 175, [1972] 2 All ER 61 at 66, where Browne J stressed the word 'solely'.
2 The persons responsible for the direction and control of a corporation or company will normally include the board of directors, and the managing director and other superior officers may also be involved: see as to the 'directing mind' of a company *Tesco Supermarkets v Nattress* [1972] AC 153 at 171, [1971] 2 All ER 127 at 132, per Lord Reid, and *H L Bolton (Engineering) Co Ltd v T J Graham & Sons Ltd* [1957] 1 QB 159 at 172, [1956] 3 All ER 624 at 630, per Denning LJ.

3 See, for example, *Rubber Improvement Ltd v Daily Telegraph Ltd* [1964] AC 234, [1963] 2 All ER 151 (company and chairman); *Broadway Approvals Ltd v Odhams Press Ltd* [1965] 2 All ER 523, [1965] 1 WLR 805 (company and managing director); *Associated Leisure Ltd v Associated Newspapers Ltd* [1970] 2 QB 450, [1970] 2 All ER 754 (company and directors); *S and K Holdings Ltd v Throgmorton Publications Ltd* [1972] 3 All ER 497, [1972] 1 WLR 1036 (company and five directors); *London Computer Operators Training Ltd v British Broadcasting Corpn* [1973] 2 All ER 170, [1973] 1 WLR 424 (company and two directors). The directors are entitled to claim damages for injury to their feelings, which is a head of damage which is not available to the corporation or company itself.

Partnerships

9.09 The partners in a firm may bring an action for defamation jointly in respect of the publication of words which are defamatory of the firm as a whole.[1] The action will be for damage done to the partnership as an entity and it seems, on the analogy of actions by limited companies and directors, that if one or more of the partners wish to claim damages in respect of injury to them as individuals (including any injury to their feelings) they should join as co-plaintiffs with the firm.

1 See *Le Fanu v Malcolmson* (1848) 1 HL Cas 637 at 669 where Lord Campbell said: 'Now suppose that several persons were in partnership as grocers, and it was alleged that they sold by short measure or false weight, or that they adulterated their goods; they might bring a joint action for that.' And see RSC Ord 81, r 1. The action may be, and usually is, brought in the firm's name.

9.10 The partners in a firm may be sued jointly in respect of any publication of defamatory matter by one partner 'acting in the ordinary course of business of the firm, or with the authority of his co-partners'.[1] The partners may also be sued jointly in accordance with the ordinary principles of vicarious liability in respect of any defamation published by a servant or agent of the partnership acting in the course of his employment. It is usual to bring the action against the partners in the firm name,[2], though the individual partner, servant or agent who made or authorised the publication should be joined as a co-defendant if doubt exists as to the liability of the firm.

1 See Partnership Act 1890, s 10. It seems, however, that even apart from s 10 the other partners will be liable for the defamation by the partner who made the publication if, for example, they approved a draft of the communication; see *Meekins v Henson* [1964] 1 QB 472 at 478, [1962] 1 All ER 899 at 902, per Winn J.
2 Partnership Act 1890, s 23 provides: 'A writ of execution shall not issue against any partnership property except on a judgment against the firm.'

Trade unions and employers' associations

9.11 A trade union, unless it is a special register body,[1] cannot bring an action in its own name[2] for damages for defamation. The reason for this inability to sue is that a trade union does not possess a legal personality. 'Unless one can attach a personality to a body it cannot sue for defamation.'[3] For many years prior to 1974 trade unions brought actions for libel on the basis that they were clothed with a quasi-corporate personality.[4] But the ability to bring such an action was lost as a consequence of the enactment of the Trade Union and Labour Relations Act 1974 which provided by s 2: (1) 'A trade union which is not a special register body shall not be, or be treated as if it were, a body corporate . . .' The effect of this provision was examined by O'Connor J in *EETPU v Times Newspapers*[5] where he held that a trade union (not being a special register body) could not bring an action for libel. He said this:

> 'The tort of libel . . . must be founded on possession of a personality which can be libelled and section 2(1) has removed that personality from the trade unions . . . There are many attributes which, but for the presence of the words "or be treated as if it were" in section 2(1), would simply confirm that a trade union enjoyed a quasi-corporate personality and could bring an action in its own name for the protection of its own reputation . . . but there it is. Parliament has deprived the trade union of the necessary personality on which an action for defamation depends . . .'

1 A special register body means an organisation whose name was entered in the special register maintained under s 84 of the Industrial Relations Act 1971; see further Trade Union and Labour Relations Act 1974, s 30(1).
2 Nor can it bring an action on behalf of the individual members of the union: see *EETPU v Times Newspapers* [1980] QB 585 at 601.
3 *EETPU v Times Newspapers* [1980] QB 585 at 595 per O'Connor J.
4 *In Bonsor v Musicians' Union* [1956] AC 104 the majority of the House of Lords appear to have treated a trade union as a quasi-corporation. For an example of an action for libel by a trade union see *NUGMW v Gillian* [1946] KB 81, [1945] 2 All ER 593.
5 [1980] QB 585.
6 [1980] QB 585 at 600–601.

9.12 An employers' association on the other hand, which may be 'either a body corporate or an unincorporated association,'[1] can bring an action for defamation. If it is a body corporate it is a legal entity and has the rights of a non-trading corporation.[2] If it is an unincorporated association it is entitled to sue because the powers given to it by s 3(2) of the Trade Union and Labour Relations Act 1974 confer on it the status of a quasi-corporation with the necessary personality to enable it to protect its reputation.[3]

1 Trade Union and Labour Relations Act, 1974, s 3(1).
2 See para 9.06, ante.
3 See *EETPU v Times Newspapers* (1980) QB 585 at 600 where O'Connor J emphasised the contrast between s 2(1) of the Trade Union and Labour Relations Act 1974 and s 3(1).

9.13 By the Trade Union and Labour Relations Act 1974, s 14 it is provided that 'no action shall lie in respect of any act alleged to have been done by or on behalf of a trade union which is not a special register body[1] or by or on behalf of an unincorporated employers' association',[2] other than actions for negligence, nuisance or breach of duty resulting in personal injury[3] and actions for breach of duty imposed in connection with the ownership, occupation, possession, control or use of property.[4] A similar but more limited immunity[5] is conferred on trade unions which are special register bodies[1] and on employers' associations which are bodies corporate 'in respect of any act alleged to have been done in connection with the regulation of relations between employers or employers' associations and workers or trade unions'.[6]

).16

plies
;, or
rs of

6 See Trade Union and Labour Relations Act 1974, s 14(1)(b).

9.14 It follows therefore that no action for defamation can be brought against a trade union which is not a special register body[1] or against an unincorporated employers' association either in the name of the union or association or against the trustees or against any members or officials on behalf of themselves and all other members of the union or association. In the case of a trade union which is a special register body or an employers' association which is a body corporate no action for defamation can be brought 'in respect of any act alleged to have been done in connection with the regulation of relations between employers or employers' associations and workers or trade unions'.[2] The section does not give any immunity, however, to individual members or officials of trade unions or employers' associations.[3]

1 See para 9.11, note 1, ante.
2 See Trade Union and Labour Relations Act 1974, s 14(1)(b).
3 Cf *Bussy v Amalgamated Society of Railway Servants and Bell* (1908) 24 TLR 437.

Unincorporated associations (other than partnerships, trade unions and employers' associations)

9.15 Unincorporated associations, other than partnerships,[1] employers' associations, and trade unions which are special register bodies,[2] cannot bring an action for defamation in the name of the association because the association does not constitute a legal entity. Nor, it seems, can some of the members of the association bring a representative action on behalf of the members as a whole in accordance with the procedure provided in RSC Ord 15, r 12. In many cases, however, where defamatory matter is published which relates to an unincorporated association, the persons who are in control of its affairs may be able to establish that the words complained of are defamatory of them as individuals.

1 See para 9.09, ante.
2 See paras 9.11–9.14, ante.

9.16 Similarly, an unincorporated association cannot be sued in an action for defamation.[1] Nor can an action be brought, it seems, against representative members on behalf of the members as a whole in accordance with RSC Ord 15, r 12.[2] The right course is to bring the action against those officers or members of the association who made or authorised the publication.[3]

1 See *London Association for Protection of Trade v Greenlands Ltd* [1916] 2 AC 15 at 20 where Lord Buckmaster LC said: 'The association consisted of some 6,200 members; it was unincorporated and consequently could not be made a defendant to the action in any capacity whatever. As an entity it could neither publish nor authorise the publication of a libel.' For the special position of partnerships, trade unions and employers' associations, see paras 9.13–9.14, ante.
2 See *Mercantile Marine Service Association v Toms* [1916] 2 KB 243, where the Court of Appeal declined to make an order allowing the chairman, vice-chairman and secretary of the Imperial Merchant Service Guild to be sued on behalf of all the members (about 15,000) of the guild in respect of an alleged libel in the Guild Gazette. See also *London Association for Protection of Trade v Greenlands Ltd* [1916] 2 AC 15 at 38–40 per Lord Parker. On the other hand in *Egger v Viscount Chelmsford* [1965] 1 QB 248 at 266, [1964] 3 All ER 406 at 413, Harman L J seems to have thought that an officer of the Kennel Club could have been sued in a representative capacity; and see [1916] 2 AC 15 at 30 per Lord Atkinson. For a detailed examination of the circumstances in which a representative action may be brought, see *John v Rees* [1970] Ch 345, [1969] 2 All ER 274.
3 See *Mercantile Marine Service Association v Toms* [1916] 2 KB 243 at 248 per Swinfen Eady LJ; *Egger v Viscount Chelmsford* [1965] 1 QB 248, [1964] 3 All ER 406.

Bankrupts

9.17   A right of action for libel or slander vested in a person who is adjudicated bankrupt does not pass to the trustee in bankruptcy although the defamation may have been the sole cause of his bankruptcy.[1] Moreover, a bankrupt may sue in respect of a defamation published during his bankruptcy. Any damages recovered by the bankrupt do not form part of his estate and can be spent by him on his living expenses. It seems probable, however, that if the damages are substantial and are invested in property, the property can be claimed by the trustee in bankruptcy.[2]

1 See *Howard v Crowther* (1841) 8 M & W 601 at 604 (an action for the seduction of a servant), where Alderson B said: 'Assignees can maintain no action for libel, although the injury occasioned thereby to the man's reputation may have been the sole cause of his bankruptcy.'
2 See *Re Wilson, ex p Vine* (1878) 8 ChD 364 at 366, where James LJ said: 'If the bankrupt had accumulated the money and had invested it in some property, that property might be reached by the trustee. But the fact that he could do that does not enable the trustee to intercept the damages before they reach the bankrupt's hands, or to prevent him, if he has got them, from spending them in the maintenance of himself and his family.'

9.18   A bankrupt may be sued for any defamation published by him, but it is to be noted that a plaintiff cannot prove in the bankruptcy for the damages or costs awarded, unless he has signed judgment before the date of the receiving order.[1] On the other hand an order of discharge does not release a bankrupt from liability to damages in respect of a defamation published by him, for such a claim is not a 'debt provable in bankruptcy'.[2]

A right of action for malicious falsehood, not being a purely personal action, passes to the trustee in bankruptcy and the bankrupt cannot sue.

1 See *Re Newman, ex p Brooke* (1876) 3 ChD 494 (damages for personal injuries).
2 See ibid.; Bankruptcy Act 1914, ss 28(2), 30(1).

CHAPTER 10

Defences: general introduction

10.01 In an action for defamation the defendant may contest the matter on the basis that the plaintiff is unable to prove a prima facie case. Thus the defendant may contend—

(a) that the words complained of were not published at all or were not published by him;

(b) that the words complained of did not refer to the plaintiff or were incapable of referring to the plaintiff;

(c) that the words complained of were not defamatory of the plaintiff or were incapable of bearing any meaning defamatory of the plaintiff.

The defendant may, in appropriate circumstances, raise one or more of these defences, but he may also, either in addition or alternatively, dispute liability on the basis that, though the plaintiff can establish the ingredients of a prima facie case, he (the defendant) has a substantive defence which defeats the plaintiff's claim.

10.02 The main defences to an action for defamation will be considered under the following headings—

(a) justification, that is, that the words are true;

(b) fair comment;

(c) absolute privilege;

(d) qualified privilege;

(e) an offer of amends under the Defamation Act 1952, s 4;

(f) leave and licence or *volenti non fit injuria*;

(g) innocent dissemination;

(h) apology and payment into court under Lord Campbell's Acts 1843 and 1845.

CHAPTER 11

Justification

INTRODUCTION

11.01   The general rule is that it is a defence to an action for libel or slander that the words are true in substance and in fact. This defence is called justification.[1] It is proposed to consider the defence under the following headings—

   (a) the basis of the defence;
   (b) the state of mind of the defendant;
   (c) the burden of proof;
   (d) the extent of the burden;
   (e) the sting of the libel;
   (f) partial justification;
   (g) justification of a meaning other than that alleged by the plaintiff;
   (h) the Rehabilitation of Offenders Act 1974;
   (i) rumour or hearsay;
   (j) reliance on facts subsequent to the publication.

1 The Faulks Committee have drawn attention to the fact that the word 'justification' can be a source of confusion and have recommended that the defence should be retitled 'truth': Cmnd 5909, paras 129, 144.

The basis of the defence

11.02   The basis of the rule that truth is a defence to an action for defamation was stated by Littledale J in *McPherson v Daniels*[1] as being that:

> 'The law will not permit a man to recover damages in respect of an injury to a character which he does not or ought not to possess.'

The rule can sometimes conflict, however, with the principle that the law of defamation is designed to protect a man's reputation, and a defendant may be able to escape liability by relying on facts of which the plaintiff's friends and acquaintances were unaware.[2]

1 (1829) 10 B & C 263 at 272.
2 As to the effect of the Rehabilitation of Offenders Act 1974, see para 11.14, post.

The state of mind of the defendant

11.03   The general rule is that the defendant's state of mind is irrelevant to the issue of justification. If the words complained of are true in substance and in fact the defendant will not be liable even though he published the words with the express intent of causing damage to the plaintiff.[1] This general rule is subject, however, to the provisions of the Rehabilitation of Offenders Act 1974.[2]

1 If the defence fails, however, such intent may affect the damages: see para 18.13, post.
2 As to the effect of the Rehabilitation of Offenders Act 1974, see para 11.14, post.

The burden of proof

11.04 The law presumes that defamatory words are false and the plaintiff need do no more than prove that defamatory words have been published of him by the defendant; it is for the defendant to prove that the words are true, if he can.

The extent of the burden

11.05 In order to succeed in a defence of justification it is necessary for the defendant to prove the truth of the words complained of not only in their literal meaning but also in such inferential or innuendo meanings as the jury may find the words to bear. Furthermore, the words in their context may amount to a general charge against the plaintiff for which the proof of one or more specific allegations may not provide an adequate defence. An example of such a general charge is provided by the case of *Bishop v Latimer*, where Byles J pointed out in the course of the hearing:[1]

> 'The libel is in general terms "how Lawyer Bishop treats his clients". It is not how he treated them in this particular case, but how he treats them generally, and even if you succeed in proving that the report is correct, so as to justify the inference that in this instance he treated his client ill, that would not answer the implied charge in the libel that he so treats his clients generally.'

1 (1861) 4 LT 775. Following the intervention by the judge the case was settled.

The sting of the libel

11.06 It is not necessary for the defendant, even at common law, to prove the truth of every detail of the words. In *Edwards v Bell*, Burrough J put the matter as follows:[1]

> 'As much must be justified as meets the sting of the charge, and if anything be contained in the charge, which does not add to the sting of it, that need not be justified.'

And in *Sutherland v Stopes*, Lord Shaw of Dunfermline said that the plea of justification was not to be considered in a 'meticulous sense' and gave the following example:[2]

> 'If I write that the defendant on March 6th took a saddle from my stable and sold it the next day and pocketed the money all without notice to me, and that in my opinion he stole the saddle, and if the facts are truly found to be that the defendant did not take the

saddle from the stable but from the harness room, and that he did not sell it the next day but a week afterwards, but nevertheless he did, without my knowledge or consent, sell my saddle so taken and pocketed the proceeds, then the whole sting of the libel may be justifiably affirmed by a jury notwithstanding these errors in detail.'

1 (1824) 1 Bing 403 at 409.
2 [1925] AC 47 at 79. It is submitted that this statement of the law is to be preferred to that of Lord Cozens-Hardy in *Maisel v Financial Times* [1915] 3 KB 336 at 339 where he said: 'Speaking generally, in an ordinary case of libel, . . . if you say of a man "he stole a hatchet on such and such a day", you must justify this particular allegation, and that is all: it is not relevant to say that he stole a hatchet the day before, or stole a hatchet the day after.'

Partial justification

11.07 Where the words complained of contain more than one charge or are otherwise severable the defendant may justify part only of the defamatory words, but at common law he remains liable to pay damages in respect of the part not justified. In *Clark v Taylor*, Tindall CJ put the matter as follows:[1]

'There can be no doubt that a defendant may justify part only of the libel containing several distinct charges. . . . But if he omits to justify a part which contains libellous matter, he is liable in damages for that which he has so omitted to justify.'

And in *Sutherland v Stopes*, Lord Shaw of Dunfermline said:[2]

'If a man says that a certain neighbour of his was guilty of manslaughter and was also a thief, it is perfectly open to take a plea in justification of either charge only.'

1 (1836) 2 Bing NC 654 at 664.
2 [1925] AC 47 at 78. Cf *Goody v Odhams Press Ltd* [1967] 1 QB 333 at 340, [1966] 3 All ER 369 at 372 per Lord Denning MR.

11.08 More recently, in *Plato Films Ltd v Speidel*, Lord Denning (when dealing with the admissibility of evidence of character in mitigation of damages) said:[1]

'[Mr Gardiner] put this instance: suppose a newspaper said of a man: "he has been convicted six times for dishonesty", but, on being sued, the newspaper finds that he has in fact only been convicted twice. The newspaper cannot justify, he said, because it cannot prove the words were true. Nor can it bring forward the two convictions in mitigation of damages because they are specific misconduct. So the plaintiff will get damages on the footing that he has never been convicted at all. If such were the law I would agree with Mr Gardiner that it would be most unjust and ought to be remedied. But it is not the law. Although the newspaper cannot justify in whole it can justify in part. It can plead that, in so far as the words meant that he had been convicted twice, they were true and thus bring the two convictions before a jury. . . . This rule is based on sound sense. Seeing that the law does not permit a defendant, in mitigation of damages, to adduce evidence which tends to justification, it must permit him to adduce the self same evidence when pleaded in partial justification. . . . If it were not so, the plaintiff would recover damages for a character which he did not possess or deserve; and this the law will not permit.'

1 [1961] AC 1090 at 1141, [1961] 1 All ER 876 at 891. See also *Clarkson v Lawson* (1830) 6 Bing 587 at 591; *Waitham v Weaver* (1822) Dow & Ry NP 10 at 11; *Vessey v Pike* (1829) 3 C & P 512.

11.09 The defence of partial justification has now been extended by statute and in certain circumstances a partial justification will provide a complete defence. Thus the Defamation Act 1952, s 5 provides:

'**Justification.** In an action for libel or slander in respect of words containing two or more distinct charges against the plaintiff, a defence of justification shall not fail by reason only that the truth of every charge is not proved if the words not proved to be true do not materially injure the plaintiff's reputation having regard to the truth of the remaining charges.'

It is to be noted, however, that this section only applies where the words complained of contain two or more distinct charges. If a defendant intends to rely on section 5 he must include a plea to that effect in his defence.[1]

1 *Moore v News of the World Ltd* [1972] 1 QB 441, [1972] 1 All ER 915.

11.10 Where the words complained of contain only one charge the position is less clear. Suppose, for example, it was alleged that a man had been convicted of rape and in fact he had been convicted of the lesser offence of indecent assault; section 5 of the Defamation Act 1952 would provide no defence nor would the case fall strictly within the old common law rule as to partial justification. Nevertheless, it is submitted that a court would not allow a plaintiff in such circumstances to recover damages on the basis that he had not been convicted of any offence involving indecency at all, and that provided it was made clear that the defence was put forward merely by way of partial justification the defendant would be entitled to put the facts before the jury.

Justification of a meaning other than that alleged by the plaintiff

11.11 Where the plaintiff contends that the words complained of bear some extended meaning or meanings other than their literal meaning, the meaning or meanings put forward should be set out in the statement of claim. It is to be remembered, however, that the question for the jury in each case where justification is set up by way of defence is whether the words are true in the meaning which the jury find the words to bear. The defendant may therefore wish to contend that the words bear some different meaning from that put forward by the plaintiff and that in the meaning contended for by the defendant the words are true. It is submitted that the defendant is able to take this course and that the older authorities to the contrary[1] would not now be followed. A defendant is not allowed, however, to set out in his defence what he says the words mean, though it is submitted that this rule needs re-examination; in many cases one of the crucial issues at the trial is the meaning of the words and it would clearly be convenient if the precise issue between the parties was placed on the record in the pleadings before the hearing.

1 See, for example, *Bremridge v Latimer* (1864) 12 WR 878; *Watkin v Hall* (1868) LR 3 QB 396 at 402.

11.12   In some cases the defendant may wish to contend that the words bear a less defamatory meaning than that alleged by the plaintiff and that in the less defamatory sense they are true. On the other hand, a defendant, with a view perhaps to introducing evidence of 'similar facts', may wish to contend that the words, which ex facie relate to a specific incident, would be understood in a wider sense, for example, as conveying a general charge of dishonesty.¹ The law on this matter appears to be at a stage of development. If the plaintiff himself pleads an inferential meaning to the effect that the words meant, for example, that he was a dishonest man or unfit to be a director, the defendant will then be free to introduce evidence of other incidents which are relevant to prove the truth of the inferential meaning.² But where the plaintiff, exercising perhaps a wise discretion, does not allege that the words impute, for example, general dishonesty, the position is less clear. It can be strongly argued that the scope of the defence of justification should not depend upon the way in which the plaintiff pleads his case and that the defendant is therefore entitled to put before the jury evidence of any facts which are relevant to justify the words in *any* meaning which they are capable of bearing.³ But it is submitted that the latitude given to the defendant is not unbounded and that he is not entitled to justify a meaning which is *wholly* distinct from that of which the plaintiff complains.

1   Sometimes it will be the plaintiff who wishes to contend that the words impute a general charge whereas the defendant will want to limit the case to a specific incident.
2   See *Maisel v Financial Times Ltd* (1915) 84 LJKB 2145; *Godman v Times Publishing Co Ltd* [1926] 2 KB 273.
3   In *Waters v Sunday Pictorial Newspapers Ltd* [1961] 2 All ER 758 at 762, [1961] 1 WLR 967 at 972, Willmer LJ, in declining to strike out part of the defence, said: 'It is impossible to say that the particulars of justification will be no answer to any conceivable meaning which a jury might find.' See also *Cadam v Beaverbrook Newspapers* [1959] 1 QB 413 at 425, [1959] 1 All ER 453 at 457, per Morris LJ; and *Slim v Daily Telegraph Ltd* [1968] 2 QB 157 at 175, per Diplock LJ.

11.13   Support for this view is to be found in *S and K Holdings Ltd v Throgmorton Publications Ltd*¹ and *London Computer Operators Training Ltd v BBC*² where the Court of Appeal declined to strike out paragraphs in the defences which sought to include as particulars of justification matters which were outside the scope of the narrower meaning of the words for which the plaintiff contended. In *London Computer Operators Training Ltd v BBC* Lord Denning MR referred to *Maisel v Financial Times*³ and continued.⁴

'An article in the ''Financial Times'' said that Mr Maisel had been arrested and charged with fraud. The plaintiff himself pleaded a wide innuendo charging generally that he was a dishonest person. The House held that the width of the innuendo extended the scope of the particulars of justification so as to admit evidence of all sorts of dishonesty. In this case, where an innuendo has not been pleaded, we look to see the full width of the meanings which the jury might reasonably put upon the words. The greater the conceivable width, the greater the scope of the particulars of justification.'

1   [1972] 3 All ER 497, [1972] 1 WLR 1036.
2   [1973] 2 All ER 170, [1973] 1 WLR 424.
3   (1915) 84 LJKB 2145.
4   [1973] 2 All ER 170 at 172, [1973] 1 WLR 424 at 427. See also ibid, per Lawton LJ at 174, 429.

The Rehabilitation of Offenders Act 1974

11.14 At common law a defence of justification provides a complete defence to an action for defamation. Accordingly, until recently the general rule was that a person could not complain in an action for libel or slander of the publication of an accurate account of offences committed by him in the past,[1] even though his friends and acquaintances knew nothing of these offences and his reputation was seriously damaged by the publication. By reason of the provisions of the Rehabilitation of Offenders Act 1974, s 8, however, a person who has been convicted of an offence and has become a rehabilitated person may be able to defeat a defence of justification in respect of certain publications about his past if he proves that the defendant was actuated by malice.

1 Even at common law, however, the plaintiff may have a remedy if the account imputes, for example, that the plaintiff is *still* unworthy of trust because of his past conviction. In *Sutherland v Stopes* [1925] AC 47 at 74, Lord Shaw of Dunfermline said: '. . . A statement of fact or of opinion which consists in the raking up of a long-buried past may, without an explanation (and, in cases which are conceivable, even with an explanation), be libellous or slanderous if written or uttered in such circumstances as to suggest that a taint upon character and conduct still subsists, and that the plaintiff is accordingly held up to ridicule, reprobation and contempt.'

11.15 Section 8 of the Rehabilitation of Offenders Act 1974 applies to any action for libel or slander[1] by a rehabilitated person[2] founded upon the publication of any matter imputing that the plaintiff has committed or been charged or prosecuted for or convicted of or sentenced for an offence which was the subject of a spent conviction.[3] In such an action the defendant is entitled to rely on the defence of justification,[4] but the defence will be defeated 'if the publication is proved to have been made with malice'.[5] Where, however, the words complained of impute some general charge, for example, that the plaintiff is 'a dishonest rogue', it seems clear that the provisions of section 8(5) do not apply.

1 That is, any action for libel or slander begun after 1 July 1975.
2 For the meaning of 'rehabilitated person' see Rehabilitation of Offenders Act 1974, s 1 in appendix 2, post. Certain sentences are excluded from rehabilitation: see ibid, s 5(1).
3 For the meaning of 'spent conviction' see Rehabilitation of Offenders Act 1974, s 1.
4 Rehabilitation of Offenders Act 1974, s 8(3).
5 Rehabilitation of Offenders Act 1974, s 8(5). See further in appendix 2, post. Since the decision in *Horrocks v Lowe* [1975] AC 135, [1974] 1 All ER 662, the question of malice in relation to a defence of qualified privilege usually resolves itself into a consideration whether or not the defendant honestly believed the truth of what he published: such a consideration would not be likely to arise where justification is pleaded and the actual truth of the words published has to be proved, though in an exceptional case the defendant might have discovered the facts after the publication and therefore had no belief in the truth of what he published at the time of publication.

Rumour or hearsay

11.16 It is no defence to an action for defamation for the defendant to prove that he was merely repeating what he had been told.[1] In *Rubber Improvement Ltd v Daily Telegraph Ltd*, Lord Devlin put the matter shortly as follows:[2]

'I agree, of course, that you cannot escape liability for defamation by putting the libel behind a prefix such as "I have been told that . . ." or "it is rumoured that . . .", and then asserting that it was true that you had been told or that it was in fact being rumoured. . . . For the purpose of the law of libel a hearsay statement is the same as a direct statement, and that is all there is to it.'

Nevertheless it remains true that words must always be considered in their context and accordingly words as repeated may bear a different meaning from that in which they would have been understood when originally published.[3] It is submitted that there may even be cases where the surrounding words or circumstances have the effect of removing any defamatory sting from the hearsay statement, but such cases are likely to be rare.[4]

1 See, for example, *Watkin v Hall* (1868) LR 3 QB 396.
2 [1964] AC 234 at 283, [1963] 2 All ER 151 at 173.
3 See *Wake v John Fairfax & Sons Ltd* [1973] 1 NSW LR 43 at 49, where the Court held: 'There can be little doubt that the nature and quality of the defamatory publication may vary, dependant upon whether it is a report of what another has said and whether it is adopted, repudiated or discounted. The purpose of the re-publication will also have a significant bearing.'
4 See para 4.11, ante.

Reliance on facts subsequent to the publication

11.17 If the words complained of contain a general charge, for example 'X is a thief', which would be understood in a general sense, the defendant is entitled to rely on facts which occur after the date of the publication if they tend to prove the truth of those words.[1]

1 See *Maisel v Financial Times Ltd* [1915] 3 KB 336; *Godman v Times Publishing Co Ltd* [1926] 2 KB 273; *Cohen v Daily Telegraph Ltd* [1968] 2 All ER 407 at 409, [1968] 1 WLR 916 at 919.

CHAPTER 12

Fair comment

INTRODUCTION

12.01 It is a defence to an action for defamation for the defendant to prove that the words complained of were published by him as fair comment[1] on a matter of public interest. The defence can be defeated, however, by proof that the defendant was actuated by express malice.[2] It is a defence of great importance and wide scope.

1 The word 'fair' in the phrase 'fair comment' can be a source of difficulty because it suggests a test of reasonableness, whereas the defence will often cover comment which would strike many people as very unfair. The Faulks Committee have recommended that the defence of 'fair comment' should be renamed simply 'comment': Cmnd 5909, para 152.
2 See para 17.10, post.

Main principles relating to the defence of fair comment

12.02 The main principles relating to the defence of fair comment may be stated as follows—

(a) the comment must be on a matter of public interest;
(b) the comment must be based on fact;
(c) the comment, though it can consist of or include inferences of fact, must be recognisable as comment;
(d) the comment must satisfy the following objective test:[1] could any fair-minded man honestly express that opinion on the proved facts?[2]
(e) even though the comment satisfies the objective test the defence can be defeated if the plaintiff proves that the defendant was actuated by express malice.

1 Some doubt has been cast on the correctness of this test by the decision of the Supreme Court of Canada in *Cherneskey v Armadale Publishers Ltd* (1978) 90 DLR (3d) 321. See further para 12.14, post.
2 It may be that where the comment contains an imputation of dishonourable or corrupt motives it is still necessary for the defendant to establish the reasonableness of his opinion; see further para 12.19, post, and the report of the Faulks Committee (Cmnd 5909) paras 161–9.

The comment must be on a matter of public interest

12.03 It is necessary for the defendant to prove that the matter on which he was commenting was one of public interest. The burden of proof lies on the defendant;

the decision is a question for the judge. The range of matters of public interest is very wide. In *London Artists Ltd v Littler*, Lord Denning MR spoke of the scope of public interest as follows:[1]

> 'There is no definition in the books as to what is a matter of public interest. All we are given is a list of examples, coupled with the statement that it is for the judge and not the jury. I would not myself confine it within narrow limits. Whenever a matter is such as to affect people at large, so that they may be legitimately interested in, or concerned at, what is going on, or what may happen to them or others; then it is a matter of public interest on which everyone is entitled to make fair comment.'

1 [1969] 2 QB 375 at 391, [1969] 2 All ER 193 at 198.

12.04 Matters which are submitted to the judgment of the public, such as literary or dramatic works, or which take place in public, such as public meetings or processions, or which relate to public affairs, such as the conduct of foreign policy, are plainly matters of public interest and present no difficulty. The fact that a matter directly concerns only one person or a limited number of persons does not prevent it from being a matter of public interest. For example, in *South Hetton Coal Co v North-Eastern News Association*[1] it was held that the insanitary conditions of a number of cottages owned by a colliery company was a matter of public interest. Indeed it is submitted that the decision in that case is far from being on the borderline and that in appropriate circumstances the treatment of, for example, any tenant by his landlord or any employee by his employer or any patient by his doctor is capable of satisfying the test propounded by Lord Denning of public concern or public interest.[2]

1 [1894] 1 QB 133.
2 In *London Artists Ltd v Littler* [1969] 2 QB 375 at 391, [1969] 2 All ER 193 at 198.

The comment must be based on fact

12.05 It is a necessary ingredient of fair comment that the comment shall be based on facts which are either stated by the commentator or indicated by him with sufficient clarity to enable the reader or listener to ascertain the matter on which the comment is being made. A defendant cannot defend a statement as comment, however, if he has not set out the facts on which he based the statement nor, at the least, indicated in general terms what those facts were.[1] In *Kemsley v Foot*, Lord Porter approved the following formulation of the law:[2]

> 'If the defendant accurately states what some public man has really done, and then asserts that "such conduct is disgraceful" this is merely an expression of his opinion, his comment on the plaintiff's conduct. So, if without setting it out, he identifies the conduct on which he comments by a clear reference. In either case, the defendant enables his readers to judge for themselves how far his opinion is well founded; and therefore, what would otherwise be an allegation of fact becomes merely a comment. But if he asserts that the plaintiff has been guilty of disgraceful conduct, and does not state what that conduct was, this is an allegation of fact for which there is no defence but privilege or truth.'

1 Where, however, the facts on which the comment is based are common knowledge, it seems that it may not be necessary either to state or to refer to them; see *O'Brien v Marquis of Salisbury* (1889) 54 JP 215 at 216, per Field J, cited in paras 12.11 and 12.13 (a), post.
2 [1952] AC 345 at 356, [1952] 1 All ER 501 at 505.

12.06   If the facts on which the comment is based are stated by the commentator the general rule of common law is that all those facts must be proved to be true. 'In a case where the facts are fully set out in the alleged libel, each fact must be justified[1] and if the defendant fails to justify one, even if it be comparatively unimportant, he fails in his defence'.[2]

1 That is, proved to be true. The use of the word 'justified' was unfortunate and it may lead to some confusion between justification and fair comment. It is important to emphasise that the defence of fair comment will not by itself protect defamatory statements of fact even if proved to be true; defamatory statements of fact can only be protected by a defence of justification.
2 *Kemsley v Foot* [1952] AC 345 at 357–8, [1952] All ER 501, at 506, per Lord Porter. But see Defamation Act 1952, s 6 and para 12.08, post.

COMMENT ON MATTER WHICH IS PROTECTED BY PRIVILEGE

12.07   Even at common law, however, this general rule is subject to an important qualification, namely, that if the stated facts are protected by privilege, expressions of opinion on those facts can be protected as fair comment even though the facts are not proved to be true. Thus if a newspaper accurately reports a Parliamentary speech or evidence given in court proceedings, and then comments on the speech or evidence, the defence of fair comment will be available notwithstanding the fact that matters stated in the speech or evidence cannot be proved to be true. This qualification was first introduced by Phillimore J in *Mangena v Wright*[1] where he said:

'If by some unfortunate error a vote in Parliament recites, or a judge giving the reasons of his judgment states, that which is derogatory to some person, and the charge is mistaken and ill-founded, and a newspaper reports such vote or judgment and proceeds in another part of its issue to comment on the character of the person in terms which would be fair if the charge were well founded, the newspaper which so reports and comments should be entitled to the protection of fair comment.'

This qualification has been approved by the Court of Appeal. In *Grech v Odhams Press* it was said:[2]

'If a statement made by a witness is fairly and accurately reported, and attributed to the witness who made it, then, no doubt, although the evidence given by the witness is afterwards shown to be false, the statement reported can be made the subject of fair comment.'

And in *London Artists Ltd v Littler* Edmund Davies LJ said:[3]

'. . . fair comment is available as a defence only in relation to facts which are either (a) true, or (b) if untrue were published on a privileged occasion.'

1 [1909] 2 KB 958.
2 [1958] 2 QB 275 at 285, [1958] 2 All ER 462 at 472, per Jenkins LJ, delivering the judgment of the court.
3 [1969] 2 QB 375 at 395, [1969] 2 All ER 193 at 201.

DEFAMATION ACT 1952, s 6

12.08   The general rule of common law that where the facts are stated in the words complained of each fact must be proved to be true has been considerably modified by statute. Thus the Defamation Act 1952, s 6 provides as follows:[1]

> **'Fair comment.** In an action for libel or slander in respect of words consisting partly of allegations of fact and partly of expression of opinion, a defence of fair comment shall not fail by reason only that the truth of every allegation of fact is not proved if the expression of opinion is fair comment having regard to such of the facts alleged or referred to in the words complained of as are proved.

1 If a defendant wishes to rely on this section he should refer to it in his defence: cf *Moore v News of World* [1972] 1 QB 441 at 448, [1972] All ER 915 at 919, per Lord Denning MR in relation to the somewhat similar provision for a defence of justification in the Defamation Act 1952, s 5.

WHERE THE FACTS ARE NOT STATED

12.09   Where, however, the facts are not stated by the commentator but merely indicated by him, the common law rule is less strict. The distinction was explained by Lord Porter in *Kemsley v Foot* as follows:[1]

> 'Where the facts are set out in the alleged libel, those to whom it is published can read them and may regard them as facts derogatory to the plaintiff; but where, as here, they are contained only in particulars and are not published to the world at large, they are not the subject matter of the comment but facts alleged to justify that comment. Twenty facts might be given in the particulars and only one justified, yet if that one fact were sufficient to support the comment so as to make it fair, a failure to prove the other nineteen would not of necessity defeat the defendant's plea.'

1 [1952] AC 345 at 358, [1952] 1 All ER 501 at 506. In the same case Lord Tucker said at 362, 508: '. . . where the facts relied on to justify the comment are contained only in the particulars it is not incumbent upon the defendant to prove the truth of every fact as stated in order to establish his plea of fair comment, but . . . he must establish sufficient facts to support the comment to the satisfaction of the jury.'

PRESENT RULES AS TO THE PROOF OF FACTS

12.10   It is submitted that since the enactment of the Defamation Act 1952, s 6, the present law as to the rules to be applied to the proof of facts in cases of fair comment may be summarised as follows—

(a) If the facts are stated by the commentator the question is: is the expression of opinion fair comment having regard to such of the facts stated in the words complained of as are proved?

(b) If the commentator merely indicates the conduct or matter on which he is commenting without stating the facts, the facts being set out for the first time in particulars of his defence in the action, the question is: is the expression of opinion fair comment having regard to such of the facts set out in the particulars as are proved?

(c) If the commentator sets out some of the facts in the words complained of and also indicates that there are other matters to which the comment is directed the question is: is the expression of opinion fair comment having regard both to

(i)   such of the facts stated in the words complained of as are proved, and

(ii) such of the additional facts set out in the particulars as are proved?[1]

1 There does not appear to be any direct authority on this point, but it is submitted that this is the correct test.

The comment, though it can include inferences of fact, must be recognisable as comment

12.11   The defence of fair comment is not restricted merely to such epithets as the commentator may apply to the subject matter commented upon, but can include inferences of fact drawn by the commentator. This point was made clear by Palles CB in *Lefroy v Burnside*, where he said:[1]

'It was contended during the argument that the statement of one fact cannot be excused as fair comment upon another fact. That proposition is, in my opinion, far too wide, and I cannot concur in it; but I think that when a matter of fact is to be excused as comment on another fact, the fact alleged and sought to be excused must be a reasonable[2] inference from the facts alleged and upon which it is a comment.'

And in *O'Brien v Marquis of Salisbury*, Field J said:[3]

'It seems to me . . . that comment may sometimes consist in the statement of a fact, and may be held to be comment if the fact so stated appears to be a deduction or conclusion[4] come to by the speaker from the facts stated or referred to by him, or in the common knowledge of the person speaking and those to whom the words are addressed and from which his conclusions may reasonably[2] be inferred.'

1 (1879) 4 LR Ir 556 at 566.
2 As to whether, in certain circumstances, the inference has to be reasonable or merely such as an honest man might draw, see further para 12.23, post.
3 (1889) 54 JP 215 at 216.
4 Compare *Clarke v Norton* [1910] VLR 494 at 499 where Cussen J said: '[Comment is] to be taken as meaning something which is or can reasonably be inferred to be a deduction, inference, conclusion, criticism, judgment, remark or observation'.

12.12   It may often be difficult to distinguish between assertions of fact on the one hand and statements which represent the inferences drawn by the commentator on the other hand. The distinction must be made, however, because, though fair comment may be available to protect a defamatory inference even though untrue, it cannot protect a defamatory statement of fact even though proved to be true unless justification also is relied upon.

12.13   There is no comprehensive statement in the decided cases as to how the distinction between a statement of fact and a statement which represents an inference drawn by the commentator is to be made, but the following rules afford some guidance—

(a) A bare statement of fact made without reference to any other facts on which it is based cannot be defended as comment. 'If a statement in words of a fact stands by itself naked, without reference, either expressed or understood, to other ante-cedent or surrounding circumstances notorious to the speaker and to those to whom the words are addressed, there will be little, if any, room for the inference that it was understood otherwise than as a bare statement of fact'.[1]

(b) If the commentator sets out or refers to other facts and then makes it clear that the relevant statement is his inference from those facts that statement can be defended as comment: '. . . if he sets out the facts correctly, and then gives his inference, stating[2] it is his inference from those facts, such inference will, as a general rule, be deemed a comment'.[3]

(c) Although the use of introductory words such as 'so in my opinion' or 'in other words' is not decisive, they are an indication that the succeeding words are comment rather than independent assertions of fact. In *Turner v MGM Pictures Ltd*, Lord Oaksey dealt with this point as follows:[4]

> 'It is true . . . that a statement which is plainly one of fact cannot be transformed into a statement of opinion merely by prefacing it with the words "in our judgment"; but the statement "that critic is completely out of touch . . . " and "her criticisms are on the whole unnecessarily harmful to the film industry" are in their very nature state-ments of opinion, and if there were any doubt as to their nature it would be removed by the words "in our judgment, based upon a considerable number of talks with Mrs. Arnot Robertson".' ·

On the other hand in *London Artists Ltd v Littler*[5] the Court of Appeal held that though the letter complained of contained the phrases 'it appears' and 'in other words', the letter as a whole imputed as a fact that there was a plot.

(d) It is necessary for the defendant to separate his comment from the statement of fact. In *Hunt v Star Newspaper Co Ltd* Fletcher Moulton LJ said:[6]

> 'Comment in order to be justifiable as fair comment must appear as comment and must not be so mixed up with facts that the reader cannot distinguish between what is report and what is comment. Any matter . . . which does not indicate with a reasonable clear-ness that it purports to be comment and not statement of fact, cannot be protected by the plea of fair comment.'

(e) A newspaper headline will seldom be treated as comment. There is little authority on this matter, but it is submitted that most headlines by their very nature would be more likely to be understood to be assertions of fact than infer-ences. In *Smith's Newspapers v Becker*, Evatt CJ said:[7]

> 'But so fortunate an avenue of escape via fair comment will seldom, if ever, be open to a newspaper which uses defamatory headlines or headings, without making it quite clear that a mere expression of opinion is being announced to the world, upon the basis of the facts to be stated in a sub-joined article. Streamer headlines, the intermingling of facts with actual or possible expressions of opinion and screaming posters are features of this age of industrialism, and praise or blame is no concern of ours. But the legal defence of fair comment will very rarely protect defamatory matter contained in such journalism, not because the motives of the proprietors are mercenary . . . , but because of the impossibility of achieving sensations and still effecting a clear separation of the facts from the defamatory expressions of opinion.'

---

1 *O'Brien v Marquis of Salisbury* (1889) 54 JP 215 at 216.
2 It is submitted, however, that it is not necessary for there to be an express statement to this effect.

3 Odgers on Libel and Slander (6th Edn) p 166, cited in *Kemsley v Foot* [1952] AC 345 at 357, [1952] 1 All ER 501 at 505.

4 [1950] 1 All ER 449 at 474. An illustration of the importance of introductory words is provided by *Dakhyl v Labouchere* [1908] 2 KB 325, n, where the House of Lords ordered a new trial on the ground of misdirection. Lord Atkinson said that the meaning which the defendant sought to put upon the words 'in other words, he is a quack of the rankest species' should have been left to the jury because the words were reasonably capable of meaning that he was 'a quack of the rankest species by reason of his connection with the Drouet Institute, and by reason of his having resorted to and adopted the quack methods of that notorious establishment'. This case is to be contrasted with *Smith's Newspapers v Becker* (1932) 47 CLR 279, where the words 'a German quack' were held to be a statement of fact.

5 [1969] 2 QB 375, [1969] 2 All ER 193.

6 [1908] 2 KB 309 at 319. See also *Kemsley v Foot* [1952] AC 345 at 356, [1952] 1 All ER 501 at 505; *London Artists Ltd v Littler* [1969] 2 QB 375 at 395, [1969] 2 All ER 193 at 202.

7 (1932) 47 CLR 279 at 303.

The general test of fair comment

12.14 It is submitted that as a general rule an expression of opinion will qualify as fair comment if it satisfies the following objective test: could any fair-minded[1] man honestly express that opinion on the proved facts? But even though the comment may satisfy the objective test, the defendant may still be liable if the plaintiff proves that in making the comment the defendant was actuated by express malice. Some doubt has now been cast, however, on the correctness of the objective test by the decision of the Supreme Court of Canada in *Cherneskey v Armadale Publishers Ltd*.[2] In that case the plaintiff complained of a letter published in the defendant's newspaper. The writers of the letter were not called to give evidence, and so there was no evidence to prove that the letter was an honest expression of their views. Moreover, as both the editor and another witness called on behalf of the defendants made it clear that the letter did not represent an expression of their opinion, the majority of the Supreme Court held that the trial judge was entitled to decide not to put the defence of fair comment to the jury. The matter was put as follows by Ritchie J:[3]

'The newspaper and its editor cannot sustain a defence of fair comment when it has been proved that the words used in the letter are not an honest expression of their opinion and there is no evidence as to the honest belief of the writers . . .
As honesty of belief is an essential component of the defence of fair comment, that defence involves at least some evidence that the material complained of was published in a spirit of fairness.'

In a powerful dissenting judgement Dickson J adopted an objective test and expressed concern at the effect of what he considered to be the majority view on the free expression of opinion. He said this:[4]

'It is not only the right but the duty of the press, in pursuit of its legitimate objectives, to act as a sounding board for the free flow of new and different ideas. It is one of the few means of getting the heterodox and controversial before the public. Many of the unorthodox points of view get newspaper space through letters to the Editor. It is one of the few ways in which the public gains access to the press. By these means various points of view, old and new grievances and proposed remedies get aired. The public interest is incidentally served by providing a safety valve for people. Newspapers will not be able to provide a forum for dissemination of ideas if they are limited to publishing opinion with which they agree.'

It would not appear, however, that the majority took the view that a newspaper could only publish defamatory comment if it was prepared to defend the comment as the honest opinion of the newspaper. The view of the majority was that there had to be *some* evidence that the words complained of constituted an honest expression of opinion. Nevertheless it is submitted that in England at any rate the balance of authority is in favour of the objective test stated at the beginning of this paragraph. The test formulated by Lord Esher MR in *Merivale v Carson* was as follows:[5]

> 'The question which the jury must consider is this—would any fair man, however prejudiced he may be, however exaggerated or obstinate his views, have said that which this criticism has said?'

This test would appear to be an objective one. So too was the test contemplated by Denning LJ in *Adams v Sunday Pictorial Newspapers (1920) Ltd* where he said:[6]

> 'If (the defendant) proves that the facts were true and that the comments, objectively considered, were fair, that is were fair when considered without regard to the state of mind of the writer I should not have thought that the plaintiff had much to complain about; nevertheless it has been held that the plaintiff can still succeed if he can prove that the comments, subjectively considered, were unfair because the writer was actuated by malice.'

1 It has been decided in this edition to include 'fair-minded' in the text. The criterion of the fair-minded man appears in many of the cases, see, e g the summing up of Diplock J in *Silkin v Beaverbrook Newspaper Ltd* [1958] 2 All ER 516 at 519, [1958] 1 WLR 743 at 748. It is submitted, however, that it is most important that the scope of the defence of fair comment should not be diminished and that the honest opinion of the prejudiced man should continue to be protected: see also para 12.15, note 3, ante.
2 (1978) 90 DLR (3d) 321. The law as stated by the majority has been reversed in some of the provinces by legislation.
3 (1978) 90 DLR (3d) 321 at 337–338.
4 (1978) 90 DLR (3d) 321 at 344.
5 (1887) 20 QBD 275 at 280.
6 [1951] 1 KB 354, [1951] 1 All ER 865. See also *Broadway Approvals v Odhams Press Ltd* [1965] 2 All ER 523, [1965] 1 WLR 805 at 535, 817, per Sellers LJ, and 539, 823, per Davies LJ, cited in para 12.27, post.

12.15   The limits of the right of comment are very wide as appears clearly from the summing up of Lord Hewart CJ in *Stopes v Sutherland*, where he said:[1]

> 'What is it that fair comment means? It means this—and I prefer to put it in words which are not my own; I refer to the famous judgment of Lord Esher MR in *Merivale v Carson*[2] "Every latitude", said Lord Esher, "must be given to opinion and to prejudice, and then an ordinary set of men with ordinary judgment must say (not whether they agree with it, but) whether any fair man would have made such a comment. Mere exaggeration, or even gross exaggeration, would not make the comment unfair. However wrong the opinion expressed may be in point of truth, or however prejudiced the writer, it may still be within the prescribed limits. The question which the jury must consider is this—would any fair[3] man, however prejudiced he may be, however exaggerated or obstinate his views, have said that which this criticism has said?" Again as Bray J said in *R v Russell*:[4] "When you come to a question of fair comment you ought to be extremely liberal, and in a matter of this kind—relating to the administration of the licensing laws—you ought to be extremely liberal because it is a matter on which men's minds are moved, in which people who do know, entertain very very strong opinions, and if they use strong language every allowance should be made in their favour. They must believe what they say, but the question whether they honestly believe it is a question for you to say. If they do believe it, and they are within anything like reasonable bounds, they come within the meaning of fair comment. If comments were made which would appear to you to have been exaggerated, it does not follow that they are not perfectly honest comments." That is the kind of maxim which

you may apply in considering whether that part of this matter which is comment is fair. Could a fair-minded man, holding a strong view, holding perhaps an obstinate view, have been capable of writing this?—which, you observe, is a totally different question from the question, do you agree with what he has said.'

1 See House of Lords, Printed Cases, 1924, p 375.
2 (1887) 20 QBD 275 at 280.
3 In *Turner v MGM Pictures Ltd* [1950] 1 All ER 449 Lord Porter said at 461: 'I should adopt (Lord Esher's) words except that I would substitute "honest" for "fair" lest some suggestion of reasonableness instead of honesty should be read in.'
4 Unreported, 2nd December 1905. The summing up of Bray J was cited by Diplock J in his summing up in *Silkin v Beaverbrook Newspapers Ltd* [1958] 2 All ER 516, [1958] 1 WLR 743.

12.16   Reference can also be made to the summing up of Diplock J in *Silkin v Beaverbrook Newspapers Ltd*.[1] In that case the plaintiff complained of a newspaper article which, he contended, meant that 'he was an insincere and hypocritical person who is prepared to sacrifice his principles for selfish reasons and personal profit and that he was unfit to participate in the debates in the House of Lords'.[2] The judge read to the jury the facts relied upon by the defendants, which it was conceded were true, and continued:[3]

'Those are the facts on which the defendants say they were commenting in the article, and those are the facts which you will bear in mind when you are asking yourselves the question in the terms in which I put it to you: not whether you agree with the comment made on those facts, but whether you think it is a comment which any man, be he prejudiced or obstinate, could honestly hold. . . .
So in considering this case, members of the jury, do not apply the test of whether you agree with it. If juries did that, freedom of speech, the right of the crank to say what he likes, would go. Would a fair-minded man holding strong views, obstinate views, prejudiced views, have been capable of making this comment? If the answer to that is yes, then your verdict in this case should be a verdict for the defendants. Such a verdict does not mean that you agree with the comment. All it means is that you think that a man might honestly hold those views on those facts.'

1 [1958] 2 All ER 516, [1958] 1 WLR 743. This is a valuable modern authority. It is to be noted, however, that no reply had been served and that therefore no issue of malice was before the jury. It is submitted therefore that the earlier part of the summing up dealing with the honesty of the writer (at 518, 747) was obiter.
2 See [1958] 2 All ER 516 at 516, [1958] 1 WLR 743 at 744.
3 [1958] 2 All ER 516 at 519–520, [1958] 1 WLR 743 at 748–9.

CRITICISMS OF ARTISTIC WORKS

12.17   In its application to criticisms of artistic (including literary) works the defence of fair comment gives very wide latitude to the commentator. Indeed, subject to any question of express malice, almost any comment is defensible as fair comment provided—

(a) the contents of the works criticised are not misrepresented; and
(b) no personal attack is made on the plaintiff.

12.18   The following statements of the law illustrate the scope of the defence in the context of artistic criticism—

(a) 'We really must not cramp observations on authors and their works. They should be liable to criticism, to exposure, and even to ridicule if their compositions be ridiculous. . . . Every man who publishes a book commits himself to the judgment of the public, and anyone may comment on his performance. If the commentator does not step aside from the works or introduce fiction for the purpose of condemnation, he exercises a fair and legitimate right.'[1]

(b) 'In the case of literary criticism it is not easy to conceive what would be outside that region,[2] unless the writer went out of his way to make a personal attack on the character of the author of the work which he was criticising. In such a case the writer would be going beyond the limits of criticism altogether and therefore beyond the limits of fair criticism.[3] *Campbell v Spottiswoode*[4] was a case of that kind, and there the jury were asked whether the criticism was fair, and they were told that, if it attacked the private character of the author, it would be going beyond the limits of fair criticism. Still there is another class of cases which, as it seems to me, the writer would be travelling out of the region of fair criticism—I mean if he imputes to the author that he has written something that in fact he has not written. That would be a mis-description of the works. There is all the difference in the world between saying that you disapprove of the character of a work, and that you think it has an evil tendency, and saying that a work treats adultery cavalierly, when in fact there is no adultery at all in the story. A jury would have the right to consider the latter beyond the limits of fair criticism.'[5]

(c) 'A critic is entitled to dip his pen in gall for the purpose of legitimate criticism; and no-one need be mealy-mouthed in denouncing what he regards as twaddle, daub or discord. English literature would be the poorer if Macaulay had not been stirred to wrath by the verses of Mr Robert Montgomery.'[6]

(d) 'In the case of criticism in matters of art, whether music, painting, literature or drama, where the private character of the person criticised is not involved, the freer criticism is the better it will be for the aesthetic welfare of the public.'[7]

(e) 'When we move in a sphere of taste, opinion, aesthetic sense or whatever we may choose to call it, we may have our pleasances, our likes and our dislikes, but, in the very nature of things the free expression of them, untainted by mis-statements of facts, can seldom be defamatory.'[8]

1 See *Carr v Hood* (1808) 1 Camp 355, n 357 per Lord Ellenborough.
2 That is, outside the limits of fair comment.
3 It is plain that the criticism need not be confined to questions of style. In *Kemsley v Foot* [1952] AC 345 at 356, [1952] 1 All ER 501 at 505, Lord Porter said: '. . . A literary work can be criticised for its treatment of life and morals as freely as it can be for bad writing, eg it can be criticised as having an immoral tendency. The fairness of the criticism does not depend upon the fact that it is confined to form or literary content.'
4 (1863) 32 LJ QB 185.
5 *Merivale v Carson* (1887) 20 QB 275 at 284 per Bowen LJ. This passage was cited by Collins MR in *McQuire v Western Morning News* [1903] 2 KB 100 at 110. The action by Mr Merivale was brought in respect of a newspaper review of a play written by the plaintiff and his wife. The action succeeded (though the jury awarded only one shilling damages) on the basis that the review imputed that the play dealt with adultery whereas in fact there was no mention of adultery at all.
6 *Gardiner v J Fairfax & Sons Pty Ltd* (1942) 42 SR (NSW) 171 at 174 per Jordan CJ.
7 *Lyon and Lyon v Daily Telegraph Ltd* [1943] 1 KB 746 at 752, [1943] 2 All ER 316 at 319 per Scott LJ.
8 *Turner v MGM Pictures Ltd* [1950] 1 All ER 449 at 464 per Lord Greene. It is submitted that by 'can seldom be defamatory' Lord Greene meant 'can seldom exceed the limits of fair comment'.

COMMENTS WHICH IMPUTE DISHONESTY OR OTHER DISHONOURABLE CONDUCT OR MOTIVES

12.19   Where the comment contains imputations to the effect that the plaintiff has acted dishonestly or dishonourably or has been inspired by some base motive, the law as to the correct test for determining whether the comment is fair is uncertain. There appear to be three possible views—

(a) The defence of fair comment does not apply at all to suggestions, even though in the form of comment, that the plaintiff has acted dishonestly or dishonourably or been prompted by some base motive. Such suggestions must be defended, if at all, by showing that they are correct inferences from the primary facts, that is, by a defence of justification.

(b) The defence of fair comment can apply to such suggestions but the defendant has to satisfy the jury that the comment was a reasonable inference from the facts commented on.

(c) The general test of fair comment applies and the question is: could any fair-minded man honestly express that opinion on the proved facts?

12.20 The strict view that suggestions of dishonesty or other dishonourable conduct or base motives can never be defended as fair comment appears to be based in the first place on the decision in *Campbell v Spottiswoode*.[1] In that case it was held that the newspaper article complained of imputed to the plaintiff that in putting forward a scheme for missions to the heathen he was in fact acting solely for the purpose of his own financial advantage and that he had made use of various subterfuges in order to obtain money from the public. Cockburn CJ drew the following distinction:[2]

'But it seems to me that a line must be drawn between hostile criticism on a man's public conduct and the motives by which that conduct may be supposed to be influenced: and that you have no right to impute to a man in his conduct as a citizen—even though it be open to ridicule or disapprobation—base, sordid, dishonest, and wicked motives, unless there is so much ground for the implication that a jury should be of the opinion not only that you may have honestly entertained some mistaken belief upon the subject but that your belief is well founded and not without cause.'[3]

Crompton J said that he agreed with Cockburn CJ and added:[4]

'If [a critic] imputes to the person he is criticising base and sordid motives which are not warranted by the facts, I cannot think for a moment that because he bona fide believes that he is publishing what is true, that is any defence in point of law. I have always in my experience heard it laid down that, although you may attack a public person for anything he has done publicly the moment you go beyond that, and impute wickedness to him, then you come within the rule with regard to all those who publish a libel, which is, that you must prove that the implications are true.'

---

1 (1863) 32 LJ QB 185.
2 (1863) 32 LJ QB 185 at 199.
3 The words 'not without cause' appear to weaken the preceding words.
4 (1863) 32 LJ QB 185 at 200–1.

12.21 Further support for the strict view is provided by the judgment of Fletcher-Moulton LJ in *Hunt v Star Newspaper Co Ltd*, where he said:[1]

'. . . Comment must not convey imputations of an evil sort except so far as the facts truly stated warrant the imputation. This is the language of Kennedy J in the case to which I have just referred.[2] It is based on the judgment in *Campbell v Spottiswoode*,[3] a case of the highest authority, and is, in my opinion, unquestionably a true statement of the law. The only portion of the statement which requires examination is the phrase ''except so far as the facts truly stated warrant the imputation''. Speaking for myself the words ''warrant the imputation'' can bear but one meaning, and that meaning is stated so plainly by Lord Atkinson in the opinion delivered by him in the case of *Dakhyl v Labouchere*[4] in the House of Lords than I cannot do better than quote his language:[5] ''Whether the personal attack in any given case can reasonably be inferred from the truly stated facts upon which it purports to be a comment is a matter of law for the determination of the judge before whom the case is tried, but if he should rule that this inference is capable of being reasonably drawn, it is for the jury to determine whether in that particular case it ought to be drawn.'' In other words a libellous imputation is not warranted by the facts unless the jury holds that it is a conclusion which ought to be drawn from those facts. Any other interpretation would amount to saying that, where facts were only sufficient to raise a suspicion of a criminal or disgraceful motive, a writer might allege such motive as a fact and protect himself under the plea of fair comment. No such latitude is allowed by English law. To allege a criminal intention or a disreputable motive as actuating an individual is to make an allegation of fact which must be supported by adequate evidence. I agree that an allegation of fact may be justified by its being an inference from other facts truly stated, but, as Lord Atkinson said in the passage just quoted, in order to warrant it the jury must be satisfied that such inference ought to be drawn from those facts.'

1 [1908] 2 KB 309 at 320.
2 *Joynt v Cycle Trade Publishing Co* [1904] 2 KB 292. A short passage from the summing up of Kennedy J is set out at 294: '. . . the comment must be such that a fair mind would use under the circumstances, and it must not mis-state facts, because a comment cannot be fair which is built upon facts which are not truly stated, and further, it does not convey imputations of an evil sort, except so far as the facts truly stated warrant the imputation'.
3 (1863) 32 LJQB 185.
4 [1908] 2 KB 325n.
5 [1908] 2 KB 325n at 329.

12.22 Furthermore, in *Homing Pigeon Publishing Co Ltd v Racing Pigeon Publishing Co Ltd* Scrutton J considered that he was obliged to take the strict view. He said that he 'would have much preferred to take the view that the phrase ''warrant the imputation'' meant ''were capable in reason of supporting the implication'' not that ''the conclusion ought to be drawn from the facts'' ',[1] but nevertheless decided that he was bound by what he regarded as the clear language of the Court of Appeal in *Hunt v Star Newspaper Co Ltd*.[2]

1 (1913) 29 TLR 389 at 390–1.
2 [1908] 2 KB 309.'See also *Greville v Wiseman* [1967] NZLR 795 at 800.

THE VIEW THAT THE EXPRESSION OF OPINION SHOULD BE REASONABLE

12.23 There is strong support for the view that in a case involving an imputation of dishonesty or of dishonourable conduct or motive the defendant has to prove that the imputation, though not necessarily the correct inference, was a *reasonable* inference from the proved facts. In *Dakhyl v Labouchere* Lord Atkinson used these words:[1]

'A personal attack may form part of a fair comment upon given facts truly stated if it be warranted by those facts—In other words, in my view, if it be a reasonable inference from those facts.'

And in *Hunt v Star Newspaper Co Ltd* Cozens-Hardy MR said:[2]

'But there still remains the question whether, if, and only if, the facts are substantially true, the comment made by the defendant, based upon those true facts, was fair and such as might, in the opinion of the jury, be reasonably made.'

1 [1908] 2 KB 325, n. This sentence occurred immediately before the passage cited by Fletcher-Moulton LJ in *Hunt v Star Newspaper Co Ltd* [1908] 2 KB 309 at 320, and it is submitted that Fletcher-Moulton LJ over-stated the effect of Lord Atkinson's speech.
2 [1908] 2 KB 309 at 317. It seems clear that both Buckley LJ in *Hunt v Star Newspaper Co Ltd* [1908] 2 KB 309 at 324, and Lord Loreburn LC (with whom Lord Robertson concurred) in *Dakhyl v Labouchere* [1908] 2 KB 325n at 327, took the view that the defence of fair comment *could* be available in a case where there was an imputation which charged the plaintiff with improper conduct. A recent authority adopting the test of a reasonable inference is the decision of Neasey J in *Porter v Mercury Newspaper* [1964] Tas SR 279 at 292 where he said: 'Whether a comment is fair depends on whether the inference is the honest expression of the opinion which the defendant held on the facts truly stated, and warranted by the facts in the sense that a fair-minded man might reasonably draw from them that inference.'

12.24 The judgment most frequently cited to support the view that the defendant must satisfy the jury as to the reasonableness of his opinion is that of Buckley LJ in *Peter Walker & Son Ltd v Hodgson* where he said:[1]

'The defendant may nevertheless succeed upon his defence of fair comment if he shows that that imputation of political bias, although defamatory, and although not proved to have been founded in truth, yet was an imputation in a matter of public interest, made fairly and bona fide and as the honest expression of the opinion which the defendant held upon the facts truly stated, and was in the opinion of the jury warranted by the facts, in the sense that a fair-minded man might upon those facts bona fide hold that opinion.'

1 [1909] 1 KB 239 at 253. See Gatley on Libel and Slander (8th Edn) para 724; report of the Faulks Committee (Cmnd 5909) para 164. It is, however, doubtful whether this passage does in fact suggest any requirement of reasonableness, as district from fair-mindedness.

12.25 It is submitted, however, that a test based on reasonableness runs counter to the whole concept of the defence of fair comment. Furthermore, it is difficult in practice to draw an accurate dividing line between cases which involve an imputation of dishonourable conduct and those which do not.

THE APPLICATION OF THE GENERAL TEST EVEN WHERE THERE ARE
IMPUTATIONS OF DISHONOURABLE CONDUCT

12.26 It is submitted that the better view is that an imputation of dishonesty or of dishonourable conduct or motives *can* be defended as fair comment provided the imputation is put forward as an expression of opinion. It seems clear that Lord Loreburn LC in *Dakhyl v Labouchere*[1] considered that such imputations were capable of being defended as fair comment. Moreover it is to be noted that in some modern cases the general test seems to have been applied without apparent hesitation. Thus, for example, in *Silkin v Beaverbrook Newspapers Ltd*[2] the plaintiff alleged that the words meant (inter alia) that 'he was an insincere and hypocritical person who was prepared to sacrifice his principles for selfish reasons of personal profit'.[3] The court was referred to several cases including *Campbell v Spottiswoode*[4] and *Hunt v Star Newspaper Co Ltd*[5] but the judge did not direct the jury that there was any burden on the defendant to prove the accuracy or reasonableness of his comment, though the plaintiff's case necessarily involved the suggestion that the words included a dishonourable motive.

1 [1908] 2 KB 325n at 329.
2 [1958] 2 All ER 516, [1958] 1 WLR 743.
3 See [1958] 2 All ER 516 at 516, [1958] 1 WLR 743 at 744.
4 (1863) 3 B & S 769.
5 [1908] 2 KB 309.

12.27 A more recent illustration is the decision in *Broadway Approvals Ltd v Odhams Press Ltd*.[1] In that case the plaintiff company alleged that the words meant that the company was 'guilty of discreditable and improper business conduct in their dealings with children'.[2] In the Court of Appeal, Sellers LJ put the matter as follows:[3]

'The comments, as well as the facts and the inferences from both fact and comment, in defamatory statements have to be proved to be true for the defence of justification to succeed but if the facts are established and the comment is fair the defence of fair comment can succeed. An honest fair expression of opinion on a matter of public interest is not actionable even though it be untrue and fail at justification. It may be said in the appropriate circumstances that a man's conduct is discreditable and it may be a fair comment to make although a jury is not prepared to find that the substance of the comment was true.'

And in the same case Davies LJ referred to the rejection by the jury of the defence of justification and continued:[4]

'But this finding is, to my mind, not in the least inconsistent with a finding that a fair minded person having the relevant facts before him might well take the view that the plaintiffs' methods were undesirable and open to strong criticism. . . . There seems to be no possible justification for the contention that the finding that the defamatory meaning ascribed by the plaintiffs to the article was not in fact justified was inconsistent with the view that the criticism voiced by the defendants could fairly be made.'

1 [1965] 2 All ER 523, [1965] 1 WLR 805.
2 See [1965] 2 All ER 523 at 531, [1965] 1 WLR 805 at 808–9.
3 [1965] 2 All ER 523 at 535, [1965] 1 WLR 805 at 817.
4 [1965] 2 All ER 523 at 539, [1965] 1 WLR 805 at 823.

12.28 It is also to be noted that in *Kemsley v Foot* Lord Porter made detailed reference to the judgment of Fletcher Moulton LJ in *Hunt v Star Newspaper Co Ltd*,[1] and seems to have taken the view that the test of honesty was a criterion of general application. Thus he said:[2]

'The facts truly stated might warrant an imputation by an honest man that the plaintiff's conduct was improper and, accordingly, the Court of Appeal sent back the case for a new trial in order that it might be ascertained (1) whether the facts stated were true, and (2) if the comment was such as an honest man might make on those facts. It was in those circumstances that Fletcher Moulton LJ gave his judgment. He was seeking to distinguish facts from comment and in effect saying that the facts alleged must be such as to warrant an honest man making the comment complained of. He had not to consider whether the facts must be set out in full or whether reference to well known or easily ascertainable facts was a sufficient statement of those relied on. In that case the facts were all set out and the only question which the court had to consider was whether, on facts assumed to be truly stated, the comment was honestly made. As the jury had been wrongly directed on this matter, the case was sent back in order that it might be ascertained whether the facts were true and, if true, whether the comment was an honest comment on facts truly stated.'

1 [1908] 2 KB 309.
2 [1952] AC 345 at 360, [1952] 1 All ER 501 at 507.

12.29   Some further guidance on this difficult point is provided by the decision of the High Court of Australia in *O'Shaughnessy v Mirror Newspapers Ltd* where, in ordering a new trial on the ground that the judge had wrongly withdrawn the issue of fact or comment from the jury, the court said:[1]

'It appears to us that the passages we have quoted could fairly have been regarded by the jury as going beyond criticism of the production and attributing a dishonourable motive to the plaintiff as a statement of fact. This is one of those cases where the critic, in making her evaluation that the production was a disaster—which, of course, she was entitled to do—did not plainly confine herself to commenting upon facts truly stated; she wrote what could, we think, have been regarded as amounting to a defamatory statement of fact, viz. that the producer dishonestly suppressed the role of other players to highlight his own role. It is not that the writer merely failed to preface what she had to say about the production with some formula such as "it seems to me"; it is rather that the jury could have found that an imputation of dishonesty was levelled against the plaintiff as the writer's explanation of what she asserted to be a waste of talent. If what was written had been no more than comment it only had to be fair, but, if it were fact, it had to be correct to defeat the plaintiff's claim. It was, we think, for the jury to decide whether there were any statements of defamatory facts and, because the issue was withdrawn from them we consider that the trial miscarried. To safeguard ourselves from too broad a generalisation we would add that it is not our view that an imputation of dishonesty is always an assertion of fact. It is part of the freedom allowed by the common law to those who comment on matters of public interest that facts truly stated can be used as the basis of an imputation of corruption or dishonesty on the part of the person involved.'

1 (1970) 45 ALJR 59 at 60.

12.30   It is submitted that the right view is that where an imputation of dis-honesty or of dishonourable conduct or motive is made such an imputation is *capable* of being defended as a fair comment and that the general test[1] should be applied. Nevertheless, in such a case it is particularly important to consider, and at the trial for the jury to be directed to consider (a) whether the imputation would be understood as a mere expression of opinion, and (b) whether, applying the objective test any fair-minded man could honestly express that opinion on the proved facts.

Furthermore, if the facts have been stated by the defendant and not merely indicated by him it is likely in the nature of things that these facts will be defamatory and accordingly defensible, if at all, by a defence of justification. It seems that the real foundation for the view that an imputation of dishonourable conduct or base motive can only be defended if they are justified is that such implications are to be regarded in all circumstances as assertions of fact. Once, however, it is conceded that such imputations *can* be comment, there seems to be no good reason for introducing a special test different from that applying to fair comment generally.

1 See para 12.14, ante.

THE MEANINGS TO WHICH THE TEST IS TO BE APPLIED

12.31   In considering whether (according to the objective test) the words used are fair comment, the test has to be applied to the meanings in which the words would be understood and not to the meaning intended by the defendant. This point emerges clearly from the judgment of Lord Esher MR in *Merivale v Carson*, where he said:[1]

'The question which the jury must consider is this—would any fair man, however prejudiced he may be, however exaggerated and obstinate his views, have said that which this criticism has said of the work that is criticised? I cannot doubt that the jury were justified in coming to the conclusion to which they did come, when once they had made up their minds as to the meaning of the words used in the article, viz. that the plaintiff had written an obscene play, and no fair man could have said that.'

1 (1887) 20 QBD 275 at 281.

12.32   It is submitted therefore that Lord Denning MR adopted the wrong approach in *Slim v Daily Telegraph Ltd* when he said:[1]

'These comments are capable of various meanings. They may strike some readers in one way and others in another way. One person may read into them implications of dishonesty, insincerity, and hypocrisy (as the judge did). Another person may only read into them implications of inconsistency and want of candour (as I would). But in considering a plea of fair comment it is not correct to canvass all the various implications which different readers may put upon the words. The important thing is to determine whether or not the writer was actuated by malice. If he was an honest man expressing his genuine opinion on a subject of public interest, then no matter that his words conveyed derogatory imputations; no matter that his opinion was wrong or exaggerated or prejudiced; and no matter it was there so expressed so that other people read all sorts of innuendo into it; nevertheless he has a good defence of fair comment. His honesty is the cardinal test.'

It is submitted that in every case, including a case where the defence of fair comment is raised, the jury has to decide as to the meaning of the words and then (where appropriate) apply the objective test of fair comment to that meaning. The meaning intended by the commentator may of course become relevant at the next stage, if and when the jury have to consider in relation to a defence of fair comment the issue of malice.

1 [1968] 2 QB 157 at 170, [1968] 1 All ER 497 at 503.

RELIANCE ON EVENTS SUBSEQUENT TO PUBLICATION

12.33   As the defence of fair comment is intended to apply to bona fide expressions of opinion, the defendant cannot rely on facts or events which take place after the date of publication. In *Cohen v Daily Telegraph Ltd* Lord Denning MR said:[1]

'In order to make good a plea of fair comment, it must be a comment on fact *existing* at the time. No man can comment on facts which may happen in the future.'

1 [1968] 2 All ER 407 at 409, [1968] 1 WLR 916 at 919. Where a defence of justification is relied on, however, a defendant is entitled to rely on subsequent facts which go to prove the truth of the words complained of.

WHETHER THE COMMENTATOR HAS TO KNOW THE FACTS

12.34   It is less clear whether the defendant is entitled to rely on facts which, though already in existence, are unknown to him. In a Scottish case, *Wheatley v Anderson*, Lord Anderson said:[1]

'The jury are entitled to know what was in a defender's mind at the time he made the comment, otherwise they will not be properly equipped for the discharge of their duty. It seems to me, however, to be quite incompetent for a defender, in support of a plea of fair comment, to aver and substantiate facts which were not in his mind at the time a comment was made, but which were discovered at a later date.'

In *Cohen v Daily Telegraph Ltd* both Lord Denning MR and Davies LJ expressed some doubt about Lord Anderson's statement of the law. It is submitted that, though logically there are strong arguments to the contrary, the better view is to allow the defendant to rely on any facts or matters existing at the time when he made his comment, provided it is clear that the defendant is genuinely exercising a right to comment.

In *Cohen v Daily Telegraph Ltd* Lord Denning MR said:[2]

'A man may comment on existing facts without having them all in the forefront of his mind at the time.'

It is submitted that it would unduly restrict the right of fair comment to place upon a defendant the burden of proving that he had at one time known each of the facts upon which he places reliance in his defence. Furthermore, the existence of such a rule would lead to difficult distinctions between the position of the original commentator and those, such as editors of newspapers and printers, who took a merely subsidiary role in the publication of the comment.

1 1927 SC 133 at 147.
2 [1968] 2 All ER 407 at 409, [1968] 1 WLR 916 at 920.

Malice

12.35 Even though the comment satisfies the objective test of fair comment, the defence of fair comment will nevertheless fail if it is found that in making the comment the defendant was actuated by express malice.[1] In *Thomas v Bradbury, Agnew & Co Ltd*, Collins MR explained this principle as follows:[2]

> 'The right [of fair comment], though shared by the public, is the right of every individual who asserts it, and is, qua him, an individual right whatever name it be called by, and comment by him which is coloured by malice cannot from his standpoint be deemed fair. He, and he only, is the person in whose motives the plaintiff in the libel action is concerned, and if he, the person sued, is proved to have allowed his view to be distorted by malice, it is quite immaterial that somebody else might without malice have written an equally damnatory criticism.'

1 See para 17.10, post.
2 [1906] 2 KB 627 at 638.

12.36 In *Adams v Sunday Pictorial Newspapers (1920) Ltd*, however, Denning LJ expressed some doubt:[1]

> 'The truth is that the burden on the defendant who pleads fair comment is already heavy enough. If he proves that the facts are true and that the comments, objectively considered, were fair, that is, if they were fair when considered without regard to the state of mind of the writer, I should not have thought that the plaintiff had much to complain about; nevertheless it has been held that the plaintiff can still succeed if he can prove that the comments, subjectively considered, were unfair because the writer was actuated by malice.'

And in *Broadway Approvals Ltd v Odhams Press Ltd*,[2] counsel for the defendants said that he wished to reserve for the decision of the House of Lords the question whether malice did in fact defeat an otherwise valid defence of fair comment. But it is submitted that the principle is now plainly established. Furthermore, it seems clear that in *Turner v MGM Pictures Ltd*[3] the House of Lords dealt with the issue of fair comment on the basis that malice was capable of destroying the defence.[4]

1 [1951] 1 KB 354 at 359–60, [1951] 1 All ER 865 at 868.
2 [1965] 2 All ER 523 at 534, [1965] 1 WLR 805 at 816. At 538, 822 Davies LJ described the submission that a defence of fair comment is not defeasible by express malice as 'a very remarkable one.'
3 [1950] 1 All ER 449. The issue of fair comment arose in relation to the telephone conversation which it was conceded was not covered by qualified privilege.
4 [1950] 1 All ER 449 at 461–2 per Lord Porter, at 470 per Lord Greene, and at 472 per Lord Oaksey.

CHAPTER 13

Absolute privilege

INTRODUCTION

13.01 The law recognises that in some circumstances the public interest requires that a person should be protected from liability for a defamatory statement even though the words cannot be proved to be true or defended as fair comment. This protection, or 'privilege' as it is called, is of two kinds—absolute and qualified. Absolute privilege is very limited in its scope but where applicable provides the defendant with complete protection. Qualified privilege on the other hand covers a great many situations, but it is a defeasible defence and will be of no avail if the plaintiff pleads and proves that the defendant in making the publication complained of was actuated by express malice.

13.02 The defence of absolute privilege applies to statements in the following categories—

(a) statements made in the course of Parliamentary proceedings;
(b) statements protected by the Parliamentary Papers Act 1840;
(c) statements made in the course of judicial or quasi-judicial proceedings;
(d) statements made by one officer of State to another in the course of duty;
(e) statements protected by the Parliamentary Commissioner Act 1967;
(f) statements made in reports by the Monopolies Commission and the Director General of Fair Trading under the Competition Act 1980.

It is probable that the defence of absolute privilege applies also to—

(g) fair and accurate reports of judicial proceedings in the United Kingdom if published contemporaneously;[1]
(h) communications between solicitor (and presumably counsel) and client.

1 See para 14.29, post.

Statements made in the course of parliamentary proceedings

13.03 No action for defamation can be brought in respect of anything said in the course of a debate in either House of Parliament.[1] It is convenient to describe statements made in such circumstances as protected by absolute privilege, but strictly speaking the protection from an action for defamation is merely part of a wider privilege[2] enshrined in article 9 of the Bill of Rights 1688, which provides:

'That the freedom of speech and debates or proceedings in Parliament ought not to be impeached or questioned in any court or place out of Parliament.'

1 In *ex p Wason* (1869) LR 4 QB 573 at 576, Cockburn CJ said: 'It is clear that statements made by members of either House of Parliament in their places in the House, though they might be untrue to their knowledge, could not be made the foundation of civil or criminal proceedings, however injurious they might be to the interest of a third person. And a conspiracy to make such statements would not make the persons guilty of it amenable to the criminal law.'
2 A plaintiff is therefore unable to rely on a speech made in Parliament as evidence of malice: *Church of Scientology of California v Johnson-Smith* [1972] 1 QB 522, [1972] 1 All ER 378.

EXTENT OF THE PRIVILEGE

13.04   The privilege extends to protect not only the proceedings in the House of Commons and House of Lords but also the proceedings in committees of either House. Moreover the protection covers not only Members themselves but also officers of either House and witnesses before committees.[1] On the other hand the privilege does not cover anything said by a Member outside Parliament,[2] though in an appropriate case such a statement may be protected by absolute[3] or qualified[4] privilege under some other head. Furthermore, though a petition to Parliament is protected by absolute privilege,[5] it seems that a letter by a member of the public to a Member of Parliament is not, even though the individual concerned may want his grievance considered by a Select Committee.[6]

1 *Goffin v Donnelly* (1881) 6 QBD 307.
2 *R v Lord Abingdon* (1794) 1 Esp 226; *R v Creevy* (1813) 1 M & S 273.
3 As to communications between Ministers of Crown, see para 13.28, post.
4 In *Beach v Freeson* [1972] 1 QB 14, [1971] 2 All ER 854, for example, it was held that a Member of Parliament was protected by qualified privilege in respect of letters to the Lord Chancellor and the Law Society communicating a constituent's complaints about the plaintiff (a solicitor). It is arguable that a letter from a Member to a Minister which is relevant to the performance by the Member of his Parliamentary duties is a proceeding in Parliament and therefore protected by absolute privilege. In *Re Parliamentary Privilege Act 1770* [1958] AC 331, [1958] 2 All ER 329, the Privy Council declined to express any opinion on the question whether a letter from a Member to the Paymaster General about the conduct of the London Electricity Board was or was not a proceeding in Parliament. It is submitted that such a communication is not a proceeding in Parliament and is protected by qualified privilege only.
5 *Lake v King* (1670) 1 Saund 131.
6 See *Rivlin v Bilainkin* [1953] 1 QB 485, [1953] 1 All ER 534.

Statements protected by the Parliamentary Papers Act 1840

13.05   All reports, papers, votes and proceedings published by order of either House of Parliament, and every verified copy, are absolutely privileged, and all proceedings will be immediately stayed on production of a certificate that such reports, etc, are published by order or under the authority of either House.[1] In *Stockdale v Hansard*[2] it was held that no privilege attached at common law to a report by the Inspectors of Prisons, even though the publication of the report had been made by order of the House of Commons. The Parliamentary Papers Act 1840 was passed as a result of this decision. A report or other document is made a

Parliamentary Paper by means of the special procedure of the motion for an unopposed return.[3]

1 Parliamentary Papers Act 1840, ss 1 and 2.
2 (1839) 9 A & E 1 at 243.
3 This special procedure cannot be used, however, while Parliament is not sitting: see Report of the Faulks Committee (Cmnd 5909) para 224.

Statements made in the course of judicial and quasi-judicial proceedings

13.06 The general rule was stated in *Royal Aquarium and Summer and Winter Garden Society v Parkinson* by Lopes LJ as follows:[1]

'The authorities establish beyond all question this: . . . that no action of libel or slander lies, whether against judges, counsel, witnesses, or parties, for words written or spoken in the course of any proceeding before any Court recognised by law, and this though the words written or spoken were written or spoken maliciously, without any justification or excuse, and from personal ill-will and anger against the person defamed.'

1 [1892] 1 QB 431 at 451.

THE REASON FOR THE GENERAL RULE

13.07 The basis of the rule is public policy, and the reason for it was explained by Fry LJ in *Munster v Lamb* in these words:[1]

'The rule of law exists, not because the conduct of those persons ought not of itself to be actionable, but because if their conduct was actionable, actions would be brought against judges and witnesses in cases in which they had not spoken with malice, in which they had not spoken with falsehood. It is not a desire to prevent actions being brought in cases where they ought to be maintained that has led to the adoption of the present rule of law; but it is the fear that if the rule were otherwise, numerous actions would be brought against persons who were merely discharging their duty. It must always be borne in mind that it is not intended to protect malicious and untruthful persons, but that it is intended to protect persons acting bona fide, who under a different rule would be liable, not perhaps to verdicts and judgments against them, but to the vexation of defending actions.'

And in *Rondel v Worsley* Lord Pearce said:[2]

'Thus, the reasons underlying the immunity of witnesses are; first, that there would otherwise be a series of retrials and, secondly, that an honest witness might be deflected by fear of the consequences.'

1 (1883) 11 QBD 588 at 607. This passage was cited by Sellers LJ in *Marrinan v Vibart* [1963] 1 QB 528 at 535, [1962] 3 All ER 380 at 382, and by Lord Reid in *Rondel v Worsley* [1969] 1 AC 191 at 229, [1967] 3 All ER 993 at 999. In *Addis v Crocker* [1961] 1 QB 11 at 28, [1960] 2 All ER 629 at 638, Pearce LJ said: 'It is clear . . . that absolute privilege is given to proceedings in courts of law in order that the judges, advocates and witnesses may perform their respective parts free from a deterrent fear of actions for defamation.'
2 [1969] 1 AC 191 at 269, [1967] 3 All ER 993 at 1025. See also *Roy v Prior* [1971] AC 470 at 480, [1970] 2 All ER 729 at 736, per Lord Wilberforce.

13.08   Absolute privilege confers protection not only against an action for libel or slander, but also against an action for conspiracy. Thus in *Marrinan v Vibart*, where the plaintiff brought an action against two police officers alleging that they had conspired to publish false statements defamatory of him in their evidence at the Central Criminal Court and at an inquiry before the Benchers of Lincoln's Inn,[1] the Court of Appeal held that the statement of claim disclosed no cause of action. Sellers LJ said:[2]

> 'It has been sought in this case to draw a difference between the action of libel and slander, the action of defamation, and that which is set up in this case, one of conspiracy. I can see no difference in the principles of the matter at all. Whatever form of action is sought to be derived from what was said or done in the course of judicial proceedings must suffer the same fate of being barred by the rule which protects witnesses in their evidence before the court and in the preparation of the evidence which is to be so given.'

1 The plaintiff also relied on statements in a report made by the defendants to the Director of Public Prosecutions; this report also was protected: see para 13.27, post.
2 [1963] 1 QB 528 at 535, [1962] 3 All ER 380 at 383.

13.09   On the other hand in *Roy v Prior* it was held that although no action would lie against a witness for words spoken in giving evidence, an action in respect of an alleged abuse of the process of the court was not to be defeated even though one step in the abuse involved the giving of evidence. Lord Morris of Borth-y-Gest explained the matter as follows:[1]

> 'If a witness gives false evidence he may be prosecuted if the crime of perjury has been committed but a civil action for damages in respect of the words spoken will not lie. . . . Nor is this rule to be circumvented by alleging a conspiracy between witnesses to make false statements. . . . This, however, does not involve that an action which is not brought in respect of evidence given in court but is brought in respect of an alleged abuse of process of court must be defeated if one step in the course of the abuse of the process of the court involved or necessitated the giving of evidence. It must often happen that a defendant who is sued for damages for malicious prosecution will have given evidence in the criminal prosecution of which the plaintiff complains. The essence of the complaint in such a case is that criminal proceedings have been instituted not only without reasonable and probable cause but also maliciously. So also in actions based upon alleged abuses of the process of the court it will often have happened that the court will have been induced to act by reason of some false evidence given by someone. In such cases the actions are not brought on or in respect of any evidence given but in respect of malicious abuse of process.'

1 [1971] AC 470 at 477–8, [1970] 2 All ER 729 at 733–4. It is to be noted that Lord Wilberforce would have allowed the action to proceed on an additional ground. At 480, 736, he said: 'The reasons why immunity is traditionally (and for this purpose I accept the tradition) conferred upon witnesses in respect of evidence given in court, are in order that they may give their evidence fearlessly and to avoid a multiplicity of actions in which the value or truth of their evidence would be tried over again. Moreover, the trial process contains in itself, in the subjection to cross-examination and confrontation with other evidence, some safeguard against careless, malicious or untruthful evidence. But none of this applies as regards such evidence as was given in support of the application for a Bench warrant. It was given ex parte: Dr Roy had no means, and no other party any interest, in challenging it: so far from the public interest requiring that it be given absolute protection, that interest requires that it should have been given carefully, responsibly and impartially.'

THE RULE APPLIES TO ALL COURTS OF LAW

13.10 Absolutely privilege undoubtedly applies to proceedings in the House of Lords, the Judicial Committee of the Privy Council, the Court of Appeal, the High Court of Justice, the Crown Court, county courts and in courts of summary jurisdiction. It also applies to proceedings before a court-martial[1] and in a coroner's court.[2]

Some guidance as to the correct method of identifying a court of law was given by Lord Scarman in *A-G v BBC,* where he said:[3]

'I would identify a court in (or "of") law, ie a court of judicature, as a body established by law to exercise, either generally or subject to defined limits, the judicial power of the state. In this context judicial power is to be contrasted with legislative and executive (ie administrative) power. If the body under review is established for a purely legislative or administrative purpose, it is part of the legislative or administrative system of the state, even though it has to perform duties which are judicial in character. Though the ubiquitous presence of the state makes itself felt in all sorts of situations never envisaged when our law was in its formative stage, the judicial power of the state exercised through judges appointed by the state remains an independent, and recognisably separate, function of government. Unless a body exercising judicial functions can be demonstrated to be part of this judicial system it is not, in my view, a court in law. I would add that the judicial system is not limited to the courts of the civil power. Courts-martial and consistory courts, (the latter since 1540) are as truly entrusted with the exercise of the judicial power of the state as are civil courts: *R v Daily Mail, ex p Farnsworth*[4] and *R v Daily Herald, ex p Bishop of Norwich.*[5]'

1 *Dawkins v Lord Rokeby* (1873) LR 8 QB 255; affd. (1875) LR 7 HL 744.
2 *Thomas v Churton* (1862) 2 B & S 475. And see *McCarey v Associated Newspapers Ltd* [1964] 2 All ER 335n, [1964] 1 WLR 855.
3 [1981] AC 303 at 359–60.
4 [1921] 2 KB 733.
5 (1932) 2 KB 402.

TRIBUNALS EXERCISING JUDICIAL AND QUASI-JUDICIAL FUNCTIONS

13.11 The doctrine of absolute privilege has been extended to 'tribunals exercising functions equivalent to those of an established court of justice'.[1] Thus, for example, absolute privilege has been held to apply to the proceedings before the following bodies—

(a) a Justice of the Peace on an application under the Lunacy Act 1890;[2]
(b) a commission issued by the bishop of a diocese under the Pluralities Acts 1838 to 1885;[3]
(c) the Disciplinary Committee constituted under the Solicitors Act;[4]
(d) the Benchers of an Inn of Court;[5]
(e) a local military tribunal under the Military Services Act 1916.[6]

1 *O'Connor v Waldron* [1935] AC 76 at 81 per Lord Atkin.
2 *Hodson v Pare* [1899] 1 QB 455.
3 *Barratt v Kearns* [1905] 1 KB 504.
4 *Addis v Crocker* [1961] 1 QB 11 [1960] 2 All ER 629. And see *Lilley v Roney* (1892) 61 LJ QB 727.
5 *Lincoln v Daniels* [1962] 1 QB 237, [1961] 3 All ER 740. It seems clear that the Disciplinary Tribunal of the Senate of the Inns of Court and the Bar will be similarly protected. And see *Re S* [1970] 1 QB 161, [1969] 1 All ER 949.
6 *Copartnership Farms v Harvey-Smith* [1918] 2 KB 405. And see *Gerhold v Baker* (1918) 35 TLR 102.

13.12   But in numerous other cases before various types of tribunals the privilege has been held to be qualified only and not absolute. Thus, for example, absolute privilege has been held not to apply to proceedings before the following bodies—

    (a) a meeting of the London County Council for granting music and dancing licences;[1]

    (b) licensing justices;[2]

    (c) a court of referees under the former Unemployment Insurance Acts;[3]

    (d) a medical referee.[4]

1 *Royal Aquarium and Summer and Winter Garden Society v Parkinson* [1892] 1 QB 431. But see note 2, infra.
2 *Attwood v Chapman* [1914] 3 KB 275. But in *R v East Riding of Yorkshire Quarter Sessions ex p Newton*. [1968] 1 QB 32 at 53, [1967] 3 All ER 118 at 121, Lord Denning MR, though stating that licensing justices were protected only by a qualified privilege, said that they were a 'magistrates' court' within the meaning of the Magistrates' Courts Act 1952. See also *Jeffrey v Evans* [1964] 1 All ER 536, [1964] 1 WLR 505. It is perhaps arguable therefore that proceedings before licensing justices are now protected by absolute privilege.
3 *Collins v Henry Whiteway & Co Ltd* [1927] 2 KB 378; *Mason v Brewis Bros Ltd* [1938] 2 All ER 420. See also *Hearts of Oak Assurance Co Ltd v A-G* [1932] AC 392.
4 *Smith v National Meter Co* [1945] KB 543, [1945] 2 All ER 35.

THE CRITERIA WHICH ARE RELEVANT TO DETERMINE WHETHER A
TRIBUNAL IS PROTECTED BY ABSOLUTE PRIVILEGE

13.13   In *Trapp v Mackie*[1] the House of Lords had to consider whether evidence given at a local inquiry before a Commissioner appointed under section 81(3) of the Education (Scotland) Act 1946 was protected by absolute privilege. In the course of their speeches Lord Diplock and Lord Fraser of Tullybelton gave important guidance as to the criteria which are relevant to determine whether a tribunal is protected by absolute privilege. Lord Diplock said:[2]

> 'Upon the immunity from suit of witnesses in respect of evidence they have given before courts of justice and tribunals acting in a manner similar to courts of justice, there is no difference between the law of Scotland and the law of England. That absolute privilege attached to words spoken or written in the course of giving evidence in proceedings in a court of justice is a rule of law, based on public policy, that has been established since earliest times. That the like privilege extends to evidence given before tribunals which, although not courts of justice, nevertheless act in a manner similar to that in which courts of justice act, was established more than a hundred years ago by the decision of this House in *Dawkins v Lord Rokeby*.[3] . . . To decide whether a tribunal acts in a manner similar to courts of justice and thus is of such a kind as will attract absolute, as distinct from qualified, privilege for witnesses when they give testimony before it, one must consider first, under what authority the tribunal acts; secondly the nature of the question into which it is its duty to inquire; thirdly the procedure adopted by it in carrying out the inquiry; and fourthly the legal consequences of the conclusion reached by the tribunal as a result of the inquiry.'[4]

Lord Diplock then considered the nature of the tribunal with which the House was concerned and continued:[5]

> 'The result of this examination of the nature of the tribunal . . . is that it shared with courts of justice the following characteristics:
>
>   (1) It was authorised by law; it was constituted pursuant to an Act of Parliament.
>   (2) It was inquiring into an issue in dispute between adverse parties of a kind similar to issues that commonly fall to be decided by courts of justice.

(3) The inquiry was held in public.

(4) Decisions as to what oral evidence should be led and what documents should be tendered or their production called for by the adverse party were left to the contending parties.

(5) Witnesses whom either of the adverse parties wished to call were compellable, under penal sanctions, to give oral evidence or to produce documents as havers; and were entitled to the same privilege to refuse to answer a question or produce a document as would apply if the inquiry were a proceeding in a court of law.

(6) The oral evidence was given upon oath; if it were false to the knowledge of the witness he would incur criminal liability for the offence of perjury.

(7) Witnesses who gave oral testimony were subject to examination-in-chief and re-examination by the party calling them and to cross-examination by the adverse party, in accordance with the normal procedure of courts of law.

(8) The adverse parties were entitled to be, and were in fact, represented by legally qualified advocates or solicitors and these were given the opportunity of addressing the tribunal on the evidence that had been led.

(9) The opinion of the tribunal as reported to the Secretary of State, even though not of itself decisive of the issue in dispute between the adverse parties, would have a major influence upon his decision either to require the education committee to reconsider its resolution to dismiss Dr Trapp or to let the matter rest.

(10) As a result of the report either of the parties to the inquiry might be ordered by the Secretary of State to pay the whole or part of the expenses of appearing at the inquiry incurred by the adverse parties; and such expenses would be recoverable in the same manner as expenses incurred in a civil action in a court of law.

I am far from suggesting either that the presence of any one of these characteristics taken in isolation would suffice to attract absolute privilege for witnesses in respect of testimony given by them before a tribunal or that the absence of any one of these characteristics would be fatal to the existence of such absolute privilege. . . . I would therefore content myself by saying that the cumulative effect of the ten characteristics that I have listed are more than enough to justify the contention . . . that the tribunal . . . was "acting in a manner as nearly as possible similar to that in which a court of justice acts in respect of an inquiry before it." '

It is proposed to consider some of these ten characteristics in a little more detail.

1 [1979] 1 All ER 489, [1979] 1 WLR 377.
2 [1979] 1 WLR 377 at 378–9.
3 (1875) LR 7 HL 744.
4 Cf the guidelines laid down by Devlin LJ in *Lincoln v Daniels* [1962] 1 QB 237, [1961] 3 All ER 740 where he said at pp 253, 746:
'It is settled that to come within the principle a tribunal must proceed in a manner that is similar to a court of justice, that its object must be to arrive at a judicial and not an administrative determination, and that it must be recognised by law.'
5 [1979] 1 WLR 377 at 383–4.

THE TRIBUNAL MUST BE RECOGNISED BY LAW

13.14   The first requirement is that the tribunal should be recognised by law.

'To attract absolute privilege . . . the tribunal, by whatever name it is described, must be "recognised by law". . . . . This is a sine qua non; the absolute privilege does not attach to purely domestic tribunals.'[1]

The phrase 'recognised by law' was used by Kelly CB in *Dawkins v Lord Rokeby*,[2] and was adopted and approved in the judgments of Fry and Lopes LJJ in *Royal*

Aquarium and Summer and Winter Garden Society v Parkinson.[3] It is clear that the recognition contemplated is not confined to tribunals which derive their authority from statute. In *Lincoln v Daniels* Devlin LJ said.[4]

'In my judgment the requirement of recognition by law is not equivalent to recognition by Act of Parliament but is capable of a wider meaning . . . there is nothing to show that the absolute privilege accorded to the court of inquiry in [*Dawkins v Lord Rokeby*[5]] depended entirely on the fact that the articles or regulations under which it was constituted had statutory force. Likewise, the absolute privilege that is accorded to the proceedings of regular courts of justice does not depend on whether the court was created or has been recognised by Act of Parliament or whether it is one set up under the prerogative, as all courts used to be, in which the judges sit as servants of the Crown, deriving their powers from the Crown as the fountain of justice.'

1 *Trapp v Mackie* [1979] 1 WLR 377 at 379 per Lord Diplock. Purely domestic tribunals include private arbitrators and club committees.
2 (1873) LR 8 QB 255 at 263.
3 [1892] 1 QB 431 at 446, 455.
4 [1962] 1 QB 237 at 253, [1961] 3 All ER 740 at 747. And at 269, 756, Danckwerts LJ said: ' "Recognised by law" surely cannot be confined to statutory recognition. The established courts of law must have acquired their powers originally from the Crown as the fountain-head of justice and not from what would properly be called a statute.' And see *Trapp v Mackie* [1979] 1 WLR 377 at 379–80 per Lord Diplock.
5 (1873) LR 8 QB 255; affd. (1875) LR 7 HL 744.

WHETHER THE TRIBUNAL IS MAKING A DECISION INTER PARTES OR A DECISION AFFECTING THE STATUS OR RIGHTS OF ANY PERSON

13.15 It is necessary to investigate the question into which it is the duty of the tribunal to inquire. If the tribunal has to 'adjudicate inter partes on the cases brought before it, and its findings and orders affect status'[1] or if the question before it 'partakes of the nature of a lis inter partes'[2] an important similarity will be established with the function of a court of law. On the other hand if the tribunal is not a body deciding between parties nor making a decision which affects criminally or otherwise the status of an individual, the tribunal, though described as a court, may be held to be exercising administrative rather than judicial functions.[3]

1 See *Addis v Crocker* [1961] 1 QB 11 at 28, [1960] 2 All ER 629 at 638, per Holroyd Pearce LJ. See also at pp 26, 636 per Hodson LJ.
2 See *Trapp v Mackie* [1979] 1 WLR 377 at 380 per Lord Diplock.
3 See, for example, *Collins v Henry Whiteway & Co Ltd* [1927] 2 KB 378 where Horridge J held that the Court of Referees constituted under the Unemployment Insurance Act 1920 was discharging administrative functions only. See also *A–G v BBC* [1981] AC 303.

13.16 It will be relevant to consider not only the nature of the question into which the tribunal is making its inquiry but also the method whereby the tribunal goes about that inquiry. In *O'Connor v Waldron* the Privy Council on an appeal from the Supreme Court of Canada decided that an enquiry under the Combines Investigation Act was not protected by absolute privilege. In the judgment of the Privy Council, Lord Atkin said:[1]

'Has then a commissioner appointed under the Combines Investigation Act attributes similar to those of a court of justice; or does he act in a manner similar to that in which such courts act? In their Lordships opinion the answer must be in the negative. . . . It is only necessary to remember that the commissioner by the Act is empowered to enter premises and examine the books, papers and records of suspected persons to see how far his functions differ from those of a judge. His conclusion is expressed in a report; it determines no rights, nor the guilt or innocence of anyone. It does not even initiate any proceedings, which have to be left to the ordinary criminal procedure. While it is true that some tribunals charged with the duty of enquiry whether an offence or breach of duty has been committed have been held entitled to judicial immunity, such as a military court of inquiry,[2] or an investigation by an ecclesiastical commission,[3] there were in those cases conditions as to the way in which the tribunal exercise its functions, and as to the effect of its decisions which led to the conclusions that such tribunals had attributes similar to those of a court of justice.'

1 [1935] AC 76 at 81.
2 *Dawkins v Lord Rokeby* (1873) LR 8 QB 255; affd. (1875) LR 7 HL 744.
3 *Barratt v Kearns* [1905] 1 KB 504.

13.17 Moreover it is clear that proceedings before the tribunal in question are not necessarily judicial or quasi-judicial proceedings merely because the decision of the tribunal affects the rights of any person or because its function cannot be regarded as administrative. In *Smith v National Meter Co Ltd* the plaintiff complained of a letter sent to a medical referee to whom a claim for compensation under the Workmen's Compensation Act 1925 had been referred. Uthwatt J rejected the contention that the letter was protected by absolute privilege, saying in the course of his judgment:[1]

'The function of the medical referee is certainly not administrative. His decision certainly affects legal rights; but that is not the test. He has to determine several facts which, apart from statutory provision, would be decided by the courts on evidence. In ascertaining facts he is not bound by the strict rules of evidence. He has to do his best on the materials before him. . . . But the substance of the task of the medical referee is to determine, on his own professional judgment and skill, medical facts.'

1 [1945] KB 543 at 547, [1945] 2 All ER 35 at 43.

WHETHER THE TRIBUNAL IS MAKING A FINAL DETERMINATION AS OPPOSED TO MAKING A REPORT TO ANOTHER BODY

13.18 It is relevant to consider the legal consequences of the conclusion reached by the tribunal as a result of the inquiry.[1] In cases where the tribunal refers its findings to another body to reach a final decision the proceedings before the tribunal may often be protected by qualified privilege only, but where the findings of the tribunal are likely to be given great weight by the decision-making body, the proceedings before the tribunal may then attract absolute privilege. In *Trapp v Mackie* Lord Diplock put the matter as follows:[2]

'Where the report of a tribunal though not necessarily decisive as a matter of legal theory nevertheless in practice has a major influence on the final decision that in law is binding and authoritative, the same considerations apply to such a tribunal as those that weigh the balance down in favour of absolute privilege for evidence given before a tribunal whose decisions are in strict law binding and authoritative in their own right.'

1 See *Trapp v Mackie* [1979] 1 WLR 377 at 379.
2 [1979] 1 WLR 377 at 383.

THE PROCEDURE OF THE TRIBUNAL

13.19   If the proceedings of the tribunal are to be protected by absolute privilege the tribunal must proceed in a manner similar to a court of justice. Accordingly it is necessary in the particular case to examine the procedure of the tribunal to see how far such procedure differs from that of a court of law.[1]

1 It is to be noted that in *Lincoln v Daniels* [1962] 1 QB 237 at 255, [1961] 3 All ER 740 at 748, Devlin LJ said: 'I appreciate that the Bench . . . conducts its proceedings with less formality than in a court of law. There are no pleadings for discovery; witnesses cannot be subpoenaed and do not give evidence on oath. These are factors to be taken into account, but I think that in any case of doubt the overriding factor is whether there will emerge from the proceedings a determination the truth and justice of which is a matter of public concern, for it is public policy that justifies absolute privilege.'

RULES AS TO EVIDENCE AND CROSS-EXAMINATION

13.20   Importance will be attached to the question whether the parties are given an opportunity to hear and consider their opponents' evidence. Thus in *Smith v National Meter Co Ltd* Uthwatt J said:[1]

'In one important aspect the proceedings differ fundamentally from a judicial proceeding. Each party is entitled to submit a statement, and a statement is made to the referee alone. Neither party is entitled to know what is therein alleged by the other. It is impossible to imagine anything less likely to find a place in a judicial proceeding.'

1 [1945] KB 543 at 548, [1945] 2 All ER 35 at 43.

PROCEEDINGS IN PRIVATE

13.21   Considerable importance will be attached to the question whether the proceedings are conducted in public or in private, because in general a tribunal having judicial functions to perform should deliberate in public.[1] But the fact that the hearing takes place in private is not conclusive.[2]

1 See *Addis v Crocker* [1961] 1 QB 11 at 30, [1960] 2 All ER 629 at 638–9, per Upjohn LJ.
2 See, for example, *Barratt v Kearns* [1905] 1 KB 504; *Addis v Crocker* [1961] 1 QB 11, [1960] 2 All ER 629.

POWER TO COMPEL THE ATTENDANCE OF WITNESSES AND TO ADMINISTER THE OATH

13.22   Importance will be attached to the fact that the tribunal has the right to obtain the assistance of the High Court to enforce the attendance of witnesses.[1] In *Addis v Crocker* Pearce LJ said:[2]

'The purpose of the High Court in lending its power to enforce the attendance of witnesses is to help the judicial process of an inferior court. It would seem anomalous and unfair that the High Court should compel the attendance of a witness before a tribunal, which may administer the oath to him, without extending to that witness the protection of privilege for the evidence which may be elicited from him.'

On the other hand in *Lincoln v Daniels*[3] the tribunal was held to be protected by absolute privilege although the attendance of witnesses could not be enforced by subpoena nor was there a requirement that evidence should be given on oath.

1 RSC Ord. 38, r 19 provides for the issue out of the Crown Office of a writ of subpoena ad testificandum or a writ of subpoena duces tecum 'in aid of an inferior court or tribunal'. See also *Soul v IRC* [1963] 1 All ER 68n, [1963] 1 WLR 112.
2 [1961] 1 QB 11 at 29, [1960] 2 All ER 629 at 638.
3 [1962] 1 QB 237, [1961] 3 All ER 740.

THE EXTENT OF THE PRIVILEGE ATTACHING TO JUDICIAL AND QUASI-JUDICIAL PROCEEDINGS

13.23 The absolute privilege extends not only to what is said in the course of the proceedings before the court or tribunal but also to the preliminary documents such as pleadings and proofs of evidence.[1] The extent of the privilege was examined by Devlin LJ in *Lincoln v Daniels*.[2]

'The absolute privilege which covers proceedings in or before a court of justice can be divided into three categories. The first category covers all matters that are done coram judice. This extends to everything that is said in the course of proceedings by judges, parties, counsel and witnesses, and includes the contents of documents put in as evidence. The second covers everything that is done from the inception of the proceedings onwards and extends to all pleadings and other documents brought into existence for the purpose of the proceedings and starting with the writ or other document which institutes the proceedings. The third category is the most difficult of the three to define. It is based on the authority of *Watson v M'Ewan*[3] in which the House of Lords held that the privilege attaching to evidence which a witness gave coram judice extended to the precognition or proof of that evidence taken by a solicitor. It is immaterial whether the proof is or is not taken in the course of proceedings. In *Beresford v White*[4] the privilege was held to attach to what was said in the course of an interview by a solicitor with a person who might or might not be in a position to be a witness on behalf of his client in contemplated proceedings.'

1 The protection is of course limited to the publication of the documents in the course of and for the purposes of the proceedings, and does not extend to publication outside unless, if the documents are read in court, their publication can be separately protected as part of a fair and accurate report of court proceedings.
2 [1962] 1 QB 237 at 257, [1961] 3 All ER 740 at 749–50.
3 [1905] AC 480.
4 (1914) 30 TLR 591.

PROCEEDINGS IN COURT OR BEFORE THE TRIBUNAL

13.24 The privilege will protect statements made in the course of the proceedings by the judge or by any member of the tribunal or by advocates or witnesses. It seems clear, however, that the witness is only protected in respect of statements made by him in his capacity as a witness. Furthermore, a witness is probably not protected in respect of a statement made in the witness box which has nothing whatever to do with the matter before the court or tribunal, though no doubt the scope of relevance would be very widely interpreted. Thus in *Seaman v Netherclift* Cockburn CJ said:[1]

'I am very far from desiring to be considered as laying down as law that what a witness states altogether out of the character and sphere of a witness, or what he may say dehors the matter in hand, is necessarily protected. I quite agree that what he says before he enters or after he has left the witness-box is not privileged, which was the question in the case before Lord Ellenborough.[2] Or if a man when in the witness-box were to take advantage of his position to utter something having no reference to the cause or matter of enquiry in order to assail the character of another, as if he were asked: Were you at York on a certain day? and he were to answer: Yes, and AB picked my pocket there; it certainly might well be said in such a case that the statement was altogether dehors the character of witness, and not within the privilege.'

And in the same case Bramwell JA said:[3]

'Suppose while the witness is in the box, a man were to come in at the door, and the witness were to exclaim "that man picked my pocket" I can hardly think that would be privileged. I can scarcely think a witness would be protected for anything he might say in the witness box, wantonly and without reference to the inquiry. I do not say he would not be protected. It might be held that it was better that everything a witness said as a witness should be protected, than that witnesses should be under the impression that what they said in the witness box might subject them to an action. I certainly should pause before I affirmed so extreme a proposition. But without affirming that, I think the words "having reference to the inquiry" ought to have a very wide and comprehensive application, and ought not to be limited to statements for which, if not true, a witness might be indicted for perjury, or the exclusion of which by the judge would give ground for a new trial; but ought to extend to that which a witness might naturally and reasonably say when giving evidence with reference to the inquiry as to which he had been called as a witness.'

1 (1876) 2 CPD 53 at 56.
2 See *Trotman v Dunn* (1815) 4 Camp 211.
3 (1876) 2 CPD 53 at 60. It is to be noted, however, that Amphlett JA said at 61: 'I can see many reasons why a witness should be absolutely protected for anything he said in the witness box.'

WRITS, PLEADINGS, AFFIDAVITS AND OTHER DOCUMENTS IN THE PROCEEDINGS

13.25 Documents which come into existence after the issue of the writ or other form of process initiating the proceedings or which are tendered in evidence in the course of the proceedings are protected by absolute privilege. The protection is of course limited to the publication for the purpose of those proceedings. It is arguable, however, that any matter contained in a pleading, affidavit or other document which was wholly irrelevant to the matter before the court would not be protected.[1]

1 It is submitted that a court might reject a claim for absolute privilege on the basis of the dicta in *Seaman v Netherclift* (1876) 2 CPD 53. The court has power under RSC Ord 18, r 19(1)(*b*) to strike out anything contained in any pleading which is 'scandalous, frivolous or vexatious' and under RSC Ord 41, r 6 to strike out of any affidavit any matter which is 'scandalous, irrelevant or otherwise oppressive.'

PROOFS OF PARTIES AND WITNESSES

13.26   Proofs of the parties and witnesses are protected by absolute privilege. If proofs of evidence were not protected a plaintiff would be able to bring an action against a witness on the basis: 'I do not bring the action against you for what you said in the witness-box, but I bring the action against you for what you told the solicitor you were about to say in the witness-box.'[1]

---

1 See *Watson v M'Ewan*[1905] AC 480 at 487 per Earl of Halsbury LC, who added: 'It is very obvious that the public policy which renders the protection of witnesses necessary for the administration of justice must as a necessary consequence involve that which is a step towards and is part of the administration of justice—namely, the preliminary examination of witnesses to find out what they can prove.' And see *Lincoln v Daniels* [1962] 1 QB 237, [1961] 3 All ER 740.

COMPLAINTS AND OTHER DOCUMENTS COMING INTO EXISTENCE WITH A
VIEW TO THE CONSIDERATION OF PROCEEDINGS

13.27   In a number of cases an action for defamation has been brought based on a letter of complaint or other document submitted to an authority responsible for considering the institution of proceedings. Such a letter is likely to be protected by qualified privilege,[1] but it seems that it will not in general[2] attract absolute privilege unless in the circumstances it is the appropriate method of instituting proceedings.[3] 'On such a point form is of the first importance; it is by form rather than by the substance of the complaint that a writ is to be distinguished from a letter before action.'[4]

---

1 See para 14.04, post.
2 The document or documents may attract absolute privilege, however, if they are in the form of proofs of witnesses. Thus in *Marrinan v Vibart* [1963] 1 QB 528, [1962] 3 All ER 380, it was held that a report by two police officers to the Director of Public Prosecutions which consisted of statements by them were protected by absolute privilege.
3 See, for example, *Lilley v Roney* (1892) 61 LJQB 727, where the letter followed the form given in the Solicitors Act Rules 1889, Sch 1.
4 See *Lincoln v Daniels* [1962] 1 QB 237 at 259, [1961] 3 All ER 740 at 750, per Devlin LJ. In that case it was held that a letter of complaint to the Bar Council was protected by qualified privilege only. See also *Szalatnay-Stacho v Fink* [1947] KB 1, [1946] 2 All ER 231, where it was held that a dossier which was sent for investigation and any action 'that may be thought proper' was too remote from actual or contemplated proceedings.

Statements made by one officer of State to another in the course of duty

13.28   Statements made by one officer of State to another in the course of duty are protected by absolute privilege. The general principle was stated by Lord Esher MR in *Chatterton v Secretary of State for India in Council* as follows:[1]

> 'If an officer of State were liable to an action of libel in respect of such a communication as this, actual malice could be alleged to rebut a plea of privilege, and it would be necessary that he should be called as a witness to deny that he acted maliciously. That he should be placed in such a position, and that his conduct should be so questioned before a jury, would clearly be against the public interest, and prejudicial to the independence necessary for the performance of his functions as an official of State. Therefore the law confers upon him an absolute privilege in such a case.'

And in *M Isaacs & Sons Ltd v Cook*[2] Roche J held that a communication could be protected by absolute privilege even though it related to commercial matters and extended the privilege to a communication by the High Commissioner of a Commonwealth government.

1   [1895] 2 QB 189 at 191. The plaintiff, a captain in the Indian Staff Corps, sued for damages for libel in respect of a statement made by the Secretary of State for India to the Parliamentary Under-Secretary for India to enable the latter to answer a question in the House of Commons.
2   [1925] 2 KB 391. The plaintiffs sued for damages for libel in respect of a report by the defendant, the High Commissioner for Australia in London, to the Prime Minister of Australia relating to the sale of Australian fruit in London.

13.29   The privilege seems to attach to communications at the highest level of the Government and the Civil Service but it is uncertain how far down the official scale the protection extends. It is submitted that the privilege should be restricted within narrow limits.[1] In *Gibbons v Duffell* the High Court of Australia held that absolute privilege did not attach to a report from an inspector of police to his superior officer concerning a subordinate: Evatt J said:[2]

'Absolute immunity from the consequences of defamation is so serious a derogation from the citizen's right to the State's protection of his good name that its existence at all can only be conceded in those few cases where overwhelmingly strong reasons of public policy of another kind cut across this elementary right of civic protection, and any extension of the area of immunity must be viewed with the most jealous suspicion and resisted until its necessity is demonstrated.'

And in *Merricks v Nott-Bower* the Court of Appeal held that it was arguable that a communication to the Commissioner of Metropolitan Police from the Deputy Commissioner was not protected by absolute privilege: Salmon LJ said:[3]

'I agree that the suggested defence of absolute privilege may well succeed at the trial, but it is by no means certain to do so. The categories of absolute privilege are not closed, but at the moment they have not been held to include a communication from one high ranking police officer to another. There is much authority upon which to found an argument that on principle such communications should be absolutely privileged; on the other hand there are the very weighty judgments in *Gibbons v Duffell*[4] which support a powerful argument the other way.'

1   It is to be noted that in *Szalatnay-Stacho v Fink* [1947] KB 1, [1946] 2 All ER 231, Mr. Gerald Slade, as counsel for the defendant, did not seek to argue that an official letter from the General Prosecutor of the Czechoslovak Military Court of Appeal to the Military Officer of the President of the Czechoslovak Government in exile in London was protected by absolute privilege under this heading as an act of State: see [1947] KB 1 at 6, 12.
2   (1932) 47 CLR 520 at 534. See also *Jackson v Magrath* (1947) 75 CLR 293.
3   [1965] 1 QB 57 at 73, [1964] 1 All ER 717 at 724–5.
4   (1932) 47 CLR 520.

REPORTS BY AN OFFICER IN THE ARMED FORCES TO HIS SUPERIOR

13.30   The protection of absolute privilege has been extended more widely in respect of communications by an officer in the armed forces to his superior officer. Thus in *Dawkins v Lord Paulet*[1] it was held that a letter from the defendant, who held the appointment of Major-General commanding the Brigade of Foot Guards in which the plaintiff was serving as a Lieutenant-Colonel, to the Adjutant-General was protected by absolute privilege. But it seems that the basis for this decision (and decisions in earlier similar cases)[2] was that a case involving questions of military discipline and military duty alone is cognizable only by a military tribunal and not by a court of law. In *Fraser v Balfour*, however, Lord Finlay LC expressed the opinion that the question whether such matters were not cognizable in a court of law was still an open question at any rate in the House of Lords, and added:[3]

> 'It involves constitutional questions of the utmost gravity and a decision upon it should be given only when the facts were before the House in a complete and satisfactory form.'

1 (1869) LR 5 QB 94.
2 See, for example, *Dawkins v Lord Rokeby* (1866) 4 F & F 806 at 841 where Willes J said: 'With respect to military men, I beg to say that I cannot conceive anything more fatal to themselves, anything more fatal to the discipline or subordination of the army, if every officer who considers himself to have been slighted by his inferiors, or every officer aggrieved by his superiors, whom, having become a soldier, he has consented to submit to, should seek to undo their judgment before a tribunal which must necessarily have but slight acquaintance with those matters upon which it is called to pronounce an opinion.'
3 (1918) 34 TLR 502. See also *Richards v Naum* [1967] 1 QB 620, [1966] 3 All ER 812, where the Court of Appeal declined to make an order that the issue of absolute privilege should be tried as a preliminary point of law in view of the uncertainty as to whether the defence of absolute privilege applied to the middle and lower ranks of the services or to the secret service or to the visiting forces of a friendly foreign power.

13.31 It seems that the category of communications which will be protected by absolute privilege under this heading as State communications or acts of State may sometimes overlap with the categories of documents which are protected from disclosure under the rule of evidence which was formerly known as Crown privilege.[1] It is submitted, however, that though there is a measure of overlap and though the questions of public interest involved are often similar this heading of absolute privilege in an action for defamation should not be confused with the rule of evidence as to the disclosure of documents.[2]

1 See *Conway v Rimmer* [1968] AC 910, [1968] 1 All ER 874; *Rogers v Secretary of State for Home Department* [1973] AC 388, [1972] 2 All ER 1057; *Norwich Pharmacal Co v Customs and Excise Comrs* [1974] AC 133, [1973] 2 All ER 943; *A. Crompton Amusement Machines Ltd v Customs and Excise Comrs (No. 2)* [1974] AC 405, [1973] 2 All ER 1169. *Burmah Oil Co Ltd v Governor & Co of The Bank of England* [1980] AC 1090; *Air Canada v Secretary of State for Trade* [1983] 2 WLR 494.
2 The absolute privilege and 'Crown' privilege cases have a similar history and a similar rationale. It seems quite plain, however, that a court might prevent the disclosure as a matter of evidence of a communication on a secret matter at quite a low level and in circumstances where this heading of absolute privilege would have no application. It may be noted that in *Conway v Rimmer* [1968] AC 910 at 967, [1968] 1 All ER 874 at 898, Lord Morris of Borth-y-Gest said: 'The decision in *Chatterton v Secretary of State for India in Council* [1895] 2 QB 189 was considerably concerned with the law of privilege in defamation cases but insofar as it related to production in evidence there was no overruling of the cases to which I have referred.'

Statements protected by the Parliamentary Commissioner Act . 1967

13.32 It seems clear that investigations carried out by the Parliamentary Commissioner are not protected by absolute privilege at common law. By statute, however, absolute privilege is conferred on certain publications by and to the Parliamentary Commissioner and on certain consequential publications as follows[1]—

(a) the publication of any matter by the Commissioner in making a report to either House of Parliament for the purposes of the Parliamentary Commissioner Act 1967;

(b) the publication of any matter by a member of the House of Commons in communicating with the Commissioner or his officers for the purposes of the Act;

(c) the publication of any matter by the Commissioner or his officers in communicating with a member of the House of Commons for the purposes of the Act;

(d) the publication by a member of the House of Commons to the person by whom a complaint was made[2] under the Act of a report or statement by the Commissioner[3] sent to the member in respect of the complaint;

(e) the publication by the Commissioner of a report[4] on a complaint to the principal officer of the department or authority concerned and to any other person alleged in the complaint to have taken or authorised the action complained of.

1 Parliamentary Commissioner Act 1967, s 10(5).
2 The communication by the complainant to a member of the House of Commons is not protected by absolute privilege, but except in unusual circumstances it would be likely to be protected by qualified privilege: cf *Beach v Freeson* [1972] 1 QB 14 at 22, [1971] 2 All ER 854 at 860, where Lane J said:

'There is no doubt at all on the evidence which I have heard that by [1969] there had been a remarkable increase in the amount of work done by Members of Parliament outside the House of Commons on behalf of their constituents. The reasons for this increase are not altogether clear but possibly it is that the private individual feels, increasingly, that he is at the mercy of huge, amorphous and unfeeling organisations who will pay no attention to his feeble cries unless they are amplified by someone in authority. The Member of Parliament in those circumstances is the obvious ally to whom to turn.'

3 That is, a report or statement under s 10(1) which provides:

'In any case where the Commissioner conducts an investigation under this Act or decides not to conduct such an investigation, he shall send to the member of the House of Commons by whom the request for investigation was made (or if he is no longer a member of that House, to such member of that House as the Commissioner thinks appropriate) a report of the results of the investigation or, as the case may be, a statement of his reasons for not conducting an investigation.'

4 That is, a report or statement under s 10(2) which provides:

'In any case where the Commissioner conducts an investigation under this Act, he shall also send a report of the results of the investigation to the principal officer of the department or authority concerned and to any other person who is alleged in the relevant complaint to have taken or authorised the action complained of.'

Statements made in reports by the Monopolies Commission and the Director General of Fair Trading

13.33 By s 16(2) of the Competition Act 1980 it is provided that 'for the purposes of the law relating to defamation, absolute privilege shall attach to any report of the [Monopolies] Commission or of the Director [of Fair Trading] under the Act.'

CHAPTER 14

Qualified privilege

INTRODUCTION

14.01 The statements to which the defence of qualified privilege applies can be conveniently grouped by reference to the following categories—

   (a) statements made in pursuance of a legal, social or moral duty to a person who has a corresponding duty or interest to receive them;
   (b) statements made for the protection or furtherance of an interest to a person who has a common or corresponding duty or interest to receive them;
   (c) statements made in the protection of a common interest to a person sharing the same interest;
   (d) fair and accurate reports[1] of judicial proceedings, however published, and whether or not published contemporaneously with the proceedings;
   (e) fair and accurate reports[1] of Parliamentary proceedings, and Parliamentary sketches;
   (f) extracts from Parliamentary papers and public registers;
   (g) certain reports published in newspapers or by broadcasting which are protected by virtue of the provisions of the Defamation Act 1952, s 7 and Schedule.

1 See para 14.29, post.

14.02 The defence of qualified privilege can be defeated if the plaintiff proves that a defendant was actuated by malice[1] in publishing the words of which complaint is made.

1 See chapter 17, post.

14.03 It is important to remember, however, that the rules as to qualified privilege which have been developed by the common law are based on a broad general principle, and that 'the circumstances that constitute a privileged occasion can themselves never be catalogued and rendered exact'.[1] The categories set out above are therefore only illustrations of the general principle and it is to be noted that in *Perera v Peiris* the Privy Council declined to decide the case before them by reference to any precise category. Lord Uthwatt explained their Lordships' approach as follows:[2]

'Both [Roman–Dutch law and the common law] accord privilege to fair reports of judicial proceedings and of proceedings in the nature of judicial proceedings and to fair reports of Parliamentary proceedings, and much time might be spent in an enquiry whether the proceedings before the commissioner fell within one or other of these categories. Their Lordships do not propose to enter on that enquiry. They prefer to relate their conclusions to the wide general principle which underlies the defence of privilege in all its aspects rather than to debate the question whether the case falls within some specific category. The wide general principle was stated by their Lordships in *Macintosh v Dun*[3] to be the "common convenience and welfare of society" or "the general interest of society,". . . . '

1 See *London Association for Protection of Trade v Greenlands Ltd* [1916] 2 AC 15 at 22 per Lord Buckmaster LC. And see *Stuart v Bell* [1891] 2 QB 341 at 346 per Lindley LJ.
2 [1949] AC 1 at 20. And in *Webb v Times Publishing Co Ltd* [1960] 2 QB 535 at 563, [1960] 2 All ER 789 at 800, Pearson J said: 'In my view, it was established by Mr. Gardiner's historical examination of the decided cases that originally and in principle there are not many different kinds of privilege,,but rather for all privilege there is the same foundation of the public interest.'
3 [1908] AC 390 at 399.

Qualified privilege which is based on a duty or interest

14.04 From the broad general principle that certain communications should be protected by qualified privilege in 'the general interest of society',[1] the courts have developed the concept that there must exist between the publisher and the publishee some duty or interest in the making of the communication. In 1855 in *Harrison v Bush* Lord Campbell CJ stated the law as follows:[2]

'A communication made bona fide upon any subject matter in which the party communicating has an interest, or in reference to which he has a duty, is privileged, if made to a person having a corresponding interest or duty, although it contain criminatory matter which, without this privilege, would be slanderous and actionable.'

And in *Pullman v Hill & Co* Lord Esher MR said:[3]

'An occasion is privileged when the person who makes the communication has a moral duty to make it to the person to whom he does make it, and the person who receives it has an interest in hearing it. Both these conditions must exist in order that the occasion may be privileged.'

1 See *Whiteley v Adams* (1863) 15 CBNS 392 at 418 per Erle CJ; *Macintosh v Dun* [1908] AC 390 at 399; *Perera v Peiris* [1949] AC 1 at 20.
2 (1856) 5 E & B 344 at 348.
3 [1891] 1 QB 524 at 528.

14.05 In *Adam v Ward* Lord Atkinson emphasised the importance of reciprocity in the following words:[1]

'It was not disputed, in this case on either side, that a privileged occasion is, in reference to qualified privilege, an occasion where the person who makes the communication has an interest or a duty, legal, social, or moral, to make it to the person to whom it is made, and the person to whom it is so made has a corresponding interest or duty to receive it. This reciprocity is essential.'

And in *Watt v Longsdon* Scrutton LJ, after considering the earlier cases, restated the law in terms which (with one important exception), are generally accepted as authoritative. He expressed the opinion[2] that qualified privilege existed where there was either:

> '(1) A duty to communicate information believed to be true to a person who has a material interest in receiving the information, or
>
> (2) an interest in the speaker to be protected by communicating information, if true, relevant to that interest, to a person honestly believed to have[3] a duty to protect that interest, or
>
> (3) a common interest in and reciprocal duty in respect of the subject matter of the communication between speaker and recipient.'

1 [1917] AC 309 at 334.
2 [1930] 1 KB 130 at 147.
3 See para 14.06, infra.

14.06 It seems clear, however, that in the second category postulated[1] by Scrutton LJ the words 'honestly believed to have', if intended to be of general application, were included in error. Thus as a general rule the question whether qualified privilege exists or not is determined by reference to the actual facts and not by reference to any belief in the mind of the publisher of the words. In *Beach v Freeson*, Lane J referred to the judgment of Lord Esher MR in *Hebditch v MacIlwaine*[2] and continued:[3]

> 'Apart from authority it seems contrary to principle that the existence of qualified privilege should depend on the mistaken belief of the defendant.'

Despite this general rule, however, it is submitted that a person to whom an inquiry is addressed is entitled to the protection of qualified privilege for his answer if he has a bona fide, though mistaken, belief that the circumstances are such as would confer a privilege. In *London Association for Protection of Trade v Greenlands* Lord Parker said:[4]

> 'It is therefore a principle of law that a person asked for information affecting the credit of another is justified in giving it, provided (1) that he bona fide believes in the truth of the information which he gives; (2) that he bona fide believes that the person making the enquiry has an interest which justifies it;. . . .'

Lord Parker was dealing with the particular question as to a person asked for information affecting the credit of another, but it is submitted that what he said can be applied to the case of any person who is asked for information and honestly believes that his interlocutor has a proper interest in receiving the information.

1 In *Watt v Longsdon* [1930] 1 KB 130 at 147.
2 [1894] 2 QB 54 at 59. And see *Phelps v Kemsley* (1942) 168 LT 18 at 20, where Goddard LJ said: 'In my opinion it is now settled that not only must the defendant use the words under a sense of duty, but there must be a duty to use them. If there be no duty, that the defendant believes there is one is not enough.'
3 [1972] 1 QB 14 at 25, [1971] 2 All ER 854 at 862.
4 [1916] 2 AC 15 at 42.

Functions of the judge and jury in relation to qualified privilege

14.07 It is a question of law for the judge whether the occasion of publication is protected by qualified privilege, but before he can reach a decision it may be necessary for the jury to make certain findings of fact. In *Hebditch v MacIlwaine*, Lord Esher MR put the matter as follows:[1]

'The question whether the occasion is privileged if the facts are not in dispute is a question of law only for the judge, not for the jury. If there are questions of fact in dispute upon which this question depends they must be left to the jury; but when the jury have found the facts, it is for the judge to say whether they constitute a privileged occasion.'

And in *Adam v Ward*, Lord Finlay LC said:[2]

'It is for the judge, and the judge alone, to determine as a matter of law whether the occasion is privileged, unless the circumtances attending it are in dispute, in which case the facts necessary to raise the question of law should be found by the jury.'

1 [1894] 2 QB 54 at 58.
2 [1917] AC 309 at 318. See also *Minter v Priest* [1930] AC 558 at 572 per Viscount Dunedin: *Bryanston Finance Ltd v de Vries* [1975] QB 703 at 738, [1975] 2 All ER 609 at 631, per Lawton LJ.

14.08   The jury will if necessary make findings of fact on such matters as to whom the words were published and as to any office held by the publisher or publishee at the time of publication. But it will be for the judge to decide whether in the light of those facts the publication was protected by qualified privilege. This decision may often be difficult where the privilege depends not on a legal duty but on a social or moral duty. In *Watt v Longsdon*, Scrutton LJ described the problem as follows:[1]

'As to legal duty, the judge should have no difficulty; the judge should know the law; but as to moral or social duties of imperfect obligation, the task is far more trouble-some. The judge has no evidence as to the view the community takes of moral or social duties. All the help the Court of Appeal can give him is contained in the judgment of Lindley LJ in *Stuart v Bell*:[2] "The question of moral or social duty being for the judge, each judge must decide it as best he can for himself. I take moral or social duty to mean a duty recognised by English people of ordinary intelligence and moral principle, but at the same time not a duty enforceable by legal proceedings, whether civil or criminal. My own conviction is that all or, at all events, a great mass of right-minded men in the position of the defendant would have considered it their duty, under the circumstances, to inform Stanley of the suspicion which had fallen on the plaintiff."[3] Is the judge merely to give his own view of moral and social duty, though he thinks a considerable portion of the community hold a different opinion? Or is he to endeavour to ascertain what view "the great mass of right-minded men" would take? It is not surprising that with such a standard both judges and text-writers treat the matter as one of great diffi-culty in which no definite line can be drawn.'

1 [1930] 1 KB 130 at 144.
2 [1891] 2 QB 341 at 350.
3 The defendant had informed Stanley (the plaintiff's employer), who was staying with the defendant as his guest, that the plaintiff was suspected of a theft at a hotel which Stanley and the plaintiff had recently visited. In an action for slander the Court of Appeal held that the occasion of the communication was privileged.

14.09   Further light is thrown on this difficult point by the judgment of Greer LJ in *Watt v Longsdon* where he said:[1]

'The only guide one can get from previous decisions is to be obtained from the judgments of the Court of Appeal in *Stuart v Bell*. There Lindley LJ says:[2] "I take moral or social duty to mean a duty recognised by English people of ordinary intelligence and moral principle, but at the same time not a duty enforceable by legal proceedings, whether civil or criminal." Would the great mass of right-minded men in the position of the defendant have considered it their duty, under the circumstances, to make the communication? Kay LJ says:[3] "The true mode of judging upon the question is to put one's self as much as possible in the position of the defendant." I think these tests are as near as one can reasonably get to the tests to be applied in forming an opinion on the question whether a privileged occasion arising out of a moral or social duty has or has not arisen.'

And in *Beach v Freeson*, Lane J referred to the judgment of Scrutton LJ in *Watt v Longsdon*[4] and continued:[5]

'The judge must, accordingly, do his best in the light of such evidence as he has, coupled with his own views[6] as to what the defendant's duties, moral or social, were in the circumstances.'

It is submitted that the effect of the authorities is that the standard to be applied by the judge is an objective standard—what would people of ordinary intelligence and moral principle have done in the circumstances?—though in setting the standard the judge has to draw on his own knowledge and experience.

1 [1930] 1 KB 130 at 153.
2 [1891] 2 QB 341 at 350.
3 [1891] 2 QB 341 at 359.
4 [1930] 1 KB 130 at 144.
5 [1972] 1 QB 14 at 24.
6 It is submitted that the words 'his own views' do not mean that the judge can apply an idiosyncratic standard of his own, but that he is to apply his view of what the ordinary right-minded man would have done.

Newspapers and broadcasting: qualified privilege for certain reports and other matter under section 7 of the Defamation Act 1952

14.10   The Defamation Act 1952, s 7[1] provides for a statutory qualified privilege[1] to protect the publication in a newspaper[2] or by broadcasting[3] of certain reports and other matter specified in the Schedule to the Act. The reports and other matter specified in the Schedule fall into two categories—

(a) statements which are privileged without explanation or contradiction; and

(b) statements which are privileged subject to explanation or contradiction.

1 Defamation Act 1952, s 7(1) is in the following terms: 'Subject to the provision of this section, the publication in a newspaper of any such report or other matter as is mentioned in the Schedule to this Act shall be privileged unless the publication is proved to be made with malice.' The section has greatly widened the scope of the qualified privilege previously afforded to certain newspaper reports by the Law of Libel Amendment Act 1888, s 4 (now repealed by the Defamation Act 1952, s 18(3)).
2 'Newspaper' is defined for the purposes of the section as meaning 'any paper containing public news or observations thereon, or consisting wholly or mainly of advertisements, which is printed for sale and is published in the United Kingdom either periodically or in parts or numbers at intervals not exceeding thirty-six days'. The intervals 'not exceeding thirty-six days' may be contrasted with the provision for intervals 'not exceeding twenty-six days' in the Newspaper Libel and Registration Act 1881, s 1, which is relevant to a defence under the Law of Libel Amendment Act 1888, s 3: see appendix 1, post.

3 Defamation Act 1952, s 9 provides: '(2) Section 7 of this Act . . . shall apply in relation to reports or matters broadcast by means of wireless telegraphy as part of any programme or service provided by means of a broadcasting station within the United Kingdom. . . . (3) In this section "broadcasting station" means any station in respect of which a licence granted by the Postmaster General under the enactments relating to wireless telegraphy is in force, being a licence which (by whatever form of words) authorises the use of the station for the purpose of providing broadcasting services for general reception.'

CONDITIONS OF THE PRIVILEGE

14.11 The privilege conferred by section 7 is a qualified privilege and can be defeated if the publication is proved to be made with malice.[1] Furthermore, it is expressly provided[2] that section 7 does not protect:

(a) any matter the publication of which is prohibited by law; or
(b) any matter which is not of public concern and the publication of which is not for the public benefit.

1 Defamation Act 1952, s 7(1).
2 Defamation Act 1952, s 7(3).

MATTER WHICH IS NOT OF PUBLIC CONCERN AND THE PUBLICATION OF WHICH IS NOT FOR THE PUBLIC BENEFIT

14.12 It seems that, as the burden of establishing the defence of qualified privilege is on the defendant, it is for the defendant to prove that the matter published is of public concern *and* that its publication is for the public benefit.[1] In practice, however, this issue appears only to have arisen where the plaintiff has sought to argue the contrary.[2] The issue is one to be decided by the judge.[3]

1 Cf *Sharman v Merritt & Hatcher Ltd* (1916) 32 TLR 360 at 361 per Shearman J.
2 See, for example, *Boston v W S Bagshaw & Sons* [1966] 2 All ER 906 at 910, [1966] 1 WLR 1126 at 1132.
3 The question whether matter is published on a privileged occasion is a question of law for the judge: see, for example, *Adam v Ward* [1917] AC 309 at 332 per Lord Dunedin. It is clear that in *Boston v W S Bagshaw & Sons* (1965) Times, 27 November, p 12 the trial judge treated the issue raised by the Defamation Act 1952, s 7(3) as a matter for his decision.

THE CONDITION AS TO EXPLANATION OR CONTRADICTION

14.13 In the case of the statements specified in Part II of the Schedule to the Defamation Act 1952, the privilege is subject to a further condition. Thus section 7(2) provides that in respect of the publication of any such report or matter as is mentioned in Part 2 of the Schedule the provisions of the section shall not be a defence 'if it is proved that the defendant has been requested by the plaintiff to publish in the newspaper[1] in which the original publication was made a reasonable letter or statement by way of explanation or contradiction, and has refused or neglected to do so, or has done so in a manner not adequate or not reasonable having regard to all the circumstances'.[2]

1 Where the offending report or other matter has been broadcast the words 'in the manner in which' are to be substituted for the words 'in the newspaper in which' in this sub-section: Defamation Act 1952, s 9(2).
2 The plaintiff should include with this request a draft of the letter or statement by way of explanation or contradiction which he wants published. A mere demand by the plaintiff for a full apology would not prevent the defendant from relying on the statutory privilege: see *Khan v Ahmed* [1957] 2 QB 149, [1957] 2 All ER 385.

MATTERS PROTECTED WITHOUT EXPLANATION OR CONTRADICTION

14.14 The reports and other matters which are protected by qualified privilege under the Defamation Act 1952, s 7 without explanation or contradiction are set out in Part 1 of the Schedule to the Act and are as follows—

Report of proceedings in a Commonwealth legislature

14.15 A fair and accurate report[1] of any proceedings in public of the legislature[2] of any part of Her Majesty's dominions outside Great Britain.[3]

1 For the meaning of 'fair and accurate report', see para 14.29, post.
2 For the meaning of 'legislature', see para 13 of the Schedule to the Act, appendix 1, post.
3 For the meaning of 'part of Her Majesty's dominions', see paras 13 and 14 of the Schedule to the Act, appendix 1, post.

Reports of proceedings of international organisations at conferences

14.16 A fair and accurate report[1] of any proceedings in public of an international organisation of which the United Kingdom or Her Majesty's Government in the United Kingdom is a member, or of any international conference to which that government sends a representative.

1 For the meaning of 'fair and accurate report', see para 14.29, post.

Reports of proceedings of an international court

14.17 A fair and accurate report[1] of any proceedings in public of an international court.

1 For the meaning of 'fair and accurate report', see para 14.29, post.

Reports of proceedings before Commonwealth courts and before courts-martial held outside the United Kingdom

14.18 A fair and accurate report[1] of any proceedings before a court exercising jurisdiction throughout any part of Her Majesty's dominions[2] outside the United Kingdom, or of any proceedings before a court-martial held outside the United Kingdom under the Naval Discipline Act, the Army Act or the Air Force Act.

1 For the meaning of 'fair and accurate report', see para 14.29, post.
2 For the meaning of 'part of Her Majesty's dominions', see Defamation Act 1952, Sch, para 13 and 14; appendix 1, post.

Report of public enquiries in the Commonwealth

14.19   A fair and accurate report[1] of any proceedings in public of a body or person appointed to hold a public inquiry by the government or legislature[2] of any part of Her Majesty's Dominions[3] outside the United Kingdom.[4]

1 For the meaning of 'fair and accurate report', see para 14.29, post.
2 For the meaning of 'legislature', see Defamation Act 1952, Sch, para 13; appendix 1, post.
3 For the meaning of 'part of Her Majesty's Dominions', see Defamation Act 1952, Sch, paras 13 and 14; appendix 1, post.
4 Reports of public inquiries in the United Kingdom are protected under Part II of the Schedule to the Defamation Act 1952: see appendix 1, post. They may also be protected by qualified privilege at common law.

Copies or extracts of public registers

14.20   A fair and accurate copy or extract from any register kept in pursuance of any Act of Parliament[1] which is open to inspection by the public or of any other document which is required by the law of any part of the United Kingdom to be open to inspection by the public.

1 'Act of Parliament' includes an Act of the Parliament of Northern Ireland: see Defamation Act 1952, Sch, para 13.

Notices and advertisements published by the courts

14.21   A notice or advertisement published by or on the authority of any court within the United Kingdom or any judge or officer of such court.

MATTERS PROTECTED SUBJECT TO EXPLANATION OR CONTRADICTION

14.22   The statements which are protected by qualified privilege under the Defamation Act 1952, s 7, subject to explanation or contradiction are set out in Part II of the Schedule to the Act. The provisions as to the publication of an explanation or contradiction at the request of the plaintiff are contained in section 7(2).[1]

1 See appendix 1, post.

Reports of the findings and decisions of various professional and other associations

14.23   A fair and accurate report[1] of the findings or decision of any of the following associations, or of any committee or governing body thereof, that is to say—

(a) an association formed in the United Kingdom for the purpose of promoting or encouraging the exercise of or interest in any art, science, religion or learning, and empowered by its constitution to exercise control over or adjudicate upon matters of interest or concern to the association, or the actions or conduct of any persons subject to such control or adjudication;

(b) an association formed in the United Kingdom for the purpose of promoting or safeguarding the interests of any trade, business, industry or profession, or of the persons carrying on or engaged in the same, and empowered by its constitution to exercise control over or adjudicate upon matters connected with the trade, business, industry or profession or the actions or conduct of those persons;

(c) an association formed in the United Kingdom for the purpose of promoting or safeguarding the interests of any game, sport or pastime to the playing or exercise of which members of the public are invited or admitted, and empowered by its constitution to exercise control over or adjudicate upon persons connected with or taking part in the game, sport or pastime;

being a finding or decision relating to a person who is a member of or is subject by virtue of any contract to the control of the association.[2]

1 For the meaning of 'fair and accurate report', see para 14.29, post.
2 See Defamation Act 1952, Sch, para 8. The effect of this paragraph is to extend a statutory qualified privilege to newspaper and broadcast reports of the findings and decisions of domestic tribunals set up by the various associations mentioned in the paragraph. Contrast the decision in *Chapman v Ellesmere* [1932] 2 KB 431.

Reports of public meetings

14.24 A fair and accurate report[1] of the proceedings at any public meeting held in the United Kingdom, that is to say, a meeting bona fide and lawfully held for a lawful purpose and for the furtherance or discussion of any matter of public concern, whether the admission to the meeting is general or restricted.[2]

1 For the meaning of 'fair and accurate report', see para 14.29, post.
2 See Defamation Act 1952, Sch, para 9. The question whether the meeting is a 'public meeting' is a question of law for the judge. It seems clear that a church or chapel service is not a public meeting and that therefore the report of a sermon would not be protected under this heading: see *Chaloner v Lansdown & Sons* (1894) 10 TLR 290.

Reports of proceedings of local authorities, tribunals, etc

14.25 A fair and accurate report[1] of the proceedings at any meeting or sitting in any part of the United Kingdom of—

(a) any local authority[2] or committee of a local authority or authorities;
(b) any justice or justices of the peace acting otherwise than as a court exercising judicial authority;
(c) any commission, tribunal, committee or person appointed for the purposes of any inquiry by Act of Parliament,[3] by Her Majesty or by a Minister of the Crown:
(d) any person appointed by a local authority to hold a local inquiry in pursuance of any Act of Parliament;
(e) any other tribunal, board, committee or body constituted by or under, and exercising functions under, an Act of Parliament; not being a meeting or sitting admission to which is denied to representatives of newspapers and other members of the public.

1 For the meaning of 'fair and accurate report', see para 14.29, post.
2 For the meaning of 'local authority', see Defamation Act 1952, Sch, para 13; appendix 1, post.
3 For the meaning of 'Act of Parliament', see Defamation Act 1952, Sch, para 13; appendix 1, post.

Reports of general meetings of companies and associations

14.26 A fair and accurate report[1] of the proceedings at a general meeting of any company or association constituted, registered, or certified by or under any Act of Parliament[2] or incorporated by Royal Charter, not being a private company within the meaning of the Companies Act 1948.

1 For the meaning of 'fair and accurate report', see para 14.29, post.
2 For the meaning of 'Act of Parliament', see Defamation Act 1952, Sch, para 13; appendix 1, post.

Copies and summaries of government notices

14.27 A copy or fair and accurate report[1] or summary of any notice or other matter issued for the information of the public by or on behalf of any government department,[2] officer of state, local authority or chief officer of police.[3] This provision was considered by the Court of Appeal in *Boston v W S Bagshaw & Sons*[4] and in *Blackshaw v Lord*.[5] In the latter case[6] Dunn LJ adopted the statement of Jordan CJ when considering a similar provision in New South Wales in *Campbell v Associated Newspapers Ltd*;[7]

'The notice or report must be of a genuinely official nature, and must be issued in such circumstances that it may fairly be regarded as issued for the information of the public. It is not, of course, for this Court to assume to lay down rules for what is, and for what is not, proper to be made the subject of a governmental or police notice or report. I see no reason for doubting that an authoritative announcement of an official character made or handed to members of the press for publication in their respective newspapers would, or at least could, constitute a notice or report issued for the information of the public, and if published in the form in which it was supplied would be published with the consent of the department, etc, supplying it. On the other hand, if the matter so supplied was such as to admit of a reasonable inference that it was mere gossip and not an official notice or report, or that an official report so supplied was not published in substantially the form in which it was issued, it would be competent to the tribunal of fact to find that the defence had not been made out.'

In *Blackshaw v Lord*, Stephenson LJ said that it might also be right to include in the ambit of the paragraph answers made by a government press officer, for example, to questions put over the telephone by a journalist. But he added:[8]

'But information which is put out on the initiative of a government department falls more easily within the paragraph than information pulled out of the mouth of an unwilling officer of the department, and . . . not every statement of fact made to a journalist by a press officer of a government department is privileged, and what is certainly outside the privilege is assumption, inference, speculation on the part of the journalist. That is not authorised; that is not official. If the assumption, inference, speculation were the press officer's, it would not be within the paragraph.'

1 For the meaning of 'fair and accurate report', see para 14.29, post.
2 Government department includes a department of the Government of Northern Ireland.
3 Defamation Act 1952, Sch, para 12.
4 [1966] 2 All ER 906, (1966) 1 WLR 1126.
5 [1983] 2 All ER 311, [1983] 3 WLR 283, CA.

6 [1983] 2 All ER 311 at 336, [1983] 3 WLR 283 at 312, CA.
7 (1948) 48 NSWSR 301 at 303.
8 [1983] 2 All ER 311 at 325, [1983] 3 WLR 283 at 299, CA.

Matters not covered by the Defamation Act 1952, s 7

14.28 It is important to emphasise that the protection conferred by section 7 of the Defamation Act 1952 only applies to reports in newspapers or broadcast for general reception. The section does not confer any protection on, for example, speakers at public meetings or at debates during meetings of local authorities, and the position of such speakers falls to be determined according to common law.[1]

Nor does the section confer any protection on the writers of books, although the statutory qualified privilege given to newspapers and broadcasts is not limited to contemporaneous reports. Furthermore, there are many important areas where the protection given by section 7 has no application at all. Thus the section has no application to, for example—

(a) the reports of any courts or bodies of the European Economic Community;
(b) any foreign legislatures or courts;[2]
(c) the proceedings of a number of important bodies such as the Council of the Stock Exchange, the Press Council and the Panel on Take-overs and Mergers.

1 Proceedings at meetings of local authorities will usually be protected by qualified privilege at common law: see, for example, *Horrocks v Lowe* [1975] AC 135, [1974] 1 All ER 662. The statutory privilege will, however, protect the speaker if sued as being responsible for the publication in the newspaper or broadcast.
2 In some circumstances reports of proceedings in foreign legislatures and courts will be protected by qualified privilege at common law: see *Webb v Times Publishing Co Ltd* [1960] 2 QB 535, [1960] 2 All ER 789.

14.29 It will be seen that there are many occasions where the protection of privilege is given to fair and accurate reports of proceedings of a public nature. The plainest example is a fair and accurate report of judicial proceedings, which is protected at common law by qualified privilege, and, if published contemporaneously in a newspaper, is protected by statute by a privilege which is almost certainly absolute.[1] The reasons for the privilege of such a report of judicial proceedings were considered by Pearson J in *Webb v Times Publishing Co Ltd*,[2] and include the fact that judicial proceedings are open to the public, that the public is concerned with the administration of justice and that it is better for the parties involved that a fair and accurate report should be published rather than that rumours should circulate. Where the privilege is conferred by statute on newspaper reports it will extend to protect all those taking part in and liable for the publication, subject of course to the question of malice where the privilege is a qualified one. Where the privilege exists at common law it seems clear that it extends to reports other than those in newspapers, for example to reports in letters or in conversation.[3] At the present day the defence has to be considered in the light of the fact that most reports which are published in the media of proceedings in Parliament, or in the courts or elsewhere do not purport to be a full account or even a precis of the whole proceedings, but are selective and concentrate on those aspects of the proceedings which are thought to be of particular interest to the public. It is submitted that short reports of this kind, or reports in the nature of sketches, will be protected provided they are neither inaccurate nor unfair to the plaintiff.[4]

1 Law of Libel Amendment Act 1888, s 3; *McCarey v Associated Newspapers Ltd* [1964] 2 All ER 335 n, [1964] 1 WLR 855.
2 [1960] 2 QB 535 at 559–562, [1960] 2 All ER 789 at 798–799.
3 In *Cook v Alexander* [1974] QB 279 at 288, [1973] 3 All ER 1037 at 1042, Lord Denning M R said (of a Parliamentary sketch): 'Such a sketch is privileged, whether spoken at the dinner table afterwards, or reported to the public at large in a newspaper.'
4 In *Cook v Alexander* [1974] QB 279 at 290, [1973] 3 All ER 1037 at 1043, Buckley L J said: '(The reporter) is I think entitled to report on the proceedings or that part of it which he selects in a manner which fairly and faithfully gives an impression of the events reported and will convey to the reader what he himself would have appreciated had he been present during the proceedings.'
   At 291, 1044, Lawton L J said: ' "Unfair" must mean unbalanced. . . . It is important to remember, however, that the balance must be in relation to the plaintiff's reputation.'

CHAPTER 15

The defence under the Defamation Act 1952, s 4

INTRODUCTION

15.01 In certain circumstances it is a defence, notwithstanding the general rule that defamation does not depend upon the intention of the defendant, for a defendant to prove that the defamation was published by him innocently and that he has made an offer of amends. This defence is provided by section 4 of the Defamation Act 1952. The defence is, however, subject to a number of conditions and in practice, in the thirty years which have elapsed since the passing of the Act, it does not seem to have provided any wide measure of additional protection to defendants.

15.02 In order for the defence to succeed the defendant has to prove—

   (a) that the words complained of were published by him innocently in relation to the person defamed;

   (b) that he has made an offer of amends as required by section 4 of the Defamation Act 1952;

   (c) that this offer of amends has been refused by the plaintiff and has not been withdrawn by the defendant.

It is necessary to consider each of these ingredients of the defence separately.

Innocent publication

15.03 In order to establish that he published the defamatory words innocently in relation to the person defamed (the complainant) the publisher[1] has to prove—

   (a) (i) that he did not intend to publish the alleged defamatory words of and concerning the complainant and did not know of circumstances by virtue of which the words might be understood to refer to him; *or*

      (ii) that the words were not defamatory on the face of them and that he (the publisher) did not know of circumstances by virtue of which they might be understood to be defamatory of the complainant; *and*

   (b) in either event, that he exercised all reasonable care in relation to the publication.

---

1 Defamation Act 1952, s 4(5). Any reference in the sub-section to 'the publisher' is to be construed as including a reference to any servant or agent of his who was concerned with the contents of the publication.

15.04 It will be seen that the provisions set out in the previous paragraph in (a) (i) apply to cases such as *E Hulton & Co v Jones*,[1] where the words, though defamatory on their face, are intended by the defendant to apply to a person other than the complainant or to a fictional character, and where the defendant can prove that he did not know of circumstances which would lead reasonable persons who knew the complainant to make an identification. The provisions in (a) (ii), on the other hand, apply to cases where the words are not even defamatory on their face but nevertheless could be understood to be defamatory of a complainant by reason of facts unknown to the defendant.[2] In all cases where an 'innocent' publication is relied upon it is for the defendant to prove that he exercised all reasonable care in relation to the publication.

1 [1910] AC 20.
2 An example of the type of case which might fall within the second category is provided by *Cassidy v Daily Mirror Newspapers* [1929] 2 KB 331, where the defendants published in a newspaper a photograph of one M.C. and a Miss X together with the words 'Mr M.C. the racehorse owner, and Miss X, whose engagement has been announced.' Unknown to the defendants M.C. was already married and his wife recovered £500 by way of damages on the basis that the publication conveyed to reasonably minded people an aspersion on her moral character.

Offer of amends

15.05 If the publisher of the words[1] alleged to be defamatory of another person claims that the words were published by him innocently in relation to that other person, he may make an offer of amends under section 4 of the Defamation Act 1952. An offer of amends means—

(a) in any case, to publish or join in the publication of a suitable correction of the words complained of, and a sufficient apology to the party aggrieved in respect of those words;

(b) where copies of a document or record containing the said words have been distributed by or with the knowledge of the person making the offer, to take such steps as are reasonably practicable on his part for notifying persons to whom copies have been so distributed that the words are alleged to be defamatory of the party aggrieved.[2]

An important limitation on the effectiveness of this defence, however, is improved by the provision that where a person has published words of which he is not the author he cannot rely on a defence under section 4 unless he proves that the words were written by the author without malice.[3]

1 Defamation Act 1952, s 16(1) provides that any reference in the Act to 'words shall be construed as including a reference to pictures, visual images, gestures and other methods of signifying meaning'.
2 Defamation Act 1952, s 4(3).
3 Defamation Act 1952, s 4(6).

15.06 It seems clear that the offer of amends has to be made in writing, because it is provided that the offer must be expressed to be made for the purposes of the section and must be accompanied by an affidavit specifying the facts relied upon by the person making it to show that the words in question were published by him innocently in relation to the party aggrieved.[1] The offer of amends (if it is to be of any value in any subsequent proceedings) has to be made as soon as practicable after the publisher of the words complained of received notice that they were, or might be, defamatory of the party aggrieved.[2]

1 Defamation Act 1952, s 4(2). For the form of a notice of an offer of amends, see 25 Court Forms (2nd Edn) (1975 issue) 97, Form 9.
2 Defamation Act 1952, s 4(1)(b).

AFFIDAVIT TO ACCOMPANY THE OFFER OF AMENDS

15.07 The contents of the affidavit which is required to accompany the offer of amends are very important, because it is provided that for the purposes of a defence under section 4(1)(b) no evidence other than evidence of facts specified in the affidavit shall be admissible on behalf of the defendant to prove that the words were published innocently by him.[1] Accordingly the affidavit has to specify the facts which are relied on to show that the publisher (and any servant or agent of his concerned with the contents of the publication) exercised all reasonable care in relation to the publication[2] and, in a case where the publisher was not the author of the words complained of, that the author of the words was not malicious.

1 Defamation Act 1952, s 4(2).
2 For the form of an affidavit to accompany an offer of amends, see 25 Court Forms (2nd Edn) (1975 issue) 97, Form 10.

ACCEPTANCE OF AN OFFER OF AMENDS

15.08 Where an offer of amends under section 4 of the Defamation Act 1952 is made, the party aggrieved may either accept the offer or reject it. If the party aggrieved accepts the offer of amends he can expect to obtain the publication of a correction and an apology and his costs. Further, where copies of the document or record containing the words complained of have been distributed by or with the knowledge of the publisher of the words, the party aggrieved can also expect that a notice shall be sent to the persons to whom copies have been distributed informing him that the words are alleged to be defamatory of him. If the party aggrieved accepts the offer of amends, however, he is not entitled[1] to any damages or to an injunction.

1 The parties can, of course, reach an agreement as to the payment of damages, but damages do not form part of the statutory remedy provided for in s 4.

15.09 In many cases the steps to be taken in fulfilment of the offer of amends will be agreed between the parties, but in default of agreement the matter is referred to and determined by a judge of the High Court, whose decision is final.[1]

1 Defamation Act 1952, s 4(4)(a). RSC Ord 82, r 8 provides: '(1) An application to the court under section 4 **of the** Defamation Act 1952 to determine any question as to the steps to be taken in fulfilment of an offer of amends made under that section must, unless the application is made in the course of proceedings for libel or slander in respect of the publication to which the offer relates, be made in chambers in the Queen's Bench Division, but only a judge may determine such question.' If an action has already been started in respect of the publication it seems clear that the matter should be referred to a judge in chambers by means of a summons in the action.

15.10   On the question of costs, section 4 makes provision for three sets of circumstances—

(a) where an action has already been started in respect of the publication;

(b) where proceedings are brought under section 4(4)(a) for the determination by a judge of the steps to be taken in fulfilment of the offer of amends;

(c) where no action has been started and no proceedings have been taken under section 4(4)(a).[1]

In each of these cases the court has power to make an order for costs against the person making the offer of amends, and this power is expressed to include the power to order the payment to the party aggrieved of costs on an indemnity basis and also of any expenses reasonably incurred or to be incurred by that party in consequence of the publication in question.[2]

1 It seems that the application to the court will be by originating summons, though RSC Ord 82, r 8 does not apply in terms to such an application.
2 Defamation Act 1952, s 4(4).

EFFECT OF ACCEPTANCE OF AN OFFER OF AMENDS

15.11   If the offer of amends is accepted by the party aggrieved and is duly performed, no proceedings for libel or slander can be taken or continued by that party against the person making the offer in respect of the publication in question. The acceptance of the offer of amends does not affect, however, any cause of action against any other person jointly responsible for the publication.[1]

1 Defamation Act 1952, s 4(1)(a).

REJECTION OF AN OFFER OF AMENDS: WHEN A STATUTORY DEFENCE IS AVAILABLE

15.12   If the offer of amends is rejected[1] and the party aggrieved brings an action for libel or slander against the person who has made the offer, it is provided that it shall be a defence for the defendant to prove—

(a) that the words complained of were published by him innocently in relation to the plaintiff;

(b) that the offer was made as soon as practicable after he received notice that the words complained of were or might be defamatory of the plaintiff;[2] and

(c) that the offer has not been withdrawn.[3]

If the defendant is not the author of the words, then he has to prove in addition—

(d) that the words were written[4] by the author without malice.[5]

---

1 The party aggrieved may wish to reject the offer of amends because, for example, he hopes to obtain damages. Before rejecting the offer, however, he will of course have to consider the matters set out in the affidavit in support and in particular the strength of the claim that all reasonable care was exercised.
2 In *Ross v Hopkinson* (1956) Times, 17 October, p 13, it was held that an offer of amends made seven weeks after the publication was not made as soon as practicable. See also 223 LT 97.
3 Defamation Act 1952, s 4(1)(b).
4 Defamation Act 1952, s 4(6). Where, for example, an action is brought against the publishers or printers of a newspaper in respect of an article by a journalist or a letter from a correspondent, it will be necessary for the publishers to prove the absence of malice in the journalist or correspondent.
5 For the meaning of malice, see para 17.03, post.

CHAPTER 16

Other defences

Leave and licence or volenti non fit injuria

16.01 It is a defence to an action for defamation to prove that the plaintiff assented to or acquiesced in the publication complained of.[1] But the evidence of assent or acquiescence must be clear and must amount to an authorisation by the plaintiff of the publication by the defendant. It is submitted therefore that an invitation to a speaker to repeat what he has said in front of witnesses or an invitation to a Member of Parliament to repeat his allegations outside the House does not constitute such an assent but is merely an indication by the prospective plaintiff that he would bring proceedings if a publication on which an action could be founded were made.

1 See *Monson v Tussauds Ltd* [1894] 1 QB 671 at 691 per Lord Halsbury, at 697 per Davey LJ; *Chapman v Ellesmere* [1932] 2 KB 431 at 463 per Slesser LJ.

Innocent dissemination

16.02 A person who acts merely as the distributor of defamatory matter may be able to rely on the defence of innocent dissemination. This defence is of importance in particular to wholesalers, booksellers, newsagents and libraries who in the absence of such a defence might be liable in respect of the publication of libels contained in books, newspapers, magazines and other reading material which they make available to the public.[1]

1 It may be noted that at common law a distributor was liable for contempt of court irrespective of knowledge if a publication distributed by him contained matter which amounted to a contempt: see *R v Griffiths ex p* [1957] 2 QB 192 [1957] 2 All ER 379. A defence of innocent publication or distribution is provided, however, by Contempt of Court Act 1981, s 3.

16.03 The matter was further considered in *Vizetelly v Mudie's Select Library Ltd.*[1] From the judgment of Romer LJ[2] in that case it is possible to formulate the following conditions which the defendant has to satisfy in order to establish the defence—

(a) that he did not know that the newspaper or other publication contained the libel complained of;

(b) that he did not know that the newspaper or other publication was of such a character that it was likely to contain libellous matter;

(c) that his lack of knowledge in respect of both the contents and the character of the newspaper or other publication was not due to any negligence on his part.

1 [1900] 2 QB 170.
2 [1900] 2 QB 170 at 179. In *Bottomley v FW Woolworth & Co Ltd* (1932) 48 TLR 521, Scrutton LJ treated the conditions laid down by Romer LJ as the correct tests to apply. It is to be noted, however, that he also said: 'It was difficult to state exactly the principles on which newsvendors, circulating libraries, the British Museum, and other institutions of that kind who did not themselves write the libels, but sold or otherwise passed on to others books and documents which in fact contained libels, were freed from responsibility.'

16.04 The liability of newsagents was considered by the Court of Appeal in *Emmens v Pottle*, where Lord Esher MR said:[1]

'I agree that the defendants are prima facie liable. They have handed to other people a newspaper in which there is a libel on the plaintiff. I am inclined to think that this called upon the defendants to shew some circumstances which absolved them from liability, not by way of privilege, but facts which shew that they did not publish the libel. . . . The proprietor of a newspaper, who publishes the paper by his servants, is the publisher of it, and he is liable for the acts of his servants. The printer of the paper prints it by his servants, and therefore he is liable for a libel contained in it.[2] But the defendants did not compose the libel on the plaintiff, they did not write it or print it; they only disseminated that which contained the libel. The question is whether, as such disseminators, they published the libel? If they had known what was in the paper, whether they were paid for circulating it or not, they would have published the libel, and would have been liable for so doing. That, I think, cannot be doubted. But here, upon the findings of the jury, we must take it that the defendants did not know that the paper contained a libel. I am not prepared to say that it would be sufficient for them to shew that they did not know of the particular libel. But the findings of the jury make it clear that the defendants did not publish the libel.[3] Taking the view of the jury to be right, that the defendants did not know that the paper was likely to contain a libel, and, still more, that they ought not to have known this, which must mean, that they ought not to have known it, having used reasonable care—the case is reduced to this, that the defendants were innocent disseminators of a thing which they were not bound to know was likely to contain a libel. That being so, I think the defendants are not liable for the libel.'

And in the same case Bowen LJ said:[4]

'A newspaper is not like a fire; a man may carry it about without being bound to suppose that it is likely to do an injury. It seems to me that the defendants are no more liable than any other innocent carrier of an article which he has no reason to suppose likely to be dangerous.'

1 (1885) 16 QBD 354 at 356–7.
2 It seems clear that the defence of innocent dissemination is not available to the printer.
3 It is submitted that it would be more accurate to say that any disseminator of a libel publishes the libel but, if he can establish the defence of innocent dissemination, he will not be responsible for that publication. In *Goldsmith v Sperrings Ltd* [1977] 2 All ER 566 at 587, [1977] 1 WLR 478 at 505, Bridge LJ said: '. . . any disseminator of defamatory matter is liable to the party defamed, subject to the defence of innocent dissemination'.
4 (1885) 16 QBD 354 at 358. In *Goldsmith v Sperrings Ltd* [1977] 2 All ER 566 at 572, [1977] 1 WLR 478 at 487, Lord Denning MR, in a dissenting judgment, was inclined to put the burden of proof on the plaintiff: 'Common sense and fairness require that no subordinate distributor—from top to bottom—should be held liable for a libel contained in it unless he knew or ought to have known that the newspaper or periodical contained a libel on the plaintiff himself; that is to say, that it contained a libel on the plaintiff which could not be justified or excused; and I should have thought that it was for the plaintiff to prove this. And the Restatement bears this out: see Restatement, Torts, 1965 Supplement, section 581, Comment.'

16.05   In *Sun Life Assurance Co of Canada v W H Smith & Son Ltd*, however, Scrutton LJ suggested that the questions for the jury should be expressed as follows:[1]

'I think it would probably be better if the questions for the jury in cases like that of *Emmens v Pottle*[2] once the libel has been established, were restricted to (1) a question whether the defendant knew and (2) a question whether the defendant ought to have known, that is to say, whether there was negligence on the part of the defendant in carrying on his business in respect of the publication of the libel.'

1 (1933) 150 LT 211 at 212.
2 (1885) 16 QBD 354.

16.06   The question of the standard of care to be exercised by the distributors was considered by the Court of Appeal in *Weldon v Times Book Club Ltd*, where Cozens-Hardy MR put the matter as follows:[1]

'It was quite impossible that distributing agents such as the respondents should be expected to read every book they had. There were some books as to which there might be a duty on the respondents or other distributing agents to examine them carefully because of their titles or the recognised propensity of their authors to scatter libels abroad. Beyond that the matter could not go. It was impossible to say there was a liability to examine the contents of books like the two in question, which were by authors of high character.'

1 (1911) 28 TLR 143 at 144. It seems that the decision in *Vizetelly v Mudie's Select Library* [1900] 2 QB 170, where the Court of Appeal declined to interfere with the verdict of the jury in favour of the plaintiff, is to be explained on the basis of the admissions made in evidence by one of the defendants' directors: see at 176 per A.L. Smith LJ. In *Bottomley v F W Woolworth & Co* (1932) 48 TLR 521, where the defendants sold remainders of American magazines at the rate of about 50,000 copies every week, Scrutton LJ described as absurd the finding of the jury that the defendants were negligent 'owing to the absence of periodical examinations of specimen magazines'.

Apology and payment into court under Lord Campbell's Act

16.07   It is provided by the Libel Act 1843, s 2[1] (as amended by the Libel Act 1845, s 2) that in an action for a libel contained in public newspaper or other periodical publication[2] it is a defence for the defendant to prove—

(a) that the publication was made without actual malice;
(b) that the publication was made without gross negligence;
(c) that an apology was published before the commencement of the action or at the earliest opportunity afterwards;[3]
(d) that a payment into court was made at the time the defence was served.

1 The Act is commonly called Lord Campbell's Act.
2 There is no definition in the Act of 'public newspaper or other periodical publication'. The Act has not been extended to broadcasting.
3 If the newspaper or periodical publication in which the libel appeared is ordinarily published at intervals exceeding one week it is open to the defendant to plead and prove as an alternative that he had offered to publish a full apology in any newspaper or periodical publication to be selected by the plaintiff.

16.08   The burden of proof is on the defendant to prove that the publication was without actual malice[1] and without gross negligence[2] and that his apology was sufficient.[3] If the defendant proves these three ingredients of the defence and that he made a payment into court at the time of serving the defence he is entitled to judgment.

1 As to the meaning of actual malice, see para 17.03, post.
2 In *Bell v Northern Constitution Ltd* [1943] NI 108, Andrews LCJ held that it was gross negligence for a news-paper to publish the announcement of a birth without making any enquiry as to the authenticity of a notice received by telephone.
3 The wording of the section is 'a full apology'. One of the issues for the jury at the trial therefore is the adequacy of the published (or, where appropriate, offered) apology.

16.09   A defence under Lord Campbell's Act is seldom if ever used in practice at the present day. In a case where a newspaper has no defence and the matter cannot be disposed of by agreement, the usual practice is for the defendant newspaper to make a payment into court under RSC Order 22 and, if thought appropriate, to publish an apology and/or serve a notice in mitigation of damages under RSC Order 82, rule 7, setting out the circumstances under which the libel was published. The advantage of a payment into court under RSC Order 22 is that the defendant would usually expect to recover his costs from the plaintiff after the date of payment in if the jury award a sum less or no greater than the sum in court, whereas if a sum is paid into court under Lord Campbell's Act and the defendant is unable to prove one or more of the necessary ingredients of the defence the plain-tiff may be awarded the costs of the action even though the jury award a smaller sum than the sum paid in.[1]

1 See *Oxley v Wilkes* [1898] 2 QB 56. Where money is paid into court under Lord Campbell's Act the defendant is entitled to refer to that fact in his defence, though (semble) the amount of the payment in should not be stated in the defence nor communicated to the court before the verdict of the jury has been given. It seems that a defendant would be entitled by giving appropriate notices to the plaintiff to rely on a payment into court both as a payment under Lord Campbell's Act and as a payment under RSC Ord 22: see *Bell v Northern Constitution Ltd* [1943] NI 108.

CHAPTER 17

Malice

INTRODUCTION

17.01 The words 'malice' and 'maliciously' are used in a number of different contexts in the law of defamation, but these uses can be conveniently grouped into two main categories—

(a) the use of the word 'maliciously' in a statement of claim;
(b) the use of the word 'malice' to denote the state of mind of the defendant which, if proved to have actuated the publication, will defeat a defence of fair comment or qualified privilege or, in certain limited circumstances, a defence of justification.

The word 'maliciously' as used in a statement of claim

17.02 In a statement of claim in an action for defamation it has been customary to plead that the words complained of were published 'falsely and maliciously'. It seems clear that such a plea is strictly speaking unnecessary.[1] The falsity of defamatory words is presumed and the burden of proving that they are true is placed on the defendant. Similarly, the publication of defamatory words is presumed to be malicious.[2] In this context, however, the word 'maliciously' does not impute a state of mind or an intention to defame[3] because the intention of the defamer is irrelevant,[4] but merely that the words were published without lawful excuse.

1 The Faulks Committee have recommended that the use of the phrase 'falsely and maliciously' should be treated as obsolete: see Cmnd 5909, para 143. It seems probable, however, that the present practice is likely to continue until changed by statute. It may be noted that the words 'falsely and maliciously' were included in precedents 32 and 33 in Schedule (B) to the Common Law Procedure Act 1852.
2 Malice in this context is sometimes referred to as malice in law.
3 It seems that in some of the earlier cases the word 'maliciously' did involve an imputation of intention. For example in *R v Lord Abingdon* (1794) 1 Esp 226, (a criminal prosecution for libel) Lord Kenyon said: 'In order to constitute libel, the mind must be in fault, and show a malicious intention to defame.'
4 See para 4.07, ante.

Express malice

17.03 The concept of express or actual malice, that is, malice in fact, is of great importance in the law of defamation because both a defence of fair comment and a defence of qualified privilege can be defeated if the plaintiff proves that when the defendant published the words complained of he was actuated by express malice. Furthermore, malice may also be relevant on the issue of damages and in certain limited circumstances in relation to a defence of justification.[1]

1 See para 11.14, ante.

17.04 The term 'express malice' has been the source of some confusion because the word 'malice' as a word in general use connotes spite or ill-will whereas the express malice which can defeat a defence of fair comment or qualified privilege can include within its ambit not only spitefulness but also a state of mind which is not 'malicious' in the ordinary sense of the word. Furthermore, in cases where the express malice relied upon does in fact involve evidence of ill-will between the parties the jury may find it difficult fully to appreciate that proof of the existence of bad feeling is not equivalent to proof that the defendant was *actuated* by malice at the time of publication.

17.05 All the earlier cases relating to express malice have now to be considered in the light of the decision of the House of Lords in *Horrocks v Lowe*. In that case the defendant was a councillor of a local authority who had published the words complained of at a council meeting and on an occasion of qualified privilege. The case was concerned therefore with the defence of qualified privilege and the effect of express malice on that defence, but the speeches in the House of Lords provide important guidance in all cases in which malice has to be considered. Lord Diplock dealt with the question of express malice in the following words:[1]

'. . . in all cases of qualified privilege there is some special reason of public policy why the law accords immunity from suit—the existence of some public or private duty, whether legal or moral, on the part of the maker of the defamatory statement which justifies his communicating it or of some interest of his own which he is entitled to protect by doing so. If he uses the occasion for some other reason he loses the protection of the privilege.

So, the motive with which the defendant on a privileged occasion made a statement defamatory of the plaintiff becomes crucial. The protection might, however, be illusory if the onus lay on him to prove that he was actuated solely by a sense of the relevant duty or a desire to protect the relevant interest. So he is entitled to be protected by the privilege unless some other dominant and improper motive on his part is proved. ''Express malice'' is the term of art descriptive of such a motive. Broadly speaking, it means malice in the popular sense of a desire to injure the person who is defamed and this is generally the motive which the plaintiff sets out to prove. But to destroy the privilege the desire to injure must be the dominant motive for the defamatory publication; knowledge that it will have that effect is not enough if the defendant is nevertheless acting in accordance with a sense of duty or in bona fide protection of his own legitimate interest.

The motive with which a person published defamatory matter can only be inferred from what he did or said or knew. If it be proved that he did not believe that what he published was true this is generally conclusive evidence of express malice, for no sense of duty or desire to protect his own legitimate interest can justify a man in telling deliberate and injurious falsehoods about another, save in the exceptional case where a person may be under a duty to pass on, without endorsing, defamatory reports made by some other person.[2]

Apart from those exceptional cases, what is required on the part of the defamer to entitle him to the protection of the privilege is positive belief in the truth of what he published or, as it is generally though tautologously termed, ''honest belief''. If he publishes untrue defamatory matter recklessly, without considering or caring whether it be true or not, he is in this, as in other branches of the law, treated as if he knew it to be false. But indifference to the truth of what he publishes is not to be equated with carelessness, impulsiveness or irrationality in arriving at a positive belief that it is true. The freedom of speech protected by the law of qualified privilege may be availed of by all sorts and conditions of men. In affording to them immunity from suit if they have acted in good faith in compliance with a legal or moral duty or in protection of a legitimate interest the law must take them as it finds them. In ordinary life it is rare indeed for people to form their beliefs by a process of logical deduction from facts ascertained by a rigorous search for all available evidence and a judicious assessment of its probative value. In greater or less degree according to their temperaments, their training, their intelligence, they are swayed by prejudice, rely on intuition instead of reasoning, leap to conclusions on inadequate evidence and fail to recognise the cogency of material which might cast doubt on the validity of the conclusions they reach. But despite the imperfection of the mental process by which the belief is arrived at it may still be ''honest'', that is, a positive belief that the conclusions they have reached are true. The law demands no more.

Even a positive belief in the truth of what is published on a privileged occasion—which is presumed unless the contrary is proved—may not be sufficient to negative express malice if it can be proved that the defendant misused the occasion for some purpose other than that for which the privilege is accorded by the law. The commonest case is where the dominant motive which actuates the defendant is not a desire to perform the relevant duty or to protect the relevant interest, but to give vent to his personal spite or illwill towards the person he defames. If this be proved, then even positive belief in the truth of what is published will not enable the defamer to avail himself of the protection of the privilege to which he would otherwise have been entitled. There may be instances of improper motives which destroy the privilege apart from personal spite. A defendant's dominant motive may have been to obtain some private advantage unconnected with the duty or the interest which constitutes the reason for the privilege. If so, he loses the benefit of the privilege despite his positive belief that what he said or wrote was true.

Judges and juries should, however, be very slow to draw the inference that a defendant was so far actuated by improper motives as to deprive him of the protection of the privilege unless they are satisfied that he did not believe that what he said or wrote was true or that he was indifferent to its truth or falsity. The motives with which human beings act are mixed. They find it difficult to hate the sin but love the sinner. Qualified privilege would be illusory, and the public interest that it is meant to serve defeated, if the protection which it affords were lost merely because a person, although acting in compliance with a duty or in protection of a legitimate interest, disliked the person whom he defamed or was indignant at what he believed to be that person's conduct and welcomed the opportunity of expressing it. It is only where his desire to comply with a relevant duty or to protect the relevant interest plays no significant part in his motives for publishing what he believes to be true that ''express malice'' can properly be found.'

1 [1975] AC 135 at 149, [1974] 1 All ER 662 at 669.
2 See paras 8.16 and 14.08, ante, and, for example, *Stuart v Bell* [1891] 2 QB 341.

EXPRESS MALICE IN RELATION TO QUALIFIED PRIVILEGE: GENERAL
PRINCIPLES

17.06 From the guidance given in *Horrocks v Lowe*[1] it is now possible to formulate the following principles to be applied where the question of express malice has
to be considered in connection with a defence of qualified privilege—

(a) The motive with which a person published defamatory matter can only be
     inferred from what he did or said or knew.[2] Evidence of the defendant's
     state of mind can therefore be tendered by either or both sides.

(b) The defendant is entitled to be protected by the privilege unless the plaintiff
     proves that the defendant had an improper motive for publishing the words
     and that the improper motive was the sole or dominant motive.[3]

(c) If the defendant did not believe that what he published was true this fact is
     generally[4] conclusive evidence of express malice, for no sense of duty or
     desire to protect his own legitimate interest can justify a man in telling
     deliberate and injurious falsehoods about another.[5]

(d) If the defendant made the publication recklessly, being indifferent to the
     truth of what he published and neither considering nor caring whether it
     was true or not, he will be treated as if he knew it to be false. But care-
     lessness or impulsiveness or irrationality in arriving at a positive belief in the
     truth of what was published does not amount to indifference to the truth.[6]

(e) Even where the defendant did believe the words to be true the plaintiff *may*
     still be able to prove that the publication was actuated by an improper
     motive, for example, a desire to injure the plaintiff or to achieve some
     personal advantage unconnected with the duty or interest which
     constitutes the reason for the privilege. But in such a case—that is, where
     the defendant believed the words to be true—judges and juries should be
     very slow to draw the inference that the sole or dominant motive for publi-
     cation was the improper motive.[7]

1 [1975] AC 135, [1974] 1 All ER 662.
2 See *Horrocks v Lowe* [1975] AC 135 at 149, [1974] 1 All ER 662 at 669, per Lord Diplock.
3 See *Horrocks v Lowe* [1975] AC 135 at 149, [1974] 1 All ER 662 at 669, per Lord Diplock.
4 In exceptional circumstances a person may be under a duty to pass on, without endorsing, defamatory reports
   made by some other person.
5 See *Horrocks v Lowe* [1975] AC 135 at 149–150, [1974] 1 All ER 662 at 669, per Lord Diplock.
6 See *Horrocks v Lowe* [1975] AC 135 at 150, [1974] 1 All ER 662 at 670, per Lord Diplock.
7 See *Horrocks v Lowe* [1975] AC 135 at 150, [1974] 1 All ER 662 at 669, per Lord Diplock.

THE PUBLICATION OF IRRELEVANT MATTER ON AN OCCASION OF
QUALIFIED PRIVILEGE

17.07 It may happen that in the course of a publication on an occasion of qualified privilege the defendant will include matter which is not relevant to the subject
matter which attracts the privilege. In such an event the question arises: is the
irrelevant matter to be treated as outside the privilege altogether or does its inclusion merely provide evidence from which malice may be inferred. In *Horrocks v
Lowe* Lord Diplock dealt with the matter as follows:[1]

'Logically it might be said that such irrelevant matter falls outside the privilege altogether. But if this were so it would involve the application by the court of an objective test of relevance to every part of the defamatory matter published on the privileged occasion; whereas, as everyone knows, ordinary human beings vary in their ability to distinguish that which is logically relevant from that which is not and few, apart from lawyers, have had any training which qualifies them to do so. So the protection afforded by the privilege would be illusory if it were lost in respect of any defamatory matter which upon logical analysis could be shown to be irrelevant to the fulfillment of the duty or the protection of the right upon which the privilege was founded. As Lord Dunedin pointed out in *Adam v Ward*[2] the proper rule as respects irrelevant defamatory matter incorporated in a statement made on a privileged occasion is to treat it as one of the factors to be taken into consideration in deciding whether, in all the circumstances, an inference that the defendant was actuated by express malice can properly be drawn. As regards irrelevant matter the test is not whether it is logically relevant but whether, in all the circumstances, it can be inferred that the defendant either did not believe it to be true or, though believing it to be true, realised that it had nothing to do with the particular duty or interest on which the privilege was based, but nevertheless seized the opportunity to drag in irrelevant defamatory matter to vent his personal spite, or for some other improper motive. Here, too, judges and juries should be slow to draw this inference.'

1 [1975] AC 135 at 151, [1974] 1 All ER 662 at 670.
2 [1917] AC 309 at 326–7.

17.08 It seems clear, however, that Lord Diplock did not mean to suggest that (subject to the question of malice) the privilege would extend to cover matter which had nothing whatever to do with the rest of the communication. In *Adam v Ward* (in the passage cited by Lord Diplock)[1] Lord Dunedin stated the position as follows:[2]

'If the defamatory statement is quite unconnected with and irrelevant to the main statement which is ex hypothesi privileged, then I think it is more accurate to say that the privilege does not extend thereto than to say, though the result may be the same, that the defamatory statement is evidence of malice.'

And in *Nevill v Fine Arts and General Insurance Co Ltd* Lord Esher MR said:[3]

'There may be an excess of the privilege in the sense that something has been published which is not within the privileged occasion at all, because it can have no reference to it. . . . But when there is only an excessive statement having reference to the privileged occasion, and which, therefore, comes within it, then the only way in which the excess is material is as being evidence of malice.'

1 See *Horrocks v Lowe* [1975] AC 135 at 151, [1974] 1 All ER 662 at 670.
2 [1917] AC 309 at 327.
3 [1895] 2 QB 156 at 170. This passage was adopted by Lord Dunedin in *Adam v Ward* [1917] AC 309 at 327.

17.09 It is submitted that the law can be stated as follows—

(a) Any matter which is in any way relevant to or connected with the subject matter which is protected by privilege will prima facie be covered by the privilege.

(b) If the defendant includes matter which is only marginally relevant such inclusion *may* provide evidence of malice as showing that the defendant was using the privileged occasion for some improper purpose.

(c) The court or jury should not apply any strict standard in determining relevance and should be slow to find malice merely because something has been included which logically is not relevant.

(d) A defamatory statement which is wholly unconnected with the subject matter which is protected by privilege will not be covered. The inclusion of this 'foreign' matter may also provide evidence that the relevant material was published with malice.[1]

---

1 See *Adam v Ward* [1917] AC 309 at 340 per Lord Atkinson. It is for the judge to rule whether any matter is irrelevant so as to fall outside the privilege: see ibid.

EXPRESS MALICE IN RELATION TO FAIR COMMENT

17.10 Though the decision in *Horrocks v Lowe*[1] related to the effect of express malice on a defence of qualified privilege it is possible from the guidance given in that case to formulate the following principles to be applied where the question of express malice has to be considered in connection with a defence of fair comment—

(a) The motive with which a person published defamatory matter can only be inferred from what he did or said or knew.[2] Evidence of the defendant's state of mind can therefore be tendered by either or both sides.

(b) The defendant is entitled to be protected by the defence of fair comment (provided the objective cost of fair comment is satisfied)[3] unless the plaintiff proves that the defendant had an improper motive for publishing the words and that the improper motive was the sole or dominant motive.[4]

(c) If the comment did not represent the honest opinion of the defendant this will generally be conclusive evidence of express malice against him.[5]

(d) Even where the comment did represent the honest opinion of the defendant the plaintiff *may* still be able to prove that the publication was actuated by an improper motive, for example, a desire to injure the plaintiff or to achieve some personal advantage. But in such a case—that is, where the comment did represent the honest opinion of the defendant—judges and juries should be very slow to draw the inference that the sole or dominant motive for publication was the improper motive.[6]

---

1 [1975] AC 135, [1974] 1 All ER 662.
2 See *Horrocks v Lowe* [1975] AC 135 at 149, [1974] 1 All ER 662 at 669, per Lord Diplock.
3 See para 12.14, ante.
4 See *Horrocks v Lowe* [1975] AC 139 at 149, [1974] 1 All ER 662 at 669, per Lord Diplock.
5 It is submitted that this would not apply, for example, to the editor, publishers or printers of a newpaper sued for defamatory comments in the newspaper by a journalist or a member of the public. It may be, however, that in such circumstances the defence of fair comment would not be available at all: see *Cherneskey v Armadale Publishers Ltd* (1978) 90 DLR (3d) 321 and para 12.14, ante.
6 See *Horrocks v Lowe* [1975] AC 135 at 150, [1974] 1 All ER 662 at 670, per Lord Diplock.

Evidence of express malice

17.11   Where a defence of qualified privilege or fair comment is raised the plaintiff may seek to defeat the defence by proof that the defendant was actuated by malice. In that event the plaintiff is required to serve a reply giving particulars of the facts and matters from which the malice is to be inferred.[1]

---

1 RSC Ord 82 r 3(3) is in the following terms: 'Where in an action for libel or slander the plaintiff alleges that the defendant maliciously published the words complained of, he need not in his statement of claim give particulars of the facts on which he relies in support of the allegation of malice, but if the defendant pleads that any of those words or matters are fair comment on a matter of public interest or were published on a privileged occasion and the plaintiff intends to allege that the defendant was actuated by express malice, he must serve a reply giving particulars of the facts and matters from which the malice is to be inferred.'

INTRINSIC EVIDENCE

17.12   The language used by the defendant *may* provide evidence that he was actuated by malice but he is allowed a wide latitude. In *Adam v Ward* Lord Atkinson, after referring to earlier authorities,[1] stated the matter in relation to the defence of qualified privilege as follows:[2]

> 'These authorities, in my view, clearly establish that a person making a communication on a privileged occasion is not restricted to the use of such language merely as is reasonably necessary to protect the interest or discharge the duty which is the foundation of his privilege; but that, on the contrary, he will be protected, even though his language should be violent or excessively strong, if, having regard to all the circumstances of the case, he might have honestly and on reasonable grounds believed that what he wrote or said was true and necessary for the purpose of his vindication, though in fact it was not so.'

---

1 *Spill v Maule* (1869) LR 4 Exch 232; *Laughton v Bishop of Sodor and Man* (1872) LR 4 PC 495; *Nevill v Fine Arts and General Insurance Co Ltd* [1895] 2 QB 156; on appeal, [1897] AC 68.
2 [1917] AC 309 at 339.

17.13   Lord Dunedin also, in *Adam v Ward*, emphasised that a wide latitude is allowed:[1]

> '. . . when considering whether the actual expression used can be held as evidence of express malice no nice scales should be used. I would particularly cite the words of the judgment of the Privy Council (in *Laughton v Bishop of Sodor and Man*):[2] ''Some expressions here used undoubtedly go beyond what was necessary for self defence, but it does not, therefore, follow that they afford evidence of malice for a jury. To submit the language of privileged communications to a strict scrutiny, and to hold all excess beyond the absolute exigency of the occasion to be evidence of malice would in effect greatly limit, if not altogether defeat, that protection which the law throws over privileged communications.'' '

---

1 [1917] AC 309 at 330.
2 (1872) LR 4 PC 495 at 508.

17.14   But the language may be so strong as to indicate that the defendant was actuated by malice, as was pointed out in *Edmondson v Birch & Co Ltd* by Collins MR where he said:[1]

'The language used may in some cases be so defamatory, and so far in excess of the occasion, as to be evidence of actual malice, and to shew that the publication of the defamatory matter was not a use, but an abuse of the privileged occasion.'

1 [1907] 1 KB 371 at 381.

17.15   In the case of fair comment too the words used may provide evidence of malice, but it seems that as a general rule language which is sufficiently strong to prove malice will also prevent the defendant from satisfying the objective test of fair comment.[1]

1 See para 12.14, ante.

EXTRINSIC EVIDENCE

17.16   Any evidence as to the state of mind of the defendant *may* be relevant on the issue whether he was actuated by express malice at the time of publication. It is proposed therefore to mention some of the headings under which such evidence may fall.

Antagonism towards the plaintiff

17.17   Any evidence tending to show that the defendant had quarrelled with the plaintiff or had threatened the plaintiff or had defamed him on other occasions, or otherwise indicating that the defendant bore some grudge or ill-will towards the plaintiff may be relevant on the issue. It is important to emphasise, however, that the existence of personal animosity does not necessarily establish that the defendant was actuated by express malice in making the publication of which complaint is made.[1]

1 See para 17.05, ante.

Indirect or improper motive

17.18   Express malice includes any indirect or improper motive. Accordingly any evidence would be relevant on the issue of malice if it tended to show that the defendant made the publication not for the purpose for which the qualified privilege existed nor in the exercise of his right to comment on a matter of public interest but, for example, in order to injure the plaintiff or some third party.[1]

1 It is not necessary that the indirect motive should be one directed at the plaintiff personally. It must be remembered, however, that in any case where an indirect or improper motive is alleged the court or jury should consider carefully whether this motive, even if proved, was the sole or dominant motive: see para 17.05, ante.

Failure to retract or apologise

17.19   It is often suggested on behalf of the plaintiff that malice is to be inferred from the fact that the defendant has failed to publish a retraction or to apologise. But as Lord Diplock pointed out in *Horrocks v Lowe:*[1]

'A refusal to apologise is at best tenuous evidence of malice, for it is consistent with a continuing belief in the truth of what one has said.'

And in *Broadway Approvals Ltd v Odhams Press Ltd* Sellers LJ said:[2]

'The failure to apologise or retract and a persistence in a plea of justification are in themselves not evidence of malice. They may be in certain circumstances but more frequently they would show sincerity and belief in what had been said and establish the best reason for the publication.'

There may be cases, however, where after publication the defendant is provided with proof that he was mistaken and that what he said was untrue: in such circumstances a failure to retract a serious charge may provide evidence that at the time of the original publication the defendant was actuated by malice.[3]

---

1 [1975] AC 135 at 154, [1974] 1 All ER 662 at 671. In *Morgan v Odhams Press* [1971] 2 All ER 1156, [1971] 1 WLR 1239 (a case where there was an issue as to whether the words referred to the plaintiff) Lord Reid said at 1164, 1247: 'To have apologised—I do not know how—might have seemed to be going some way towards admitting that they had defamed the appellant.'
2 [1965] 2 All ER 523 at 533, [1965] 1 WLR 805 at 814. In that case the defendants' defence of justification failed but they succeeded on the issue of fair comment: Davies LJ said at 540, 824: 'The jury have in effect found that the comment would have been fair if made by a non-malicious person. How then could a failure to apologise make the comment unfair or render its publication malicious?'
3 If a defendant repeats an allegation after he is satisfied as to its falsity he will not be able to rely on his honest belief, and the inference may be that he was actuated by malice not only in relation to the repetition but also in relation to the original publication.

The effect of the malice of another person

17.20   Where defamatory matter is published in circumstances in which a number of persons may be liable in respect of the publication and the question arises whether the publication was actuated by express malice, it is necessary to consider the position of each person separately. In the first place it is clear that the ordinary rules as to vicarious liability apply and that an employer or principal will be liable if his employee or agent was actuated by malice in making a defamatory publication within the scope of his employment or agency.[1] Apart from cases of vicarious liability, however, a defendant who is entitled to the protection of qualified privilege will not lose that protection merely because a co-publisher was actuated by express malice.[2] Moreover, it is submitted that the same principle will be applied where more than one person takes part in a publication to which a defence of fair comment is relevant, and that, for example, the editor or printers of a newspaper can rely on the defence of fair comment—provided the comment satisfies the objective test[3] and they are innocent of malice—even though the author of the article was malicious.[4]

---

1 *Egger v Viscount Chelmsford* [1965] 1 QB 248, [1964] 3 All ER 406; *Riddick v Thames Board Mills Ltd* [1977] 3 All ER 677 at 693, [1977] 3 WLR 63 at 79 per Stephenson LJ. On the other hand it seems that an innocent employee or agent is not infected by the malice of his employer or principal: see *Egger v Viscount Chelmsford*,

supra, where dicta to the contrary effect in *Adam v Ward* [1917] AC 309 were regarded as obiter and erroneous.
2 See, for example, *Egger v Viscount Chelmsford* [1965] 1 QB 248, [1964] 3 All ER 406.
3 See para 12.14, ante.
4 See *Egger v Viscount Chelmsford* [1965] 1 QB 248 at 265, [1964] 3 All ER 406 at 412, per Lord Denning MR; but for a contrary view see ibid at 269, 415, per Davies LJ.

CHAPTER 18

Damages

INTRODUCTION

18.01 In an action for defamation the only relief which the plaintiff can obtain from a court, apart from an injunction in appropriate circumstances to prevent repetition of the libel or slander,[1] is an award of damages. The principles governing such awards are therefore of great importance.

1 For the principles governing the grant of an interlocutory injunction, see para 19.02, post.

18.02 The general rule is that in actions for defamation, as in other actions for tort, the damages are to be assessed on a compensatory basis. In certain circumstances, however, exemplary (or punitive) damages can be awarded. The broad headings under which the subject of damages will be examined will be—

(a) compensatory damages, which may include special damages, and, if aggravating circumstances exist, aggravated damages;
(b) exemplary damages.[1]

1 See paras 18.25–18.27, post.

Compensatory damages

BASIC RULE: COMPENSATION NOT PUNISHMENT

18.03 The basic rule of common law is that in civil actions damages are awarded as compensation for injury, not as punishment for wrongdoing.[1] Accordingly in most actions for defamation the damages have to be assessed on a compensatory basis.[2]

1 It is to be noted, however, that Lord Wilberforce in his dissenting speech in *Cassell & Co Ltd v Broome* [1972] AC 1027 at 1114, [1972] 1 All ER 801 at 860, said: 'It cannot lightly be taken for granted, even as a matter of theory, that the purpose of the law of tort is compensation, still less that it ought to be . . . or that there is something inappropriate or illogical or anomalous . . . in including a punitive element in civil damages'.
2 For cases where exemplary damages can be awarded see paras 18.25–18.27, post.

THE PURPOSE OF COMPENSATORY DAMAGES

18.04 The purpose of an award of compensatory damages is to restore the plaintiff, as far as money can do so, to the position he would have been in if the tort had not been committed. This principle of restitutio in integrum was stated by Lord Blackburn in *Livingstone v Rawyards Coal Co* as follows:[1]

> 'Where any injury is to be compensated by damages, in settling the sum of money to be given for reparation of damages you should as nearly as possible get at that sum of money which would put the party who has been injured, or who has suffered, in the same position as he would have been in if he had not sustained the wrong for which he is now getting his compensation or reparation.'

1 (1880) 5 App Cas 25 at 39.

18.05 In many actions for tort the principle of restitutio in integrum is an adequate guide to the estimation of damage because the damage suffered can be estimated by relation to some material loss. But in some actions, including actions for defamation and most actions for personal injuries, the assessment of damages will include a substantial subjective element, because neither physical pain nor the damage to a reputation are convertible by the use of any yardstick into a sum of money. Whereas, however, the awards made by the courts in actions for personal injuries for pain and suffering and loss of amenity have over the years achieved some measure of uniformity, awards in defamation actions cannot be said even to approximate to any conventional scale.

THE SUBJECTIVE ELEMENT, AND WHETHER A COMPARISON CAN BE MADE
WITH AWARDS FOR PERSONAL INJURIES

18.06 There has been some judicial criticism of the fact that awards of damages in actions for defamation may often seem disproportionate to awards made for serious personal injuries. Thus in *McCarey v Associated Newspapers Ltd* Diplock LJ said:[1]

> 'I do not believe that the law today is more jealous of a man's reputation than of his life or limb. That is the scale of values of the duel. Of course, the injuries in the two kinds of case are very different, but each has as its main consequences pain or grief, annoyance or unhappiness, to the plaintiff. In this court recently we refused by a majority to disturb a verdict of a jury awarding £2,000 to a woman thirty years of age who had, after considerable suffering for many months and two operations in hospital, had a leg amputated below the knee and her knee permanently immobilised. In that case it was the view of the Court of Appeal that a proper measure of damages, had the award been made by a judge, would have been in the neighbourhood of £4,000 to £6,000, a figure which is in scale with the amount of damages which are commonly awarded (and have been approved by this court) in serious physical injury cases. If £2,000 is not inappropriate, or if £4,000 to £6,000 is appropriate, compensation for a life-long injury of that character which has its physical effect every day of the plaintiff's future life, and £9,000 is the appropriate award for the injury done to the plaintiff in this case, then I can only say that the scale of values is wrong, and if that is the law, so much the worse for the law. But I do not accept that that higher scale of values in defamation cases is sanctioned by the law. It is, I think, legitimate as an aid to considering whether the award of damages by a jury is so large that no reasonable jury would have arrived at that figure if they had applied proper principles, to bear in mind the kind of figures which are proper, and have been held to be proper, in cases of disabling physical injury.'

1 [1965] 2 QB 86 at 109, [1964] 3 All ER 947 at 960. See also *Groom v Crocker* [1939] 1 KB 194 at 231, [1938] 2 All ER 394 at 419, where Mackinnon LJ said: 'In the course of some twelve years at nisi prius I have been struck by the contrast between the frequent niggardliness of verdicts in cases of personal injury and the invariable profuseness in claims for defamation. A soiled reputation seems assured of more liberal assuagement than a compound fracture'; and *Broadway Approvals Ltd v Odhams Press Ltd* [1965] 2 All ER 523 at 536, [1965] 1 WLR 805 at 818 where Sellers LJ said: 'If Santo had lost a leg, a great deprivation which nothing could restore, it is unlikely that he would have received more than about half of the sum awarded by the jury for the injury to his reputation' (Santo had been awarded £10,000).

18.07   There does not seem to be, however, any general trend to relate damages in actions for defamation to awards made in cases involving personal injury. Moreover, the large subjective element in an award of damages in an action for defamation makes it difficult to draw a fair comparison with awards in other types of action. In *Cassell & Co Ltd v Broome* Lord Hailsham of St Marylebone LC said:[1]

'In almost all actions of breach of contract, and in many actions for tort, the principle of restitutio in integrum is an adequate and fairly easy guide to the estimation of damage, because the damage suffered can be estimated by relation to some material loss. It is true that where loss includes a pre-estimate of future losses, or an estimate of past losses which cannot in the nature of things be exactly computed, some subjective element must enter in. But the estimate is in things commensurable with one another, and convertible at least in principle to the English currency in which all sums of damages must ultimately be expressed.[2] In many torts, however, the subjective element is more difficult. The pain and suffering endured, and the future loss of amenity, in a personal injuries case are not in the nature of things convertible into legal tender. . . . Nor, so far as I can judge, is there any purely rational test by which a judge can calculate what sum, greater or smaller, is appropriate. What is surprising is not that there is difference of opinion about such matters, but that in most cases professional opinion gravitates so closely to a conventional scale. Nevertheless in all actions in which damages, purely compensatory in character, are awarded for suffering, from the purely pecuniary point of view the plaintiff may be better off. The principle of restitutio in integrum, which compels the use of money as its sole instrument for restoring the status quo, necessarily involves a factor larger than any pecuniary loss. In actions of defamation and in any other actions where damages for loss of reputation are involved, the principle of restitutio in integrum has necessarily an even more highly subjective element. Such actions involve a money award which may put the plaintiff in a purely financial sense in a much stronger position than he was before the wrong. Not merely can he recover the estimated sum of his past and future losses, but, in case the libel, driven underground, emerges from its lurking place at some future date, he must be able to point to a sum awarded by a jury sufficient to convince a bystander of the baselessness of the charge. As Windeyer J well said in *Uren v John Fairfax & Sons Pty Ltd*:[3]

''It seems to me that, properly speaking, a man defamed does not get compensation *for* his damaged reputation. He gets damages *because* he was injured in his reputation, that is simply because he was publicly defamed. For this reason, compensation by damages operates in two ways—as a vindication of the plaintiff to the public and as consolation to him for a wrong done. Compensation is here a solatium rather than a monetary recompense for harm measurable in money.''

This is why it is not necessarily fair to compare awards of damages in this field with damages for personal injuries.[4] Quite obviously, the award must include factors for injury to the feelings, the anxiety and uncertainty undergone in the litigation, the absence of apology, or the reaffirmation of the truth of the matters complained of, or the malice of the defendant. The bad conduct of the plaintiff himself may also enter into the matter, where he has provoked the libel, or where perhaps he has libelled the defendant in reply. What is awarded is thus a figure which cannot be arrived at by any purely objective computation. This is what is meant when the damages in defamation are described as being ''at large''.'

1 [1972] AC 1027 at 1070, [1972] 1 All ER 801 at 823.
2 In certain circumstances claims in contract for a liquidated sum can be made in a foreign currency: see *Miliangos v George Frank (Textiles) Ltd* [1976] AC 443, [1975] 3 All ER 801; Administration of Justice Act 1977, s 4.
3 [1967] 117 CLR 118 at 150.
4 In *Lewis v Daily Telegraph Ltd* [1963] 1 QB 340 at 381, [1962] 2 All ER 698 at 717, Pearce LJ said: 'I do not derive help from considering personal injury cases.' And see *Blackshaw v Lord* [1983] 2 All ER 311, [1983] 3 WLR 283 at 331, 305–6, per Stephenson LJ, and 340, 317 per Fox LJ.

DAMAGES CAN FALL WITHIN A WIDE BRACKET

18.08 In *Cassell & Co Ltd v Broome* Lord Reid referred to the wide bracket within which damages in a defamation action can fall:[1]

'Damages for any tort are or ought to be fixed at a sum which will compensate the plaintiff, so far as money can do it, for all the injury which he has suffered. Where the injury is material and has been ascertained it is generally possible to assess damages with some precision. But that is not so where he has been caused mental distress or when his reputation has been attacked—where, to use the traditional phrase, he has been held up to hatred, ridicule or contempt. Not only is it impossible to ascertain how far other peoples minds have been affected, it is almost impossible to equate the damage to a sum of money. Any one person trying to fix a sum as compensation will probably find in his mind a wide bracket within which any sum could be regarded by him as not unreasonable—and different people will come to different conclusions. So in the end there will probably be a wide gap between the sum which on an objective view could be regarded as the least and the sum which could be regarded as the most to which the plaintiff is entitled as compensation.'

Furthermore, it is only quite recently that there has been any detailed analysis by the courts of the damages awarded in cases where, as in defamation actions, the damages are said to be 'at large'. Lord Diplock commented on this point as follows:[2]

'It may seem remarkable that there had not previously been[3] any judicial analysis, even as elementary as this, of the constituent elements of the compound "damages at large" but it has to be remembered that at common law the assessment of damages was the exclusive function of the jury, and, despite growing exceptions from the mid-19th century onwards, nearly all actions for torts in which damages were at large were tried by jury until after 1933. The assessment of damages was an arcanum of the jury box into which judges hesitated to peer; and it does not appear to have been their practice to give any direction to the jury as to how they should arrive at the amount of damages they should award, beyond some general exhortation to do their best in a manner which was peculiarly within their sphere.'[4]

1 [1972] AC 1027 at 1085, [1972] 1 All ER 801 at 836.
2 [1972] AC 1027 at 1125, [1972] 1 All ER 801 at 869.
3 Lord Diplock was referring to the analysis by Lord Devlin in *Rookes v Barnard* [1964] AC 1129 at 1221 et seq, [1964] 1 All ER 367 at 407 et seq.
4 It is for consideration whether the jury should be given more guidance as to the range of figures within which they should keep. Following the decision in *Savalas v Associated Newspapers* (1976) Times, 16 June, p 1, the foreman of the jury wrote to *The Times* newspaper as follows: 'It is no betrayal of the secrets of the jury room to confess that, with the other jurors, I entered the Royal Courts of Justice on June 14th with not the remotest idea what compensation is paid for anything except perhaps a dented boot and wing; haloes are outside our normal terms of reference. Apparently that is why we were asked. If that is so, the court had the outcome it deserved from the appointed procedure.' (*The Times*, 22 June 1976). But the present law is that the judge should not mention any figure to the jury as being an appropriate award: see *Montereale v Longmans Green & Co Ltd* (1965) 109 Sol Jo 215.

18.09   The fact that the damages can fall within a wide bracket means that it is very difficult for a defendant to disturb the award made by a jury. In *Blackshaw v Lord*, Stephenson LJ referred to the problem in these terms:[1]

> 'The extent of the subjective element in such injury as a libelled plaintiff may suffer, where, as here, the defendants' conduct does not mitigate but aggravates the damage, and the impossibility of ascertaining how wide and deep and long-lasting will be the damage to the libelled plaintiff's reputation, and the impossibility of converting either into money, have been so stressed by judges in that and other cases that counsel were unable to point to any case in the last 18 years since *McCarey v Associated Newspapers Ltd*[2] where this court had interfered with a jury's award of damages for defamation. We still have the power to reduce an excessive award but can we ever exercise it, at any rate in the absence of any plain misdirection by the trial judge? Are there any circumstances in which the size of the sum awarded is by itself so clearly and ridiculously disproportionate to the injury, even when aggravated, that this court can exercise its apparently obsolescent power and order a new trial as it did in *Rubber Improvement Ltd v Daily Telegraph Ltd*[3] . . . in the hope that another jury may not award the same sum, as well they may, an objection pointed out, for example, by Scrutton LJ in *Youssoupoff v MGM Pictures Ltd*.'[4]

1 [1983] 2 All ER 311 at 328, [1983] 3 WLR 283 at 302–3.
2 [1965] 2 QB 86, [1964] 3 All ER 947.
3 [1964] AC 234, [1963] 2 All ER 151, HL.
4 (1934) 50 TLR 581 at 585.

Factors to be taken into account in awarding compensatory damages

18.10   The large subjective element in an award of damages in a defamation action makes it impossible to put forward any objective standards by which to gauge the *right* figure in any particular case. Nevertheless, it is possible to identify the factors which can properly be taken into account in assessing damages. The seriousness of the libel is of course always a relevant consideration; the other factors will be considered under the following headings—

(a) special damage;
(b) injury to the plaintiff's feelings including aggravating factors;
(c) extent of the publication;
(d) mitigating factors.

SPECIAL DAMAGE

18.11   Special damage for the purpose of the law of defamation[1] may be defined as any material or temporal loss which is either a pecuniary loss or is capable of being estimated in money. Thus, for example, a plaintiff is entitled in an action for defamation to recover as special damage any pecuniary loss suffered as a result of losing his employment or a contract because of the publication of the defamatory matter. Furthermore, special damage can include the loss not only of a specific contract or of any specific customers but also a general loss of business. Where, however, the plaintiff wishes to claim special damage he must give particulars of his loss in the pleadings and give discovery of any relevant documents. Special damage is not confined to business or similar loss but may include, for example, the loss of hospitality from friends, provided such loss is capable of being estimated in money.[2]

1 The phrase 'special damage' is used in various senses in the law: see *Ratcliffe v Evans* [1892] 2 QB 524 at 528 per Bowen LJ.
2 See *Davies v Solomon* (1871) LR 7 QB 112.

18.12 In *Lewis v Daily Telegraph Ltd*, where the plaintiff company and its chairman and managing director brought an action for libel in respect of an article which stated the Fraud Squad were inquiring into the affairs of the company, Pearce LJ said:[1]

'If a person libelled has suffered specific damage he can plead it as special damage and recover it. That claim will then have the advantage (or disadvantage) of a careful scrutiny, supported by documents and oral evidence from which a court can decide whether in truth a decline of business resulted from the libel. The plaintiffs would then have to give particulars and facts and figures to support it. The plaintiffs or their accountants could produce figures of turnover and graphs showing any sudden downward tendency, such as, for instance, that in the week after the libel orders noticeably declined and so forth. Managers, salesmen and others could give supporting evidence. Evidence could be called to show that the price of the shares in the stock market had declined.[2] And the defendants would have an opportunity of calling evidence to counter the plaintiffs' claim for special damage.'

1 [1963] 1 QB 340 at 376, [1962] 2 All ER 698 at 714. And see *Calvet v Tomkies*, [1963] 3 All ER 610 at 613, [1963] 1 WLR 1397 at 1400, where Russell LJ said: 'If evidence of actual loss of earnings or decline in business, even without any figures mentioned, is to be put forward in a case such as this, as at present advised, I for my part am inclined to think that it should be pleaded with consequential discovery.' See also Lord Denning MR at 611, 1399.
2 A decline in the price of the shares would be evidence of damage to the goodwill of the company.

INJURY TO THE PLAINTIFF'S FEELINGS INCLUDING AGGRAVATING FACTORS

18.13 In cases where the plaintiff is an individual, one of the most important factors in the assessment of damages is the effect of the libel on the plaintiff's feelings. In *McCarey v Associated Newspapers Ltd (No 2)* Pearson LJ dealt with the various elements in compensatory damages as follows:[1]

'Compensatory damages, in a case in which they are at large, may include several different kinds of compensation to the injured plaintiff. They may include not only actual pecuniary loss and anticipated pecuniary loss or any social disadvantages which result, or may be thought likely to result, from the wrong which has been done. They may also include the natural injury to his feelings—the natural grief and distress which he may have felt at having been spoken of in defamatory terms, and if there has been any kind of high-handed, oppressive, insulting or contumelious behaviour by the defendant which increases the mental pain and suffering caused by the defamation and may constitute injury to the plaintiff's pride and self-confidence, those are proper elements to be taken into account in a case where the damages are at large.'

And in *Cassell & Co Ltd v Broome* Lord Reid said:[2]

> '[The defendant] may have behaved in a high-handed, malicious, insulting or oppressive manner in committing the tort or he or his counsel may at the trial have aggravated the injury by what they there said. That would justify going to the top of the bracket and awarding as damages the largest sum that could fairly be regarded as compensation.'

1 [1965] 2 QB 86 at 104, [1964] 3 All ER 947 at 957.
2 [1972] AC 1027 at 1085, [1972] 1 All ER 801 at 836.

18.14 Where the behaviour of the defendant has increased the injury to the plaintiff's feelings flowing naturally from the publication of the defamatory matter itself, the jury are entitled to include in their award an element of 'aggravated damages'. It is important to emphasise, however, that the sum to be awarded is a single sum and that aggravated damages are intended as compensation for the plaintiff and not as a form of punishment of the defendant. Among the factors that are likely to increase the damages are—

(a) a failure to apologise;[1]
(b) an unsuccessful plea of justification.[2]

1 See, for example, *Cassell & Co Ltd v Broome* [1972] AC 1027 at 1071, [1972] 1 All ER 801 at 824, per Lord Hailsham. Though a failure to apologise may provide little or no evidence of malice (see para 17.19, ante) it is likely to increase the affront to the plaintiff.
2 See, for example, *Cassell & Co Ltd v Broome* [1972] AC 1027 at 1071, [1972] 1 All ER 801 at 824, per Lord Hailsham and at 1125, 870 per Lord Diplock; *Associated Leisure Ltd v Associated Newspapers Ltd* [1970] 2 QB 450 at 455, [1970] 2 All ER 754 at 757, per Lord Denning MR.

EXTENT OF THE PUBLICATION

18.15 In many cases an important factor in the assessment of damages will be the extent of the publication. Thus whereas a limited publication to one or two individuals may lead to a very modest award of damages, particularly if the publishees are not influenced by the publication or may disbelieve it, a publication in a national newspaper or by means of television or radio may lead to a very substantial award because the defamatory material is likely to come to the notice of a very large number of people including many who are friends or acquaintances of the plaintiff. On the other hand the gravity of the matter cannot always be assessed by reference to the extent of the publication and certainly not in any direct ratio to the number of persons to whom the defamatory material is published. Thus a publication by letter to an employer or to a limited circle of the plaintiff's friends may be no less damaging than the publication of similar material in an article in a newspaper. Moreover, where a true innuendo is relied upon, or where only persons with knowledge of special facts would identify the plaintiff, it is submitted that the jury should be warned that the only relevant publication is to the persons with the special knowledge.[1]

1 This submission would seem to be consistent with *Fullam v Newcastle Chronicle and Journal Ltd* [1977] 3 All ER 32, [1977] 1 WLR 651.

MITIGATING FACTORS

18.16   There are a number of matters which the court or jury is entitled to take into account as mitigating factors to reduce the damages which would otherwise be appropriate. The main factors may be listed as follows—

    (a) the reputation of the plaintiff;
    (b) the behaviour of the plaintiff towards the defendant and in the action;
    (c) any apology tendered by the defendant;
    (d) other facts negativing malice on the part of the defendant;
    (e) sums received by the plaintiff in respect of similar publications.

THE REPUTATION OF THE PLAINTIFF

18.17   In an action for defamation the plaintiff complains of injury to his reputation caused by the publication of the alleged libel or slander. As a matter of commonsense therefore it is relevant to consider the reputation[1] which the plaintiff bore before the publication took place. Indeed before 1852 it was the practice for the plaintiff to plead in his declaration by way of preparatory averment that he was a man of good reputation, and it was open to the defendant in answer to this averment to call general evidence that the plaintiff was a man of bad reputation.[2] In *Scott v Sampson*[3] Cave J put the matter as follows:

> '. . . it seems most material that the jury who have to award those damages should know, if the fact is so, that he is a man of no reputation. . . . On principle, therefore, it would seem that general evidence of reputation should be admitted.'

1   The word 'reputation' is used in preference to 'character' as the latter word is liable to cause confusion. It is to be noted, however, that the word 'character' is used in RSC Order 82, rule 7.
2   See *Earl of Leicester v Walter* (1809) 2 Camp 251; *Thompson v Nye* (1850) 16 QB 175 at 180 per Erle J. This evidence could be tendered under the general issue: by way of contrast the truth of the allegation complained of had to be specially pleaded: see *Underwood v Parks* (1743) 2 Stra 1200.
3   (1882) 8 QBD 491 at 503. See also the passage in Starkie on Slander and Libel (2nd Edn) vol 2 p 88 (written in 1830), cited by Lord Denning in *Plato Films Ltd v Speidel* [1961] AC 1090 at 1137, [1961] 1 All ER 876 at 888.

18.18   But though the rule as to the admission of general evidence of bad reputation is of long standing it has proved a source of difficulty in practice.[1] It is submitted that the present law can be summarised as follows—

    (a) As a general rule the plaintiff cannot be cross-examined about specific acts of misconduct other than those (if any) which are pleaded in support of a defence 'of justification or fair comment', nor can any evidence of such acts be tendered in chief by the defendant. To this general rule there are two partial exceptions:
    (i) Cross-examination as to credit. Where the credit of the plaintiff as a witness is relevant he can be cross-examined as to credit and (subject to the proviso stated below) in the course of this cross-examination questions can be asked which may relate to specific acts of misconduct.[2]
    (ii) Cross-examination as to and evidence of previous convictions. Subject to the proviso stated below, the plaintiff can be cross-examined about, and

evidence can be tendered relating to, any previous convictions which are relevant to that aspect of his reputation with which the case is concerned.[3] These exceptions are both subject to the important proviso, however, that unless justification is pleaded[4] no questions can be asked or evidence adduced which tend in any way to prove the truth of the words complained of.[5] Furthermore, evidence in chief of any previous convictions can only be put forward if the provisions of RSC Order 82, rule 7 are complied with.[6]

(b) Evidence of rumours that the plaintiff has committed either the specific acts of misconduct alleged in the words complained of or any other acts of misconduct is irrelevant and inadmissible.[7] In *Scott v Sampson* Cave J put the matter as follows:[8]

'If these rumours and suspicions have in fact affected the plaintiff's reputation, that may be proved by general evidence of reputation. If they have not affected it, they are not relevant to the issue.'

(c) The plaintiff may always be cross-examined as to his general reputation. In addition the defendant is entitled to tender evidence of the plaintiff's bad reputation[9] provided:
(i) he has pleaded justification; or
(ii) he has served at least seven days before the trial a notice in mitigation of damages in accordance with RSC Order 82, rule 7.[10]

1 The rule was examined in detail in *Scott v Sampson* (1882) 8 QBD 491; *Hobbs v Tinling* [1929] 2 KB 1 and *Plato Films Ltd v Speidel* [1961] AC 1090, [1961] 1 All ER 876. And see *Goody v Odhams Press* [1967] 1 QB 333, [1966] 3 All ER 369.
2 The defendant will of course be bound by the plaintiff's answers.
3 See *Goody v Odhams Press* [1967] 1 QB 333, [1966] 3 All ER 369. It must be emphasised, however, that evidence of previous convictions is admissible because 'it is evidence—and the most cogent evidence—that the plaintiff in fact has a bad reputation': ibid at 343, 374 per Salmon LJ. And at 340, 372 Lord Denning MR said: 'I think that previous convictions are admissible. They stand in a class by themselves. They are the raw material upon which bad reputation is built up. They have taken place in open court. They are matters of public knowledge. They are accepted by people generally as giving the best guide to his reputation and standing. They must of course be relevant, in this sense, that they must be convictions in the relevant section of his life and have taken place within a relevant period such as to affect his current reputation. . . . They are very different from previous instances of misconduct, for these have not been tried out or resulted in convictions or come before a court of law.'
4 In *Goody v Odhams Press* [1967] 1 QB 333, [1966] 3 All ER 369, there was a plea of partial justification.
5 In *Watt v Watt* [1905] AC 115 at 118 Lord Halsbury said: 'Even in mitigation of damages it is well settled you cannot go into evidence which, if proved, would constitute a justification. Nor does it appear to me that it makes any difference that the evidence is offered in cross-examination'. See also *Hobbs v Tinling* [1929] 2 KB 1 at 18 per Scrutton LJ. In addition, regard must be had to the provisions of the Rehabilitation of Offenders Act 1974; see appendix 2.
6 The rule requires that unless justification is pleaded a notice giving particulars of the relevant matters relied on should be served at least seven days before the trial.
7 The rule as to previous convictions seems at first sight to be an exception, but evidence of such convictions is admitted as evidence of general reputation.
8 (1882) 8 QBD 491 at 503. The point had been left open in *Thompson v Nye* (1850) 16 QB 175. In *Plato Films Ltd v Speidel* [1961] AC 1090 at 1136, [1961] 1 All ER 876 at 888, Lord Denning said: 'Rumour is a lying jade, begotten by gossip out of hearsay, and is not fit to be admitted to audience in a court of law.'
9 It seems clear, however, that the evidence should be directed to the relevant section of the plaintiff's reputation: see for example *Plato Films Ltd v Speidel* [1961] AC 1090 at 1140, [1961] 1 All ER 876 at 890, per Lord Denning.
10. RSC Ord 82, r 7 provides: 'In an action for libel or slander, in which the defendant does not by his defence assert the truth of the statement complained of, the defendant shall not be entitled on the trial to give evidence in chief, with a view to mitigation of damages, as to the circumstances under which the libel or slander was published, or as to the character of the plaintiff, without the leave of the judge, unless seven days at least before the trial he furnishes particulars to the plaintiff of the matters as to which he intends to give evidence'.

18.19   In practice, however, it is seldom easy to adduce any impressive 'general' evidence of bad reputation, though the speech of Lord Denning in *Plato Films Ltd v Speidel* provides helpful guidance as to the kind of evidence which is admissible to show bad or good reputation, as the case may be:[1]

'In order to arrive at a man's character and reputation, you should call those who know him and have had dealings with him: for they provide the only sound foundation on which to build. . . . If it is evidence of *good* character, a witness of good standing is called, such as a clergyman, a schoolmaster or an employer, and is asked such questions as these: "What are you? How long have you known him? Have you known him well? Have you had an opportunity of observing his conduct? What character has he borne during that time for honesty, morality or loyalty?" (according to the nature of the case). "As far as you know, has he deserved that character?". . . . But the witness cannot be asked questions in examination-in-chief about particular facts so as to illustrate the plaintiff's good behaviour on particular occasions. In cross-examination, however, he may be asked what are the grounds of his belief, and he may be asked as to particular facts known to him tending to shake it. If it is evidence of *bad* character which is given (such as that a man is a reputed thief or a woman is a common prostitute), the evidence often takes the form of a police officer who knows him being called and saying: "I know the defendant and have known him (or her) for some time. He is a well known pickpocket" or "She is a common prostitute", or as the case may be.[2] In such cases the witness usually speaks from his own observation and knowledge. The greater his personal knowledge, the more valuable his evidence. . . .   When general evidence of bad character is given, a witness cannot in chief give particular instances: though he can, of course, in cross-examination be asked the grounds of his belief and on what it is based.' When evidence of good or bad character is given, it should be directed to that sector of a man's character which is relevant. Thus, if the libel imputes theft, the relevant sector in his character for honesty, not his character as a motorist. . . . It is for the judge to rule what is the relevant sector.'

1 [1961] AC 1090 at 1138–40, [1961] 1 All ER 876 at 889–90. See also *Hobbs v Tinling* [1929] 2 KB 1 at 17 per Scrutton LJ: 'The defendant may mitigate damages by giving evidence to prove that the plaintiff is a man of bad general reputation, and the plaintiff may rebut it by "coming prepared with friends who have known him to prove that his reputation has been good" (*Scott v Sampson* (1882) 8 QBD 491 at 503 per Cave J)'.
2 It has been found in practice, however, that police forces are very reluctant to provide witnesses to give evidence of this nature.

THE BEHAVIOUR OF THE PLAINTIFF TOWARDS THE DEFENDANT AND IN THE ACTION

18.20   The behaviour of the plaintiff himself is relevant on the issue of damages. In *Cassell & Co Ltd v Broome* Lord Hailsham of St Marylebone LC said that the damages could be reduced if the plaintiff had behaved badly, 'as for instance by provoking[1] the defendant, or defaming him in return'. He continued:[2]

'In all such cases it must be appropriate to say with Lord Esher MR in *Praed v Graham*.[3] ". . . in actions of libel . . . the jury in assessing damages are entitled to look at the whole conduct of the defendant" (I would personally add "and of the plaintiff") "from the time the libel was published down to the time they give their verdict. They may consider what his conduct has been before action, after action, and in court during the trial".'

In addition it is to be remembered that in some circumstances a previous defamation by the plaintiff concerning the defendant may provide the defendant with a defence of qualified privilege on the basis that a person who is attacked is entitled to make a reply if he does so in good faith.[4]

1 If the provocation or other conduct of the defendant forms part of the 'circumstances under which the libel or slander was published' the defendant must bear in mind the provisions of RSC Ord 82, r 7.
2 [1972] AC 1027 at 1071, [1972] 1 All ER 801 at 824.
3 (1889) 24 QBD 53.
4 See, for example, *Turner v MGM Pictures Ltd* [1950] 1 All ER 449 at 470 per Lord Oaksey.

ANY APOLOGY TENDERED BY THE DEFENDANT

18.21 An apology does not provide a defence to an action for defamation[1] but unless it is wholly inadequate or insincere or made at too late a stage it is an important factor to be taken into account in assessing the damages. Thus a proper apology is almost certain to reduce the injury to the plaintiff's feelings and may well lessen the damage to his reputation. It is not the usual practice at the present time to make use of the statutory provision for giving notice of an apology contained in the Libel Act 1843, s 1.[2] An apology is sometimes pleaded in the defence, however, and there does not appear to be any objection to giving a notice similar to a notice under RSC Order 82, rule 7 that the defendant intends to rely on a previous apology in mitigation of damages.

1 It is to be noted, however, that 'a sufficient apology to the party aggrieved' is a necessary element of an offer of amends under Defamation Act 1952, s 4: see further para 15.05, ante.
2 Libel Act 1843, s 1 provides: 'In any action for defamation it shall be lawful for the defendant (after notice in writing of his intention so to do, duly given to the plaintiff at the time of filing or delivering the plea in such action) to give in evidence, in mitigation of damages, that he made or offered an apology to the plaintiff for such defamation before the commencement of the action, or as soon afterwards as he had an opportunity of doing so, in case the action shall have been commenced before there was an opportunity of making or offering such apology'.

OTHER FACTS NEGATIVING MALICE ON THE PART OF THE DEFENDANT

18.22 Though the honest belief by the defendant in the truth of what he published does not by itself provide any defence to an action for defamation it *may* be a relevant factor in the assessment of damages. The defendant may therefore wish to rely on his own bona fides (for example, he may have received the information from a reliable source and have made such checks as he could), or on other circumstances, to reduce the damages which would otherwise be appropriate. It is to be remembered, however, that if the facts on which he wishes to rely form part of 'the circumstances under which the libel or slander was published' he must comply with RSC Order 82, rule 7[1] if he wishes to give evidence of those facts in chief.

1 See para 18.18, note 10, ante.

AGGRAVATED AND EXEMPLARY DAMAGES WHERE THERE IS MORE THAN
ONE DEFENDANT

18.23   It is to be remembered that the plaintiff is entitled to a single award only
in respect of any single publication of a libel or slander even though the publication
was made by a number of persons. This rule may have important consequences
where there are two or more defendants and the behaviour of some but not all the
defendants has been such as to give rise to the possibility of an award of aggravated
or exemplary[1] damages.

1 The word 'exemplary' is used in preference to 'punitive': cf *Cassell & Co Ltd v Broome* [1972] AC 1027 at
[1972] 1 All ER 801 at 826, per Lord Hailsham of St Marylebone LC.

18.24   In *Cassell & Co Ltd v Broome* Lord Hailsham of St Marylebone LC stated
the law as follows:[1]

> 'I think . . . that awards of punitive damages in respect of joint publications should
> reflect only the lowest figure for which any of them can be held liable. This seems to me
> to flow inexorably both from the principle that only one sum may be awarded in a
> single proceeding for a joint tort, and from the authorities[2] . . . I think that the
> inescapable conclusion to be drawn from those authorities is that only one sum can be
> awarded by way of exemplary damages where the plaintiff elects to sue more than one
> defendant in the same action in respect of the same publication, and that this sum must
> represent the highest *common* factor, that is, the *lowest* sum for which any of the
> defendants can be held liable on this score. Although we were concerned with
> exemplary damages, I would think that the same principle applies generally and in
> particular to aggravated damages,[3] and that dicta or apparent dicta to the contrary can
> be disregarded. . . . Plaintiffs who wish to differentiate between the defendants can do
> so in various ways, for example, by electing to sue the more guilty only, by com-
> mencing separate proceedings against each and then consolidating,[4] or, in the case of a
> book or newspaper article, by suing separately in the same proceedings for the publi-
> cation of the manuscript to the publisher by the author.'

Accordingly a plaintiff who is aware that the culpability of the defendants responsible for a joint publication is not uniform should be careful to sue only the most
guilty or to bring separate proceedings.[5]

1 [1972] AC 1027 at 1063, [1972] 1 All ER 801 at 817.
2 For a list of the authorities, see [1972] AC 1027 at 1063, [1972] 1 All ER 801 at 817.
3 In *Egger v Viscount Chelmsford* [1965] 1 QB 248 at 263, [1964] 3 All ER 406 at 411, Lord Denning MR said: 'I
   think that the jury should be directed not to give anything in the nature of aggravated damages in a verdict
   which will affect the one who was innocent of malice. In short, the innocent parties to a joint publication
   ought not to be affected by the malice of the malicious one.'
4 It is doubtful whether this suggestion would in fact assist the plaintiff, since the effect of consolidation under
   RSC ord 4 r 10 in that the consolidated actions are thenceforth treated as one action; while an order for consolidation under s 5 of the Law of Libel Amendment Act 1888, which requires the jury to apportion the
   damages amongst the defendants, can only be made on the application of two or more of the *defendants*.
5 The Defamation Act in Singapore contains a special provision to enable separate awards to be made against
   different defendants; see appendix 5.

Exemplary damages

18.25   As has already been stated,[1] the basic rule of common law is that in civil
actions damages are awarded as compensation for injury, not as punishment for

wrongdoing. In three sets of circumstances, however, exemplary (or punitive) damages may be awarded

(a) where the plaintiff has been injured by oppressive, arbitrary or unconstitutional action by servants of the Government;[2]

(b) where the defendant has deliberately committed a tort with the intention of gaining some advantage which he calculates will outweigh any sum which he will have to pay to the plaintiff by way of compensation;

(c) where exemplary damages are expressly authorised by statute.[3]

1 See para 18.03, ante.
2 It seems that servants of the Government will include local government officers and other persons, such as the police, exercising governmental functions; see *Cassell & Co Ltd v Broome* [1972] AC 1027 at 1088, [1972] 1 All ER 801 at 838, per Lord Reid.
3 It may be noted that in *Rookes v Barnard* [1964] AC 1129 at 1225, [1964] 1 All ER 367 at 410 Lord Devlin said he expressed no view on whether the Copyright Act 1956 authorised an award of exemplary, as distinct from aggravated, damages. In *Cassell & Co Ltd v Broome* [1972] AC 1027 at 1134, [1972] 1 All ER 801 at 877, Lord Kilbrandon said that in his opinion s 17(3) of the Copyright Act did not authorise an award of exemplary damages.

18.26   The principles governing the award of exemplary damages in civil actions were examined by Lord Devlin in his speech in *Rookes v Barnard*,[1] where he set out the categories of case in which such an award can be made. Having considered the first category—oppressive, arbitrary or unconstitutional action by the servants of the Government[2]—he continued:[3]

'Cases in the second category are those in which the defendant's conduct has been calculated by him to make a profit for himself which may well exceed the compensation payable to the plaintiff. . . . It is a factor also that is taken into account in damages for libel; one man should not be allowed to sell another man's reputation for profit. Where a defendant with a cynical disregard for a plaintiff's rights has calculated that the money to be made out of his wrongdoing will probably exceed the damages at risk, it is necessary for the law to show that it cannot be broken with impunity. This category is not confined to moneymaking in the strict sense. It extends to cases in which the defendant is seeking to gain at the expense of the plaintiff some object—perhaps some property which he covets—which either he could not obtain at all or not obtain except at a price greater than he wants to put down. Exemplary damages can properly be awarded whenever it is necessary to teach a wrongdoer that tort does not pay.'

The guidance provided by Lord Devlin on exemplary damages was considered in detail and with specific reference to an action for defamation in the seven speeches in the House of Lords in *Cassell & Co Ltd v Broome*,[4] where a majority of the House upheld an award of exemplary damages to the plaintiff.

1 [1964] AC 1129, [1964] 1 All ER 367. This decision has not been followed in Australia: see *Australian Consolidated Press Ltd v Uren* [1969] 1 AC 590, [1967] 3 All ER 523.
2 See para 18.25, note 2, ante.
3 [1964] AC 1129 at 1226, [1964] 1 All ER 367 at 410.
4 [1972] AC 1027, [1972] 1 All ER 801.

18.27   It is submitted that the present law as to the award of exemplary damages in actions for defamation can be stated as follows—

(a) Exemplary damages can only[1] be awarded if the plaintiff proves[2] that the defendant when he made the publication knew that he was committing a tort or was reckless whether his action was tortious or not, and decided to publish because the prospects of material advantage outweighed the prospects of material loss.[3] 'What is necessary is that the tortious act must be done with guilty knowledge for the motive that the chances of economic advantage outweigh the chances of economic, or perhaps physical, penalty.'[4]

(b) The mere fact that a libel is committed in the course of a business carried on for profit, for example the business of a newspaper publisher, is not by itself sufficient to justify an award of exemplary damages.[5]

(c) If the case is one where exemplary damages *can* be awarded the court or jury should consider whether the sum which it proposes to award by way of compensatory damages is sufficient not only for the purpose of compensating the plaintiff but also for the purpose of punishing the defendant. It is only if the sum proposed by way of compensatory damages (which may include an element of aggravated damages) is insufficient that the court or jury should add to it enough 'to bring it up to a sum sufficient as punishment'.[6]

(d) The sum awarded as damages should be a single sum which will include, where appropriate, any elements of aggravated or exemplary damages.[7]

(e) The plaintiff can only recover exemplary damages if he is the victim of the punishable behaviour.[8]

(f) A jury should be warned of the danger of an excessive award.[9]

(g) The means of the parties, though irrelevant to the issue of compensatory damages, can be taken into account in awarding exemplary damages.[10]

(h) Where a number of persons are sued the question of exemplary damages has to be considered by reference to the least guilty of the defendants.[11]

1 It is possible, however, that in appropriate circumstances a claim for exemplary damages in an action for defamation could be included in the first of Lord Devlin's categories on the basis that the publication constituted an oppressive, arbitrary or unconstitutional action by a servant of Government.
2 The burden of proof is on the plaintiff and if the evidence is insufficient the judge should withdraw the matter from the jury: *Cassell & Co Ltd v Broome* [1972] AC 1027 at 1081, [1972] 1 All ER 801 at 833, per Lord Hailsham LC. RSC Order 8(3) provides: 'A claim for exemplary damages must be specifically pleaded together with the facts on which the party pleading relies'.
3 See *Cassell & Co Ltd v Broome* [1972] AC 1027 at 1079, [1972] 1 All ER 801 at 831, per Lord Hailsham LC. At 1088, 839, Lord Reid said: 'The jury were fully entitled to hold that the appellants knew when they committed this tort that passages in this book were highly defamatory of the respondent and could not be justified as true and that it could properly be inferred that they thought that it would pay them to publish the book and risk the consequences of any action the respondent might take. It matters not whether they thought that they could escape with moderate damages or that the enormous expenses involved in fighting an action of this kind would prevent the respondent from pressing his claim.'
4 It is to be noted that in *Cassell & Co Ltd v Broome* [1972] AC 1027 at 1119, [1972] 1 All ER 801 at 864 Lord Wilberforce said: 'I am far from convinced that Lord Devlin ever intended . . . to limit punitive damages in defamation actions to cases where a "profit motive" is shown.'
5 *Manson v Associated Newspapers Ltd* [1965] 2 All ER 954, [1965] 1 WLR 1038; *McCarey v Associated Newspapers Ltd* [1965] 2 QB 86, [1964] 3 All ER 947; *Broadway Approvals Ltd v Odhams Press Ltd* [1965] 2 All ER 523, [1965] 1 WLR 805; *Cassell & Co Ltd v Broome* [1972] at 1079, [1972] 1 All ER 801 at 831, per Lord Hailsham LC.
6 See *Cassell & Co Ltd v Broome* [1972] AC 1027 at 1089, [1972] 1 All ER 801 at 839, per Lord Reid. It is most important to emphasise that before making *any* punitive award the court or jury must first take into account the punitive effect of the compensatory damages: see ibid. at 1059–1061, 814–816, per Lord Hailsham LC.
7 *Cassell & Co Ltd v Broome* [1972] AC 1027 at 1072, [1972] 1 All ER 801 at 825, per Lord Hailsham LC. It seems that it is permissible to ask the jury to state what lesser sum they would have awarded if they had confined themselves to compensatory damages: see ibid. at 1082, 833, per Lord Hailsham LC.

8 *Rookes v Barnard* [1964] AC 1129 at 1227, [1964] 1 All ER 367 at 411; and see *Cassell & Co Ltd v Broome* [1972] AC 1027 at 1081, [1972] 1 All ER 801 at 833, per Lord Hailsham LC.

9 *Cassell & Co Ltd v Broome* [1972] AC 1027 at 1081, [1972] 1 All ER 801 at 833, per Lord Hailsham LC.

10 *Rookes v Barnard* [1964] AC 1129 at 1228, [1964] 1 All ER 367 at 411; and see *Cassell & Co Ltd v Broome* [1972] AC 1027 at 1081, [1972] 1 All ER 801 at 833, per Lord Hailsham LC.

11 *Cassell & Co Ltd v Broome* [1972] AC 1027 at 1063, [1972] 1 All ER 801 at 817, per Lord Hailsham LC, and at 1090, 840, per Lord Reid.

CHAPTER 19

Injunctions

INTRODUCTION

19.01 The court has jurisdiction[1] to grant an injunction either before or at the trial to prevent any further publication by the defendant of the libel or slander of which the plaintiff complains. Before the trial, however, it is a jurisdiction which is exercised with great caution. It is proposed to consider the subject of inter-locutory injunctions under the following headings—

- (a) general principles;
- (b) ex parte applications;
- (c) applications quia timet;
- (d) undertaking as to damages.

---

1 Before the Common Law Procedure Act 1854, the jurisdiction to grant relief by way of an injunction was only exercisable by the Court of Chancery and by the Court of Exchequer in equity. The first reported case in which an injunction was granted in an action for defamation was *Saxby v Easterbrook and Hannaford* (1878) 3 CPD 339, though in that case the injunction was only granted after the plaintiff had obtained a verdict from the jury.

Interlocutory injunctions

GENERAL PRINCIPLES   *In conjunction with* 18.01.

19.02 In many cases where defamatory matter has been published the most important immediate step from the point of view of the plaintiff is to prevent any further publication.[1] The court has jurisdiction to grant an injunction to prevent any further publication where the plaintiff can establish—

- (a) a prima facie case of libel or slander;
- (b) that the defendant threatens or intends to make a further publication;
- (c) that if a further publication is made the plaintiff will suffer an injury which cannot be fully compensated in damages.

Even if these conditions are satisfied, however, the general rule is that an inter-locutory injunction will not be granted if there is any doubt as to whether the words are defamatory, or if the defendant swears that he will be able to justify the words complained of, or if the defendant swears that he intends to rely on any other recognised defence, such as qualified privilege or fair comment.[2] Moreover, an injunction will not be granted if the plaintiff has delayed making an application to the court.

1 An application for an interlocutory injunction is usually made in the Queen's Bench Division by summons to a judge in chambers. Exceptionally the plaintiff proceeds by way of motion in the Chancery Division.
2 It is possible though very unlikely that a court would be willing to decide on an interim application that the defence of qualified privilege or fair comment was bound to fail because the defendant was clearly actuated by express malice in making the publication.

19.03 The classic exposition of the law with regard to the grant of interlocutory injunctions in actions for defamation was given by Lord Esher MR in *Coulson v Coulson*, where he said:[1]

'It could not be denied that the court had jurisdiction to grant an interim injunction before trial. It was, however, a most delicate jurisdiction to exercise, because, though Fox's Act only applied to indictments and informations for libel, the practice under that Act had been followed in civil actions for libel, that the question of libel or no libel was for the jury. It was for the jury and not for the court to construe the document and to say whether it was a libel or not. To justify the court in granting an interim injunction it must come to a decision upon the question of libel or no libel before the jury decided whether it was a libel or not. Therefore, the jurisdiction was of a delicate nature. It ought only to be exercised in the clearest cases, where any jury would say that the matter complained of was libellous, and where, if the jury did not so find, the court would set aside the verdict as unreasonable. The court must also be satisfied that in all probability the alleged libel was untrue, and, if written on a privileged occasion, that there was malice on the part of the defendant. It followed from those three rules that the court could only on the rarest occasions exercise the jurisdiction.'

1 (1887) 3 TLR 846. In *Bonnard v Perryman* [1891] 2 Ch 269 at 284 Lord Coleridge CJ, in delivering the considered judgment of the Court of Appeal, said: 'We entirely approve of and desire to adopt as our view the language of Lord Esher in *Coulson v Coulson*.'

19.04 In *Fraser v Evans* Lord Denning MR explained the practice with regard to the grant of interlocutory injunctions as follows:[1]

'The court will not restrain the publication of an article, even though it is defamatory, when the defendant says he intends to justify it or to make fair comment on a matter of public interest. That has been established for many years ever since *Bonnard v Perryman*.[2] The reason sometimes given is that the defences of justification and fair comment are for the jury, which is the constitutional tribunal, and not for the judge. But a better reason is the importance in the public interest that the truth should out. As the court said in that case: "The right of free speech is one which it is for the public interest that individuals should possess, and, indeed, that they should exercise without impediment, so long as no wrongful act is done." There is no wrong done if it is true, or if it is fair comment on a matter of public interest. The court will not prejudice the issue by granting an injunction in advance of publication.'

1 [1969] 1 QB 349 at 360, [1969] 1 All ER 8 at 10.
2 [1891] 2 Ch 269.

19.05 In *Harakas v Baltic Mercantile and Shipping Exchange Ltd*,[1] the Court of Appeal considered a case involving the International Maritime Bureau which was set up in 1980 to combat maritime fraud. Lord Denning MR said this:[2]

'This Court never grants an injunction in respect of libel when it is said by the defendant that the words are true and that he is going to justify them.[3] So also when an occasion is protected by qualified privilege this Court never grants an injunction to restrain the slander or libel—to prevent a person from exercising that privilege—unless it is shown that what the defendant proposes to say is known by him to be untrue so that it is clearly malicious. So long as he proposes to say what he honestly believes to be true, no injunction should be granted against him. That was made clear in *Quartz Hill Consolidated Gold Mining Co v Beall*.[4] When there is a bureau of this kind—which is specially charged with the responsibility of obtaining information and giving it to those interested, to warn them of possible dangers—it is very important that they should be able to give information to people who are properly interested: so long as it is done honestly and in good faith.'

1 [1982] 2 All ER 701, [1982] 1 WLR 958.
2 [1982] 1 WLR 958 at 960.
3 Cf *Schering Chemicals Ltd v Falkman Ltd* [1982] QB 1 at 18.
4 [1882] 20 ChD 501.

THE EFFECT OF THE DECISION IN AMERICAN CYANAMID

19.06 In *American Cyanamid Co v Ethicon Ltd* the House of Lords had occasion to consider (in an action for the alleged infringement of a patent) the practice of the courts as to the grant of interlocutory injunctions. The House laid down some general guidelines which can be summarised as follows:[1]

(a) It is no part of the court's function on the hearing of an application for an interlocutory injunction to try to resolve conflicts of evidence or to decide difficult questions of law.

(b) Unless it is clear that the plaintiff has no real prospect of obtaining a permanent injunction at trial the court should first consider whether damages would be an adequate remedy for the plaintiff if an injunction was not granted and whether the defendant would be in a financial position to pay them. No interlocutory injunction should normally be granted, however strong the plaintiff's case, if damages would be an adequate remedy and the defendant has the means to pay.

(c) If damages would not provide an adequate remedy for the plaintiff[2] the court should then consider whether, if the defendant succeeded at the trial, damages under the plaintiff's undertaking would be an adequate remedy for the defendant and whether the plaintiff would be able to pay such damages.[3]

(d) If there is doubt as to the adequacy of the respective remedies in damages the court should then consider any other factors which throw light on the question whether the balance of convenience lies in favour of granting or refusing the interlocutory relief that is sought.

(e) Where other factors appear to be evenly balanced it is a counsel of prudence to take such measures as are calculated to preserve the status quo.[4]

1 [1975] AC 396 at 406–408, [1975] 1 All ER 504 at 509–11.
2 Or (semble) if the defendant is unable to pay the damages.
3 If damages under the plaintiff's undertaking would be an inadequate remedy or if the plaintiff would be unable to pay such damages it seems that the court would normally refuse the interlocutory injunction.
4 See [1975] AC 396 at 408, [1975] 1 All ER 504 at 511.

19.07   It is to be noted, however, that in the *American Cyanamid* case no reference was made to the rules governing the grant of interlocutory injunctions in
actions for defamation. Moreover, though the guidelines laid down by the House
of Lords appear to be of general application, it seems clear that the previous
practice is still followed in actions for defamation. In *Bestobell Paints Ltd v Bigg*,
Oliver J said:[1]

> 'There is an old and well established principle which is still applied in modern times and
> which is in no way affected by the recent decision by the House of Lords in *American
> Cyanamid Corpn v Ethicon*, that no interlocutory injunction will be granted in defama-
> tion proceedings, where the defendant announces his intention of justifying, to restrain
> him from publishing the alleged defamatory statement unless its truth or untruth has
> been determined at the trial, except in cases where the statement is obviously untruth-
> ful and libellous. That was established towards the end of the last century and it has
> been asserted over and over again . . . an interlocutory restraint in any case that is not
> obvious would operate as an unjust fetter on the right of free speech and the defendant's
> liberty (if he is right) to speak the truth.'

The same view has been taken both in Australia[2] and New Zealand[3] that the
principle expounded in *Bonnard v Perryman*[4] as to the grant of interlocutory
injunctions in actions for defamation has survived the decision in *American
Cyanamid*.

1 [1975] FSR 421. See also *J Trevor & Sons v PR Soloman* (1977) Times, 16 December, CA; *Herbage v Times
   Newspapers* (1981) Times, 1 May, CA; *Hubbard v Pitt* [1976] QB 142 at 174, 178, 186, [1975] 3 All ER 1 at 6,
   10, 17; *Schering Chemicals Ltd v Falkman Ltd* [1982] QB 1 at 16.
2 See *Edelsten v John Fairfax & Sons Ltd* [1978] 1 NSWLR 685.
3 See *McSweeney v Berryman* [1980] 2 NZLR 168.
4 [1891] 2 Ch 269.

EX PARTE APPLICATIONS

19.08   In an urgent case the party complaining that defamatory matter has been
published of him can apply to the court ex parte. The application is made to the
judge in chambers and can be made as soon as the writ is issued, or, where the
application has to be made after court hours or at weekends, even before the writ is
issued.[1] The application should be supported by evidence on affidavit.[2] It is most
important that the affidavits should be frank and accurate as the court may decline
to continue the injunction when the matter is heard inter partes on the short
ground that full disclosure of the relevant facts was not made at the time of the
grant of the ex parte order.[2]

1 See, for example, *Fraser v Evans* [1969] 1 QB 349, [1969] 1 All ER 8. There may be other exceptional circumstances justifying an ex parte application before the issue of the writ. The court will require an undertaking
   that the writ will be issued at the earliest opportunity and that the affidavit in support will be filed.
2 For the contents of an affidavit in support of an ex parte application for an injunction: see Practice Note (Judge
   in Chambers: Procedure) [1983] 1 All ER 1119 at 1120, [1983] 1 WLR 433 at 434. in Appendix 3, post.

AN APPLICATION QUIA TIMET

19.09 The court has jurisdiction to grant an injunction quia timet before any publication of the defamatory matter takes place.[1] In most cases, however, where the plaintiff is aware that defamatory matter is to be published about him he will not know the actual words which will be used and in these circumstances no injunction is likely to be granted. It is to be remembered that 'no one can obtain a quia timet order by merely saying 'Timeo'; he must aver and prove that what is going on is calculated to infringe his rights.'[2]

1 See, for example, *Fraser v Evans* [1969] 2 QB 349, [1969] 1 All ER 8. As a general rule an application quia timet is more appropriate to a threatened publication of defamatory matter in a book or magazine rather than in a newspaper or broadcast. Thus a book or magazine is likely to be in its final form in sufficient time before publication for the plaintiff to take some action, whereas if the threatened publication is to be in a newspaper or broadcast the plaintiff may find it impossible to put before the court the precise words of which he complains.
2 *A–G for Dominion of Canada v Ritchie Contracting and Supply Co Ltd* [1919] AC 999 at 1005 per Lord Dunedin.

UNDERTAKING AS TO DAMAGES

19.10 In all cases in which an interlocutory injunction is granted (except where the order is in the nature of a final order),[1] the plaintiff is required as a condition of the grant of the injunction to give an undertaking as to damages.[2] The purpose of the undertaking is to provide for the compensation of the defendant for any loss sustained by him by reason of the injunction if it should be held at the trial that the plaintiff had not been entitled to restrain the defendant.[3] Accordingly where a plaintiff is seeking to restrain, for example, the whole edition of a national newspaper he will wish to consider carefully his potential liability in damages before making an application.

1 *Fenner v Wilson* [1893] 2 Ch 656.
2 See generally as to the practice: Supreme Court Practice, RSC Ord 29, r 1 and notes. It seems that this kind of undertaking was invented by Knight Bruce LJ when Vice-Chancellor: see *Smith v Day* (1882) 21 Ch D 421 at 424.
3 The court may order an inquiry as to damages if the plaintiff fails on the merits at the trial or if it is established before trial that an injunction ought not to have been granted in the first instance: see *Ushers Brewery v P S King & Co* [1972] Ch 148, [1971] 2 All ER 468.

CHAPTER 20

Criminal libel

INTRODUCTION

20.01 The publication of a libel, provided that it is a serious libel,[1] is a criminal offence as well as an actionable wrong. Some aspects of the offence of criminal libel[2] were considered by the House of Lords in *Gleaves v Deakin*,[3] and it is plain from the speeches in that case that the publication of a libel which is merely trivial is not a criminal offence. Viscount Dilhorne dealt with the matter as folows:[4]

> 'It was thought at one time that the distinction between a libel for which civil proceedings might be brought and a criminal libel which might be the subject of a prosecution lay in the criminal libel having a tendency to disturb or provoke a breach of the peace: see *R v Labouchere*.[5] In *R v Wicks*[6] du Parcq J, delivering the judgment of the Court of Criminal Appeal, said:[7] ''. . . a criminal prosecution for libel ought not to be instituted and, if instituted, will probably be regarded with disfavour by judge and jury, when the libel complained of is of so trivial a character as to be unlikely either to disturb the peace of the community or seriously to affect the reputation of the person defamed.'' He went on to cite the following passage from the judgment of Mansfield CJ in *Thorley v Lord Kerry*:[8] ''There is no doubt that this was a libel, for which the plaintiff in error might have been indicted and punished; because, though the words impute no punishable crimes, they contain that sort of imputation which is calculated to vilify a man and bring him, as the books say, into hatred, contempt, and ridicule; for all words of that description an indictment lies, . . .'' This, du Parcq J said, remained the law.
> A criminal libel must be serious libel. If the libel is of such a character as to be likely to disturb the peace of the community or to provoke a breach of the peace, then it is not to be regarded as trivial. But to hold as du Parcq J, did, in my view rightly, that the existence of such a tendency suffices to show that the libel is a serious one, is a very different thing from saying that proof of its existence is necessary to establish guilt of the offence.'

The principle that the libel must be serious to warrant criminal proceedings was also underlined by Lord Scarman:[9]

> 'It is, however, not every libel that warrants a criminal prosecution. To warrant prosecution the libel must be sufficiently serious to require the intervention of the Crown in the public interest[10]. . . . The libel must be more than of a trivial character: it must be such as to provoke anger or cause resentment. . . . In my judgment, the references in the case law to reputation, outrage, cruelty or tendency to disturb the peace are no more than illustrations of the various factors which either alone or in combination contribute to the gravity of the libel. The essential feature of a criminal libel remains—as in the past—the publication of a grave, not trivial, libel.'

Moreover when the trial of Mr Deakin took place at the Central Criminal Court in 1981[11] Comyn J directed the jury that a criminal libel was 'a written statement so serious in itself, and so greatly affecting a person's character and reputation, as to justify invoking criminal law and punishment instead of, or as well as, the civil law and damages.'

1　The publication of a slander has not been a crime at common law for several centuries. The statutory offence of scandalum magnatum was abolished by the Statute Law Revision Act 1887.
2　A valuable summary of the present law of criminal libel is set out in the Law Commission Working Paper No 84, Criminal Libel, Part III.
3　[1980] AC 477.
4　[1980] AC 477, 486–7.
5　(1884) 12 QBD 320 at 322 per Lord Coleridge CJ.
6　[1936] 1 All ER 384.
7　[1936] 1 All ER 384 at 386.
8　(1812) 4 Taunt 355 at 364.
9　In *Gleaves v Deakin* [1980] AC 477 at 494–5.
10　The prosecution may be brought by a private individual. Under the Prosecution of Offences Act 1979, s 4, however, the Director of Public Prosecutions has the power to take over the conduct of the proceedings. In a proper case this power may be exercised with a view to bringing the prosecution to an end: see, for example, *Raymond v A-G* [1982] QB 839 (a private prosecution for alleged perjury and other offences).
11　See Times newspaper, 25 February 1981. Mr Deakin and his co-defendants were acquitted.
12　The Law Commission in Working Paper No 84, para 6.10 have questioned whether 'seriousness' is an appropriate limitation on the offence.

20.02　In practice, however, criminal proceedings for libel are relatively ·uncommon.[1] On the other hand criminal proceedings can be brought in some cases where a civil action would not lie. Thus a prosecution for libel can be brought though the only publication is to the person defamed, whereas in a civil action it is necessary to prove publication to a third party. Moreover, whereas in a civil action truth provides a complete defence unless the case is one to which the Rehabilitation of Offenders Act 1974 applies and malice is proved,[2] in criminal proceedings the defendant has to plead and prove not only the truth of what was published but that the publication was for the public benefit.[3]

1　The Criminal Statistics for England and Wales disclose the following figures: see Cmnd 8668

	Cases considered by the police	Defendants found guilty
1973	19	3
1974	16	3
1975	9	—
1976	6	—
1977	5	—
1978	3	2
1979	5	—
1980	4	—
1981	5	2

2　See para 11.14, ante.
3　See Libel Act 1843, s 6.

Libels in newspapers—special provisions

20.03　It was provided by the Newspaper Libel and Registration Act 1881, s 3 that leave to institute a criminal prosecution for defamatory libel against a newspaper had to be obtained from the Director of Public Prosecutions. This restriction on prosecutions proved to be of little value in practice, however, and the law was changed by the Law of Libel Amendment Act 1888, s 8, which repealed the earlier provision and substituted the following:[1]

> 'No criminal prosecution shall be commenced against any proprietor, publisher, editor, or any person responsible for the publication of a newspaper for any libel published therein without the order of a Judge at Chambers being first had and obtained. Such application shall be made on notice to the person accused, who shall have an opportunity of being heard against it.'

1 In *Gleaves v Deakin* [1980] AC 477 at 488 Viscount Dilhorne said that he did not regard it as very desirable that judges should have any responsibility for the institution of prosecutions and favoured a reform whereby 'no prosecution for criminal libel could be brought without the leave of the Attorney-General or of the Director of Public Prosecutions'. Other members of the House supported a change in the law so as to require the leave of the Attorney-General. Lord Diplock emphasised that the Attorney-General would be able to consider whether the prosecution was necessary on any of the grounds specified in article 10.2 of the European Convention for the Protection of Human Rights and Fundamental Freedoms (1953) (Cmnd 8969): see p 484.

20.04 The following points relating to this statutory restriction on the prosecution of newspaper libels require to be noted—

(a) The word 'newspaper' means 'any newspaper containing public news, intelligence, or occurrences, or any remarks or observations therein printed for sale, and published in England or Ireland periodically, or in parts or numbers at intervals not exceeding twenty-six days between the publication of any two such papers, parts or numbers; also any paper printed in order to be dispersed, and made public weekly or oftener, or at intervals not exceeding twenty-six days, containing only or principally advertisements.'[1] It follows therefore that leave is not required in the case of, for example, a book or a monthly magazine nor is it required where the publication in question was in the course of a television or radio broadcast.

(b) The restriction does not apply to anyone except the proprietor,[2] publisher, editor or a person who is responsible for the publication of a newspaper. Accordingly an application for leave is not necessary where the intended prosecution is against the author of a newspaper article.[3]

(c) There is no appeal from the decision of the judge whether he makes the order or refuses it.[4]

1 See the Newspaper Libel and Registration Act 1881, s 1, as applied by the Law of Libel Amendment Act 1888, s 1.
2 For the definition of proprietor see the Newspaper Libel and Registration Act 1881, s 1.
3 No application for leave would be necessary, it seems, in the case of a prosecution against the printers or distributors. In practice, however, it is probable that any prosecution would be brought also against the publisher or editor and that if proceedings were intended against the printers or distributors they would be included in the application. It is to be noted that in *Goldsmith v Pressdram Ltd* [1977] QB 83, [1977] 2 All ER 557, leave to bring proceedings against the distributors was included in the application to the judge.
4 *ex p Pullbrook* [1892] 1 QB 86; *Goldsmith v Pressdram Ltd* [1977] QB 83, [1977] 2 All ER 557.

FACTORS TO BE TAKEN INTO ACCOUNT BY THE JUDGE

20.05 In deciding whether to give leave to institute a criminal prosecution for defamatory libel in a newspaper as required by the Law of Libel Amendment Act

1888, s. 8, the judge has to exercise his discretion having regard to all the circumstances of the case. In *Goldsmith v Pressdram Ltd* Wien J declined to lay down principles to show how the discretion should be exercised because to do so 'would have the inevitable effect of diminishing the ambit of the discretion that must be open to every judge who hears an application of this sort'.[1] But having declined to lay down guiding principles for the exercise of discretion Wien J continued as follows:[1]

> 'For the benefit of the parties in this case, and for my own benefit as well, I think I ought to state that there are principles that can be extracted from all the cases that have been cited, that should influence me one way or the other in this particular case. . . . First, before a discretion can be exercised in favour of an applicant who wishes to institute criminal proceedings in respect of a libel, which he contends is criminal, there must be a clear prima facie case. What I mean by that is that there must be a case to go before a criminal court that is so clear at first sight that it is beyond argument that there is a case to answer. Secondly, the libel must be a serious one – so serious that it is proper for the criminal law to be invoked. It may be a relevant factor that it is unusually likely for the libel to provoke a breach of the peace, although that is not a necessary ingredient at all. Thirdly, the question of the public interest must be taken into account, so that the judge has to ask himself the question, "Does the public interest *require* the institution of criminal proceedings?" What is not appropriate, in my judgment, is the question whether damages might or might not afford an adequate remedy to a complainant. I consider that the question is irrelevant. Once one arrives at the conclusion that the criminal law ought to be invoked then it is not a private case between individuals: the state has an interest and the state has a part in it.'

1 [1977] QB 83 at 88, [1977] 2 All ER 557 at 562.

20.06 The approach formulated by Wien J was adopted by Taylor J in *Desmond v Thorne*[1] where he agreed[2] that it was undesirable to attempt to lay down detailed criteria for the exercise of an unfettered discretion. Furthermore, in considering how to exercise his discretion in a case involving an article in *The Sunday People* which the complainant asserted portrayed him as (inter alia) 'a habitually violent drunken bully,' Taylor J said this:[2]

> 'I have no doubt that in considering whether there is a clear prima facie case I must look at all the circumstances. Likewise in considering whether the public interest requires the institution of criminal proceedings. Adopting that approach and applying the principles to the facts of the present case, I am far from satisfied that there is here a case so clear as to be, beyond argument, a case to answer. The admitted facts take much of the sting out of the article. The applicant's own script contains passages which tend to confirm both the tenor and some of the detail of the article. The affidavit evidence, not only of the respondents but of independent witnesses, further tends to undermine the reliability of the evidence for the applicant. Furthermore, I am quite satisfied that this is not a case in which the public interest requires the institution of criminal proceedings.'

1 [1982] 3 All ER 268, [1983] 1 WLR 163.
2 [1982] 3 All ER 268 at 272, [1983] 1 WLR 163 at 169.

Committal proceedings

20.07 Criminal libel is triable only on indictment in the Crown Court.[1] It is a Class 3 offence. Except in a case of a newspaper libel, to which the Newspaper

Libel and Registration Act 1881, s 4 applies,[2] the examining justices on the committal proceedings are not to enquire into the truth of the libel on the reputation of the complainant. Their task was described by Lord Scarman in *Gleaves v Deakin*[3] as follows:

'In my judgment, therefore, an examining magistrate, if satisfied that the libel has been published and is serious, must commit the defendant, leaving to the jury at trial the issue of public benefit, which includes questions as to truth and as to the character and reputation of the person defamed. '

1 S 5 of the Newspaper Libel and Registration Act 1881, which provided for the summary trial in certain circumstances of trivial libels in newspapers was repealed by the Criminal Law Act 1977, s 65 and Sch 13.
2 See para 20.08.
3 [1980] AC 477 at 496.

20.08 Where, however, the libel was published in a newspaper and the proceedings are against 'a proprietor, publisher, an editor, or any person responsible for the publication' of the newspaper the special provision contained in the Newspaper Libel and Registration Act 1881 applies. Section 4 is in these terms:

'A court of summary jurisdiction, upon the hearing of a charge against a proprietor, publisher, or editor, or any person responsible for the publication of a newspaper, for a libel published therein, may receive evidence as to the publication being for the public benefit, and as to the matters charged in the libel being true, and as to the report being fair and accurate, and published without malice, and as to any matter which under this or any other Act, or otherwise, might be given in evidence by way of defence by the person charged on his trial on indictment,[1] and the court, if of the opinion after hearing such evidence that there is a strong or probable presumption that the jury on the trial would acquit the person charged, may dismiss the case'.

It will be seen that in cases to which his section applies the court of summary jurisdiction may receive evidence as to the truth of the matters published. In other cases, however, except where the charge involves an allegation that the defendant knew the libel to be false,[2] such evidence is not admissible because it is only on a trial or indictment that the defendant may raise the defence of truth and that the publication was for the public benefit.[3]

1 For the defences available on indictment, see para 20.14, post.
2 See Libel Act 1843, s 4, and para 20.03, ante.
3 See Libel Act 1843, s 6; *R v Carden* (1879) 5 QBD 1.

Defences to a prosecution for criminal libel

20.09 The defences[1] to criminal proceedings for a defamatory libel are—

(a) that the words complained of are true, and that it was for the public benefit that they should be published;

(b) that the words complained of are fair comment on a matter of public interest;

(c) that the occasion of publication of the words complained of was privileged;

(d) that the publication was made without the authority or knowledge of the defendant, and did not arise from want of due care or caution on his part.

1 It will be for the prosecution to prove that the words were published by the defendant, and were sufficiently serious to warrant criminal proceedings.

TRUTH AND THAT PUBLICATION WAS FOR THE PUBLIC BENEFIT

20.10 At common law a defendant was not entitled to set up the truth of the words complained of by the way of defence to criminal proceedings. In 1843, however, the Libel Act 1843, s 6 effected an important change in the law by providing as follows:

> '. . . On the trial of any indictment or information[1] for a defamatory libel, the defendant having pleaded such plea as hereinafter mentioned, the truth of the matters charged may be inquired into, but shall not amount to a defence, unless it was for the public benefit that the said matters charged should be published; and . . . to entitle the defendant to give evidence of the truth of such matters charged as a defence to such indictment or information it shall be necessary for the defendant, in pleading to the said indictment or information, to allege the truth of the said matters charged in the manner now required in pleading a justification for an action of defamation, and further to allege that it was for the public benefit that the said matters charged should be published, and the particular fact or facts by reason whereof it was for the public benefit that the said matters charged should be published, to which plea the prosecutor shall be at liberty to reply generally, denying the whole thereof . . .'[2]

1 Criminal informations were abolished by the Criminal Law Act 1967, s 6(6).
2 The Libel Act 1843, s 6 also provided—
  (a) that if the defendant is convicted the court can take into account in aggravation or mitigation of the sentence the fact that the plea of truth and that the publication was for the public benefit has been made and also the evidence given to prove or disprove the plea;
  (b) that the truth of the matters cannot be inquired into unless there is a plea of justification;
  (c) that the defendant may in addition to the plea of justification enter a plea of not guilty;
  (d) that nothing in the Act is to take away or prejudice any defence available to the defendant under the plea of not guilty.

20.11 It will be seen therefore that a defendant can set up a defence of justification to a charge of criminal libel but that the defence is subject to certain conditions—

(a) In addition to proving the truth of the words complained of the defendant has to prove that the publication of the words was for the public benefit.
(b) The defence cannot be set up unless the defendant enters an express plea of justification.[1]
(c) The defence cannot be set up except on a trial on indictment.[2]

It is also to be noted that the Defamation Act 1952, s 5 does not apply to criminal proceedings so that where the libel contains several distinct charges the defendant has to prove each of these charges.[3]

1 The plea is in writing and should set out the facts relied on in support of the plea of justification that it was for the public benefit that the defamatory matters charged in the indictment should be published and the facts

relied on to prove the publication was for the public benefit. The prosecution can enter a replication denying the matters set out in the plea of justification, but it seems that a replication is not necessary as where no replication is filed the defendant is not entitled to be acquitted on the basis that the justification has not been traversed: *R v Seham Yousry* (1914) 84 LJ KB 1272. Forms of pleas of justification and replication are contained in the Indictment Rules 1916 (SR & O 1916 No 282).

2 Except under s 4 of the Newspaper Libel and Registration Act 1881: see para 20.08, ante.
3 *R v Newman* (1853) 1 E & B 558. Where, however, the libel contains a general charge, for example, 'X is a thief', the defence of justification could succeed though the defendant succeeded in proving some only of the acts of theft set out in the plea: cf. *R v Labouchere* (1880) 14 Cox C C 419. Furthermore, a defendant may be able to persuade the jury that the charges he cannot prove are not serious having regard to those he can prove and that he should be acquitted. In *Gleaves v Deakin* [1980] AC 477, 493 Lord Edmund-Davies said that the law should be changed so that section 5 was made applicable to criminal proceedings.

FAIR COMMENT

20.12   It seems clear that the defence of fair comment can be set up in answer to a charge of criminal libel under the general plea of not guilty.[1] Until the latter part of the nineteenth century, however, fair comment was generally regarded as a species of qualified privilege. Furthermore, in the early civil cases the concept of fair comment developed in relation to the criticism of art and literature,[2] whereas more recently, and particularly in the present century, the defence has been extended to cover matters of public interest over a very wide range, and to inferences of fact as well as mere expressions of opinion. There is no modern authority which provides any guidance on the application of fair comment to a charge of criminal libel, but it is submitted that in a case where the defendant intends to rely on the defence of fair comment he should file a plea setting out the facts on which the comment is based and identifying the relevant matter of public interest.[3] It is to be noted that the Defamation Act 1952, s 6 does not apply to criminal proceedings.

1 It should perhaps be noted, however, that in *Goldsmith v Pressdram Ltd* [1977] QB 83 at 90, Wien J said: 'I do not have to decide whether or not a defence of fair comment is available in criminal proceedings.'
2 See, for example, *Dibdin v Swan* (1793) 1 Esp 27.
3 It is to be remembered that the Libel Act 1843, s 6 provides '. . . that the truth of the matters charged in the alleged libel complained of . . . shall in no case be inquired into without . . . [a] plea of justification'. Nevertheless, it is submitted that notwithstanding this provision evidence can be given of the truth of non-defamatory facts or of facts which are not contained in the libel charged even without a plea of justification. If the facts were defamatory and were published as part of the libel they would not in any event be protected by a defence of fair comment.

ABSOLUTE AND QUALIFIED PRIVILEGE

20.13   In general the law as to the defences of absolute and qualified privilege is the same for criminal libel as for a civil action.[1] It is to be noted, however, that the Defamation Act 1952 does not apply to criminal proceedings.[2] Accordingly, the statutory protection afforded to certain newspaper reports under the Defamation Act 1952, s 7[3] is not available in criminal proceedings. It is submitted, however, that the provisions of the Law of Libel Amendment Act 1888, s 4 are still in force for the purpose of criminal libel because, it is suggested, the combined effect of the Defamation Act 1952, s 17(2) and s 18(3) was to limit the repeal of s 4 of the 1888 Act to its application to civil proceedings.[4] The Law of Libel Amendment Act 1888, s 4 is in the following terms:

'**Newspaper reports of proceedings of public meetings and of certain bodies and persons privileged.**—A fair and accurate report published in any newspaper of the proceedings of a public meeting,[5] or (except where neither the public nor any newspaper reporter is admitted) of any meeting of a vestry, town council, school board, board of guardians, board or local authority formed or constituted under the provisions of any Act of Parliament, or of any committee appointed by any of the above-mentioned bodies,[6] or of any meeting of any commissioners authorised to act by letters patent, Act of Parliament, warrant under the Royal Sign Manual, or other lawful warrant or authority,[7] select committees of either House of Parliament, . . . and the publication at the request of any Government office or department, officer of state, commissioner of police, or chief constable, of any notice or report issued by them for the information of the public[8] shall be privileged, unless it shall be proved that such report or publication was published or made maliciously:[9] Provided that nothing in this section shall authorise the publication of any blasphemous or indecent matter:[10] Provided also, that the protection intended to be afforded by this section shall not be available as a defence in any proceedings if it shall be proved that the defendant has been requested to insert in the newspaper in which the report or other publication complained of appeared a reasonable letter or statement by way of contradiction or explanation of such report or other publication, and has refused or neglected to insert the same:[11] Provided further, that nothing in this section contained shall be deemed or construed to limit or abridge any privilege now by law existing,[12] or to protect the publication of any matter not of public concern and the publication of which is not for the public benefit.'[13]

In any event it is to be noted that s 3 of the 1888 Act[14] was not repealed by the Defamation Act 1952, and that seemingly the statutory privilege conferred by that section on newspaper reports of court proceedings is available in criminal proceedings.

1 See for example *R v Rule* [1937] 2 KB 375 [1937] 2 All ER 772.
2 Defamation Act 1952, s 17(2) provided: 'Nothing in this Act affects the law relating to criminal libel.'
3 See also Defamation Act 1952, s 9(2) (extension of s 7 to broadcast reports), and Schedule. For the meaning of 'newspaper' in the Law of Libel Amendment Act 1888, see para 20.05, ante.
4 Defamation Act 1952, s 18(3) provided: 'Sections four and six of the Law of Libel Amendment Act 1888 are hereby repealed.' Section 18(3) was itself repealed by the Statute Law (Repeals) Act 1974, but such repeal did not effect any revival of the earlier section. Defamation Act 1952, s 17(2), however, provided: 'Nothing in this Act affects the law relating to criminal libel, and it is submitted that this provision (notwithstanding s 7(4) and s 18(3)) had the effect of excluding criminal libel from the ambit of the repeal of the law of Libel Amendment Act 1888, s 4. See also *Swift v Pannell* (1883) 24 Ch D 210, and D.B. Murray, When is a Repeal not a Repeal?, 16 MLR 50. It is submitted that the repeal effected by s 18(3) should be regarded as a consequential repeal following on the enactment of the provisions contained in s 7 and the Schedule.
5 'Public meeting' is defined for the purposes of the section as 'any meeting bona fide and lawfully held for a lawful purpose, and for the furtherance or discussion of any matter of public concern, whether the admission thereto be general or restricted'. Cf Defamation Act 1952, Schedule, Part II, para 9.
6 Cf Defamation Act 1952, Schedule, Part II, para 10(a).
7 Cf Defamation Act 1952, Schedule, Part II, para 10(c).
8 Cf Defamation Act 1952, Schedule, Part II, para 12.
9 Cf Defamation Act 1952, s 7(1).
10 Cf Defamation Act 1952, s 7(3).
11 Cf Defamation Act 1952, s 7(2).
12 Cf Defamation Act 1952, s 7(4).
13 Cf Defamation Act 1952, s 7(3).
14 See appendix 1.

PUBLICATION WITHOUT AUTHORITY

20.14 In civil actions for libel published by an employee or agent the general rule of tort applies whereby the employer or principal is jointly and severally liable with the employee or agent for torts committed with the former's consent or express or implied authority. The Libel Act 1843, s 7, however, provides a special defence in criminal proceedings as follows:

'. . . Whensoever, upon the trial of any indictment or information[1] for the publication of a libel, upon the plea of not guilty, evidence shall have been given which shall establish a presumptive case of publication against the defendant by the act of any other person by his authority, it shall be competent to such defendant to prove that such publication was made without his authority, consent or knowledge, and that the said publication did not arise from want of due care or caution on his part'.

It seems that the employer or principal will be able to escape liability under this section, provided he exercised due care, unless it is proved that he actually authorised or knew of the libel. Thus it has been held that a proprietor of a newspaper is not criminally liable for a libel which has been inserted in it without his knowledge or consent merely because he has given the editor a general authority to publish what he thinks appropriate.[2]

1 Criminal informations were abolished by the Criminal Law Act 1967, s 6(6).
2 *R v Holbrook* (1877) 3 QBD 60; *R v Holbrook* (1878) 4 QBD 42. Cf *R v Allison* (1888) 59 LT 933.

Penalties

20.15 Offences of defamatory libel fall into two main categories—those which involve knowledge on the part of the defendant of the falsity of the defamatory publication, and those which do not. Thus, though the publication of a defamatory libel is a common law offence, the maximum penalties[1] which are prescribed by statute depend on the state of knowledge of the defendant. The Libel Act 1843, s 4 provides as follows:

'**Publication of libel known to be false**—if any person shall maliciously publish any defamatory libel, knowing the same to be false,[2] every such person, being convicted thereof, shall be liable to be imprisoned . . . for any term not exceeding two years, and to pay such fine as the court shall award.'

Where, however, the defendant did not know that the libel was false a lesser penalty is prescribed. The Libel Act 1843, s 5 provides:

'**Publication of libel**—if any person shall maliciously publish any defamatory libel, every such person, being convicted thereof, shall be liable to fine or imprisonment or both, as the court may award, such imprisonment not to exceed the term of one year.'

1 At common law before 1843 there was no limit to the term of imprisonment which could be imposed for the publication of a defamatory libel.
2 Knowledge of falsity may be inferred by the jury on proof that the defendant had means of knowledge: *R v Wicks* [1936] 1 All ER 384. If the prosecution fail to prove the scienter required for s 4 the defendant may nevertheless be convicted for publishing a defamatory libel and sentenced in accordance with s 5.

APPENDIX 1

Statutes

This appendix contains the text of the following Acts—

Libel Act 1792
Criminal Libel Act 1819
Parliamentary Papers Act 1840
Libel Act 1843
Libel Act 1845
Newspaper Libel and Registration Act 1881
Law of Libel Amendment Act 1888
Slander of Women Act 1891
Defamation Act 1952

LIBEL ACT 1792

(32 Geo 3 c 60)
An Act to remove Doubts respecting the Functions of Juries in Cases of Libel

Whereas doubts have arisen whether on the trial of an indictment or information for the making or publishing any libel, where an issue or issues are joined between the King and the defendant or defendants, on the plea of not guilty pleaded, it be competent to the jury impanelled to try the same to give their verdict upon the whole matter in issue:

1. On the trial of an indictment for a libel the jury may give a general verdict upon the whole matter put in issue

On every such trial the jury sworn to try the issue may give a general verdict of guilty or not guilty upon the whole matter put in issue upon such indictment or information, and shall not be required or directed by the court or judge before whom such indictment or information shall be tried to find the defendant or defendants guilty merely on the proof of the publication by such defendant or defendants of the paper charged to be a libel, and of the sense ascribed to the same in such indictment or information.

2. The court shall give their opinion and directions

Provided always, that on every such trial the court or judge before whom such indictment or information shall be tried shall, according to their or his discretion, give their or his opinion and directions to the jury on the matter in issue between the King and the defendant or defendants, in like manner as in other criminal cases.

3. Jury may find a special verdict

Provided also, that nothing herein contained shall extend or be construed to extend to prevent the jury from finding a special verdict, in their discretion, as in other criminal cases.

4. Defendant found guilty may move in arrest of judgment as before this Act

Provided also, that in case the jury shall find the defendant or defendants guilty it shall and may be lawful for the said defendant or defendants to move in arrest of judgment, on such ground and in such manner as by law he or they might have done before the passing of this Act, any thing herein contained to the contrary notwithstanding.

CRIMINAL LIBEL ACT 1819

(60 Geo 3 & 1 Geo 4 c 8)

An Act for the more effectual Prevention and Punishment of blasphemous and seditious Libels   [30th December 1819]

1. After verdict, etc, against any person for composing, etc, a blasphemous or seditious libel, the court may make order for the seizure of copies of the libel in possession of such person, etc

. . . In every case in which any verdict or judgment by default shall be had against any person for composing, printing, or publishing any blasphemous libel, or any seditious libel tending to bring into hatred or contempt the person of his Majesty . . . or the government and constitution of the United Kingdom as by law established, or either House of Parliament, or to excite his Majesty's subjects to attempt the alteration of any matter in Church or State as by law established, otherwise than by lawful means, it shall be lawful for the judge or the court before whom or in which such verdict shall have been given, or the court in which such judgment by default shall be had, to make an order for the seizure and carrying away and detaining in safe custody, in such manner as shall be directed in such order, all copies of the libel which shall be in the possession of the person against whom such verdict or judgment shall have been had, or in the possession of any other person named in the order for his use, evidence upon oath having been previously given to the satisfaction of such court or judge, that a copy or copies of the said libel is or are in the possession of such other person for the use of the person against whom such verdict or judgment shall have been had as aforesaid; and in every such case it shall be lawful for any justice of the peace, or for any constable or other peace officer, acting under any such order, or for any person or persons acting with or in aid of any such justice of the peace, constable, or other peace officer, to search for any copies of such libel in any house, building, or other place whatsoever belonging to the person against whom any such verdict or judgment shall have been had, or to any other person so named, in whose possession any copies of any such libel, belonging to the person against whom any such verdict or judgment shall have been had, shall be; and in case admission shall be refused or not obtained within a reasonable time after it shall have been first demanded, to enter by force by day into any such house, building, or place whatsoever, and to carry away all copies of the libel there found, and to detain the same in safe custody, until the same shall be restored under the provisions of this Act, or disposed of according to any further order made in relation thereto.

The words omitted were repealed by the SLR Act 1890.

2. Copies of libels so seized shall be restored if judgment is arrested, etc; but shall otherwise be disposed of as the court shall direct

. . . If in any such case as aforesaid judgment shall be arrested, or if, after judgment shall have been entered, the same shall be reversed upon any writ of error, all copies so seized shall be forthwith returned to the person or persons from whom the same shall have been so taken as aforesaid, free of all charge and expence, and without the payment of any fees whatever; and in every case in which final judgment shall be entered upon the verdict so found against the person or persons charged with having composed, printed, or published such libel, then all copies so seized shall be disposed of as the court in which such judgment shall be given shall order and direct.

The words omitted were repealed by the SLR Act 1888.

3–11. (*Ss 3 and 10 apply to Scotland; ss 4 and 7 repealed by the Criminal Law Act 1967, s 10(2) and Sch 3, Part I, and the Criminal Law Act (Northern Ireland) 1967, s 15(2) and Sch 2; ss 5 and 6 rep. by 11 Geo 4 & 1 Will 4 c 73 (1830), s 1; ss 8 and 9 rep. by the Public Authorities Protection Act 1893, s 2 and Schedule; s 11 repealed by the SLR Act 1873.*)

PARLIAMENTARY PAPERS ACT 1840

(3 & 4 Vict c 9)

An Act to give summary Protection to Persons employed in the Publication of Parliamentary Papers   [14th April 1840]

1. Proceedings, criminal or civil, against persons for publication of papers printed by order of Parliament, to be stayed upon delivery of a certificate and affidavit to the effect that such publication is by order of either House of Parliament

. . . It shall and may be lawful for any person or persons who now is or are, or hereafter shall be, a defendant or defendants in any civil or criminal proceeding commenced or prosecuted in any manner soever, for or on account or in respect of the publication of any such report, paper, votes, or proceedings by such person or persons, or by his, her, or their servant or servants, by or under the authority of either House of Parliament, to bring before the court in which such proceeding shall have been or shall be so commenced or prosecuted, or before any judge of the same (if one of the superior courts at Westminster), first giving twenty-four hours notice of his intention so to do to the prosecutor or plaintiff in such proceeding, a certificate under the hand of the lord high chancellor of Great Britain, or the lord keeper of the great seal, or of the speaker of the House of Lords, for the time being, or of the clerk of the Parliaments, or of the speaker of the House of Commons, or of the clerk of the same house, stating that the report, paper, votes, or proceedings, as the case may be, in respect whereof such civil or criminal proceeding shall have been commenced or prosecuted, was published by such person or persons, or by his, her, or their servant or servants, by order or under the authority of the House of Lords or of the House of Commons, as the case may be, together with an affidavit verifying such certificate; and such court or judge shall thereupon immediately stay such civil or criminal proceeding; and the same, and every writ or process issued therein, shall be and shall be deemed and taken to be finally put an end to, determined, and superseded by virtue of this Act.

The words omitted were repealed by the SLR (No 2) Act 1890.

2. Proceedings to be stayed when commenced in respect of a copy of an authenticated report, etc.

. . . In case of any civil or criminal proceeding hereafter to be commenced or prosecuted for or on account or in respect of the publication of any copy of such report, paper, votes, or proceedings, it shall be lawful for the defendant or defendants at any stage of the proceedings to lay before the court or judge such report, paper, votes, or proceedings and such copy, with an affidavit verifying such report, paper, votes, or proceedings, and the correctness of such copy, and the court or judge shall immediately stay such civil or criminal proceeding; and the same, and every writ or process issued therein, shall be and shall be deemed and taken to be finally put an end to, determined, and superseded by virtue of this Act.

The words omitted were repealed by the SLR (No 2) Act 1888.

3. In proceedings for printing any extract or abstract of a paper, it may be shown that such extract was bona fide made

. . . It shall be lawful in any civil or criminal proceeding to be commenced or prosecuted for printing any extract from or abstract of such report, paper, votes, or proceedings, to give in evidence . . . such report, paper, votes, or proceedings, and to show that such extract or abstract was published bona fide and without malice; and if such shall be the opinion of the jury, a verdict of not guilty shall be entered for the defendant or defendants.

The words omitted were repealed by the SLR (No 2) Act 1888, and by the SLR Act 1958.

4. Act not to affect the privileges of Parliament

Provided always . . . that nothing herein contained shall be deemed or taken, or held or construed, directly or indirectly, by implication or otherwise, to affect the privileges of Parliament in any manner whatsoever.

The words omitted were repealed by the SLR (No 2) Act 1888.

LIBEL ACT 1843

(6 & 7 Vict c 96)

An Act to amend the Law respecting defamatory Words and Libel

[24th August 1843]

1. Offer of an apology admissible in evidence in mitigation of damages in action for defamation

. . . In any action for defamation it shall be lawful for the defendant (after notice in writing of his intention so to do, duly given to the plaintiff at the time of filing or delivering the plea in such action,) to give in evidence, in mitigation of damages, that he made or offered an apology to the plaintiff for such defamation before the commencement of the action, or as soon afterwards as he had an opportunity of doing so, in case the action shall have been commenced before there was an opportunity of making or offering such apology.

The words omitted were repealed by the SLR Act 1891.

2. In an action against a newspaper for libel, the defendant may plead that it was inserted without malice and without negligence, and that he has published or offered to publish an apology

. . . In an action for libel contained in any public newspaper or other periodical publication it shall be competent to the defendant to plead that such libel was inserted in such newspaper or other periodical publication without actual malice, and without gross negligence, and that before the commencement of the action, or at the earliest opportunity afterwards, he inserted in such newspaper or other periodical publication a full apology for the said libel, or, if the newspaper or periodical publication in which the said libel appeared should be ordinarily published at intervals exceeding one week, had offered to publish the said apology in any newspaper or periodical publication to be selected by the plaintiff in such action; . . . and . . . to such plea to such action it shall be competent to the plaintiff to reply generally, denying the whole of such plea.

The words omitted were repealed by the SLR Act 1891, and the SLR Act 1892.

3. (*Repealed by the Larceny Act* 1916, *s* 48 *and Schedule.*)

4. Publication of libel known to be false

. . . If any person shall maliciously publish any defamatory libel, knowing the same to be false, every such person, being convicted thereof, shall be liable to be imprisoned in the common gaol or house of correction for any term not exceeding two years, and to pay such fine as the court shall award.

The words omitted were repealed by the SLR Act 1891.

5. Publication of libel

. . . If any person shall maliciously publish any defamatory libel, every such person, being convicted thereof, shall be liable to fine or imprisonment or both, as the court may award, such imprisonment not to exceed the term of one year.

The words omitted were repealed by the SLR Act 1891.

6. On trial of indictment defendant may plead the truth of the matters charged, and that their publication was for the public benefit, and thereupon the truth of the matter charged may be inquired into—On conviction of defendant the court may consider whether his guilt is aggravated or mitigated by such plea—Defendant may also plead not guilty—Defences open to defendant under plea of not guilty not prejudiced

. . . On the trial of any indictment or information for a defamatory libel, the defendant having pleaded such plea as hereinafter mentioned, the truth of the matters charged may be inquired into, but shall not amount to a defence, unless it was for the public benefit that the said matters charged should be published; and . . . to entitle the defendant to give evidence of the truth of such matters charged as a defence to such indictment or information it shall be necessary for the defendant, in pleading to the said indictment or information, to allege the truth of the said matters charged in the manner now required in pleading a justification to an action for defamation, and further to allege that it was for the public benefit that the said matters charged should be published, and the particular fact or facts by reason whereof it was for the public benefit that the said matters charged should be published, to which plea the prosecutor shall be at liberty to reply generally, denying the whole thereof; and . . . if after such plea the defendant shall be convicted on such indictment or information it shall be competent to the court, in pronouncing sentence, to consider whether the guilt of the defendant is aggravated or mitigated by the said plea, and by the evidence given to prove or to disprove the same: Provided always, that the truth of the matters charged in the alleged libel complained of by such indictment or information shall in no case be inquired into without such plea of justification: Provided also, that in addition to such plea it shall be competent to the defendant to plead a plea of not guilty: Provided also, that nothing in this Act contained shall take away or prejudice any defence under the plea of not guilty which it is now competent to the defendant to make under such plea to any action or indictment or information for defamatory words or libel.

The words omitted were repealed by the SLR Act 1891.

7. Defendant may produce evidence to rebut primâ facie case of publication by his agent

. . . Whensoever, upon the trial of any indictment or information for the publication of a libel, under the plea of not guilty, evidence shall have been given which shall establish a presumptive case of publication against the defendant by the act of any other person by his authority, it shall be competent to such defendant to prove that such publication was made without his authority, consent, or knowledge, and that the said publication did not arise from want of due care or caution on his part.

The words omitted were repealed by the SLR Act 1891.

8. (*Repealed by the Costs in Criminal Cases Act* 1908, *s* 10 *and Schedule.*)

9. Interpretation of Act

. . . Wherever throughout this Act, in describing the plaintiff or the defendant, or the party affected or intended to be affected by the offence, words are used importing the singular number or the masculine gender only, yet they shall be understood to include several persons as well as one person, and females as well as males, unless when the nature of the provision or the context of the Act shall exclude such construction.

The words omitted were repealed by the SLR Act 1891.

10. Extent of Act

. . . Nothing in this Act contained shall extend to Scotland.

The words omitted were repealed by the SLR Act 1874 (No. 2).

LIBEL ACT 1845

(8 & 9 Vict c 75)

An Act to amend an Act passed in the Session of Parliament held in the Sixth and Seventh Years of the Reign of Her present Majesty, intituled 'An Act to amend the Law respecting defamatory Words and Libel' [31st July 1845]

1. (*Repealed by the SLR Act* 1892.)

2. Defendant not to plead matters allowed by 6 & 7 Vict c 96, without payment into court

. . . It shall not be competent to any defendant in such action, whether in England or in Ireland, to file any such plea, without at the same time making a payment of money into court by way of amends . . . but every such plea so filed without payment of money into court shall be deemed a nullity, and may be treated as such by the plaintiff in the action.

The words omitted were repealed by the SLR Act 1891.

NEWSPAPER LIBEL AND REGISTRATION ACT 1881

(44 & 45 Vict c 60)

An Act to amend the Law of Newspaper Libel, and to provide for the Registration of Newspaper Proprietors   [27th August 1881]

1. Interpretation

In the construction of this Act, unless there is anything in the subject or context repugnant thereto, the several words and phrases herein-after mentioned shall have and include the meanings following; (that is to say,)

The word 'registrar' shall mean in England the registrar for the time being of joint stock companies, or such person as the Board of Trade may for the time being authorise in that behalf, and in Ireland the assistant registrar for the time being of joint stock companies for Ireland, or such person as the Board of Trade may for the time being authorise in that behalf.

The phrase 'registry office' shall mean the principal office for the time being of the registrar in England or Ireland, as the case may be, or such other office as the Board of Trade may from time to time appoint.

The word 'newspaper' shall mean any paper containing public news, intelligence, or occurrences, or any remarks or observations therein printed for sale, and published in England or Ireland periodically, or in parts or numbers at intervals not exceeding twenty-six days between the publication of any two such papers, parts, or numbers.

Also any paper printed in order to be dispersed, and made public weekly or oftener, or at intervals not exceeding twenty-six days, containing only or principally advertisements.

The word 'occupation' when applied to any person shall mean his trade or following, and if none, then his rank or usual title, as esquire, gentleman.

The phrase 'place of residence' shall include the street, square, or place where the person to whom it refers shall reside, and the number (if any) or other designation of the house in which he shall so reside.

The word 'proprietor' shall mean and include as well the sole proprietor of any newspaper, as also in the case of a divided proprietorship the persons who, as partners or otherwise, represent and are responsible for any share or interest in the newspaper as between themselves and the persons in like manner representing or responsible for the other shares or interests therein, and no other person.

2, 3. (*Repealed by the Law of Libel Amendment Act* 1888, *ss* 2 *and* 8.)

4. Inquiry as to libel being for public benefit or being true

A court of summary jurisdiction upon the hearing of a charge against a proprietor, publisher, or editor, or any person responsible for the publication of a newspaper, for a libel published therein, may receive evidence as to the publication being for the public benefit, and as to the matters charged in the libel being true, and as to the report being fair and accurate, and published without malice, and as to any matter which under this or any other Act, or otherwise, might be given in evidence by way of defence by the person charged on his trial on indictment, and the court, if of opinion after hearing such evidence that there is a strong or probable presumption that the jury on the trial would acquit the person charged, may dismiss the case.

5. Provision as to summary conviction for libel

If a court of summary jurisdiction upon the hearing of a charge against a proprietor, publisher, editor, or any person responsible for the publication of a newspaper for a libel published therein is of opinion that though the person charged is shown to have been guilty the libel was of a trivial character, and that the offence may be adequately punished by virtue of the powers of this section, the court shall cause the charge to be reduced into writing and read to the person charged, and then address a question to him to the following effect 'Do you desire to be tried by a jury or do you consent to the case being dealt with summarily?' and, if such person assents to the case being dealt with summarily, the court may summarily convict him and adjudge him to pay a fine not exceeding fifty pounds.

Section twenty-seven of the Summary Jurisdiction Act 1879 shall, so far as is consistent with the tenor thereof, apply to every such proceeding as if it were herein enacted and extended to Ireland, and as if the Summary Jurisdiction Acts were therein referred to instead of the Summary Jurisdiction Act 1848.

This section is repealed as to England and Wales by the Criminal Law Act 1977, ss 17, 65 and Sch 13.

6. (*Repealed by the Administration of Justice (Miscellaneous Provisions) Act* 1933, *s* 10(3) *and Sched.* 3, *and the Criminal Justice Act (Northern Ireland)* 1945, *s* 4 *and Sch* 4.)

7. Registration of the names of only a portion of the proprietors of a newspaper

Where, in the opinion of the Board of Trade, inconvenience would arise or be caused in any case from the registry of the names of all the proprietors of the newspaper (either owing to minority, coverture, absence from the United Kingdom, minute subdivision of shares, or other special circumstances), it shall be lawful for the Board of Trade to authorise the registration of such newspaper in the name or names of some one or more responsible 'representative proprietors.'

8. Register of newspaper proprietors to be established

A register of the proprietors of newspapers as defined by this Act shall be established under the superintendence of the registrar.

9. Annual Returns

It shall be the duty of the printers and publishers for the time being of every newspaper to make or cause to be made to the Registry Office . . . in the month of July in every year, a return of the following particulars according to the Schedule A hereunto annexed; that is to say,
   (a) The title of a newspaper:
   (b) The names of all the proprietors of such newspaper together with their respective occupations, place of business (if any), and places of residence.

The words omitted were repealed by the SLR Act 1894.

10. Penalty for omission to make annual returns

If within the further period of one month after the time hereinbefore appointed for the making of any return as to any newspaper such return be not made, then each printer and publisher of such newspaper shall, on conviction thereof, be liable to a penalty not exceeding [£50] and also to be directed by a summary order to make a return within a specified time.

Amended by the Criminal Law Act 1977, s 31(6).

11. Power to party to make return

Any party to a transfer or transmission of or dealing with any share of or interest in any newspaper whereby any person ceases to be a proprietor or any new proprietor is introduced may at any time make or cause to be made to the Registry Office a return according to the Schedule B hereunto annexed and containing the particulars therein set forth.

12. Penalty for wilful misrepresentation in or omission from return

If any person shall knowingly and wilfully make or cause to be made any return by this Act required or permitted to be made in which shall be inserted or set forth the name of any person as a proprietor of a newspaper who shall not be a proprietor thereof, or in which there shall be any misrepresentation, or from which there shall be any omission in respect of any of the particulars by this Act required to be contained therein whereby such return shall be misleading, or if any proprietor of a newspaper shall knowingly and wilfully permit any such return to be made which shall be misleading as to any of the particulars with reference to his own name, occupation, place of business (if any), or place of residence, then and in every such case every such offender being convicted thereof shall be liable to a penalty not exceeding one hundred pounds.

13. Registrar to enter returns in register

It shall be the duty of the registrar and he is hereby required forthwith to register every return made in conformity with the provisions of this Act in a book to be kept for that purpose at the Registry Office and called 'the register of newspaper proprietors,' and all persons shall be at liberty to search and inspect the said book from time to time during the hours of business at the Registry Office, and any person may require a copy of any entry in or an extract from the book to be certified by the registrar or his deputy for the time being or under the official seal of the registrar.

14. Fees payable for registrar's services

There shall be paid in respect of the receipt and entry of returns made in conformity with the provisions of this Act, and for the inspection of the register of newspaper proprietors, and for certified copies of any entry therein, and in respect of any other services to be performed by the registrar, such fees (if any) as the Board of Trade with the approval of the Treasury may direct and as they shall deem requisite to defray as well the additional expenses of the Registry Office caused by the provisions of this Act, as also the further remunerations and salaries (if any) of the registrar, and of any other persons employed under him in the execution of this Act, and such fees shall be dealt with as the Treasury may direct.

15. Copies of entries in and extracts from register to be evidence

Every copy of an entry in or extract from the register of newspaper proprietors, purporting to be certified by the registrar or his deputy for the time being, or under the official seal of the registrar, shall be received as conclusive evidence of the contents of the said register of newspaper proprietors, so far as the same appear in such copy or extract without proof of the signature thereto or of the seal of office affixed thereto, and every such certified copy or extract shall in all proceedings, civil or criminal, be accepted as sufficient primâ facie evidence of all the matters and things thereby appearing, unless and until the contrary thereof be shown.

16. Recovery of penalties and enforcement of orders

All penalties under this Act may be recovered before a court of summary jurisdiction in manner provided by the Summary Jurisdiction Acts.

Summary orders under this Act may be made by a court of summary jurisdiction . . .

The words omitted were repealed by the Courts Act 1971, s 56, Sch 11, Part IV.

17. (*Repealed by the SLR Act 1894.*)

18. Newspapers belonging to joint stock companies

The provisions as to the registration of newspaper proprietors contained in this Act shall not apply to the case of any newspaper which belongs to a joint stock company duly incorporated under and subject to the provisions of the Companies Acts 1862 to 1879.

Companies Acts 1862 to 1879: see now Companies Act 1948.

19. Extent

This Act shall not extend to Scotland.

20. Short title

This Act may for all purposes be cited as the Newspaper Libel and Registration Act 1881.

THE SCHEDULES TO WHICH THIS ACT REFERS

SCHEDULE A   Section 9

RETURN made pursuant to the Newspaper Libel and Registration Act 1881

Title of the Newspaper	Names of the Proprietors	Occupations of the Proprietors	Places of business (if any) of the Proprietors	Places of Residence of the Proprietors

SCHEDULE B   Section 11

RETURN made pursuant to the Newspaper Libel and Registration Act 1881

Title of Newspaper	Names of Persons who cease to be Proprietors	Names of Persons who become Proprietors	Occupation of new Proprietors	Places of business (if any) of new Proprietors	Places of Residence of new Proprietors

LAW OF LIBEL AMENDMENT ACT 1888

(51 & 52 Vict c 64)

An Act to amend the Law of Libel   [24th December 1888]

1. Interpretation

In the construction of this Act the word 'newspaper' shall have the same meaning as in the Newspaper Libel and Registration Act 1881.

2. (*Repealed by the SLR Act* 1908.)

3. Newspaper reports of proceedings in court privileged

A fair and accurate report in any newspaper of proceedings publicly heard before any court exercising judicial authority shall, if published contemporaneously with such proceedings, be privileged: Provided that nothing in this section shall authorise the publication of any blasphemous or indecent matter.

4. (*Repealed by the Defamation Act* 1952, *s* 18(3), *and the Defamation Act* (*Northern Ireland*) 1955, *s* 16(2).) [*But see para* 20.13, *ante*.]

5. Consolidation of actions

It shall be competent for a judge or the court, upon an application by or on behalf of two or more defendants in actions in respect to the same, or substantially the same, libel brought by one and the same person, to make an order for the consolidation of such actions, so that they shall be tried together; and after such order has been made, and before the trial of the said actions, the defendants in any new actions instituted in respect of the same, or substantially the same, libel shall also be entitled to be joined in a common action upon a joint application being made by such new defendants and the defendants in the actions already consolidated.

In a consolidated action under this section the jury shall assess the whole amount of the damages (if any) in one sum, but a separate verdict shall be taken for or against each defendant in the same way as if the actions consolidated had been tried separately; and if the jury shall have found a verdict against the defendant or defendants in more than one of the actions so consolidated, they shall proceed to apportion the amount of damages which they shall have so found between and against the said last-mentioned defendants; and the judge at the trial, if he awards to the plaintiff the costs of the action, shall thereupon make such order as he shall deem just for the apportionment of such costs between and against such defendants.

6, 7. (*S* 6 *repealed by the Defamation Act* 1952, *s* 18(3), *and the Defamation Act* (*Northern Ireland*) 1955, *s* 16(2); *s* 7 *repealed by the Indictments Act* 1915, *s* 9 *and Sch* 2, *and the Indictments Act* (*Northern Ireland*) 1945, *s* 9(3) *and Sch* 2.)

8. Order of Judge required for prosecution of newspaper proprietor, etc

. . . No criminal prosecution shall be commenced against any proprietor, publisher, editor, or any person responsible for the publication of a newspaper for any libel published therein without the order of a Judge at Chambers being first had and obtained.

Such application shall be made on notice to the person accused, who shall have an opportunity of being heard against such application.

The words omitted from this section, which repealed the Newspaper Libel and Registration Act 1881, s 3, were themselves repealed by the SLR Act 1908.

9. Person proceeded against criminally a competent witness

Every person charged with the offence of libel before any court of criminal juris-diction, and the husband or wife of the person so charged, shall be competent, but not compellable, witnesses on every hearing at every stage of such charge.

10. Extent of Act

This Act shall not apply to Scotland.

11. Short title

This Act may be cited as the Law of Libel Amendment Act 1888.

SLANDER OF WOMEN ACT 1891

(54 & 55 Vict c 51)

An Act to amend the Law relating to the Slander of Women

[5th August 1891]

1. Amendment of law

Words spoken and published . . . which impute unchastity or adultery to any woman or girl shall not require special damage to render them actionable.

Provided always, that in any action for words spoken and made actionable by this Act, a plaintiff shall not recover more costs than damages, unless the judge shall certify that there was reasonable ground for bringing the action.

The words omitted from this section were repealed by the SLR Act 1908.

2. Short title and extent

This Act may be cited as the Slander of Woman Act 1891, and shall not apply to Scotland.

DEFAMATION ACT 1952

(15 & 16 Geo 6 & 1 Eliz 2 c 66)

An Act to amend the law relating to libel and slander and other malicious falsehoods

[30th October 1952]

1. Broadcast statements

For the purposes of the law of libel and slander, the broadcasting of words by means of wireless telegraphy shall be treated as publication in permanent form.

2. Slander affecting official, professional or business reputation

In an action for slander in respect of words calculated to disparage the plaintiff in any office, profession, calling, trade or business held or carried on by him at the time of the publication, it shall not be necessary to allege or prove special damage, whether or not the words are spoken of the plaintiff in the way of his office, profession, calling, trade or business.

3. Slander of title, & c

(1) In an action for slander of title, slander of goods or other malicious falsehood, it shall not be necessary to allege or prove special damage—

  (a) if the words upon which the action is founded are calculated to cause pecuniary damage to the plaintiff and are published in writing or other permanent form; or
  (b) if the said words are calculated to cause pecuniary damage to the plaintiff in respect of any office, profession, calling, trade or business held or carried on by him at the time of the publication.

(2) Section one of this Act shall apply for the purposes of this section as it applies for the purposes of the law of libel and slander.

4. Unintentional defamation

(1) A person who has published words alleged to be defamatory of another person may, if he claims that the words were published by him innocently in relation to that other person, make an offer of amends under this section; and in any such case—

  (a) if the offer is accepted by the party aggrieved and is duly performed, no proceedings for libel or slander shall be taken or continued by that party against the person making the offer in respect of the publication in question (but without prejudice to any cause of action against any other person jointly responsible for that publication);
  (b) if the offer is not accepted by the party aggrieved, then, except as otherwise provided by this section, it shall be a defence, in any proceedings by him for libel or slander against the person making the offer in respect of the publication in question, to prove that the words complained of were published by the defendant innocently in relation to the plaintiff and that the offer was made as soon as practicable after the defendant received notice that they were or might be defamatory of the plaintiff, and has not been withdrawn.

(2) An offer of amends under this section must be expressed to be made for the purposes of this section, and must be accompanied by an affidavit specifying the facts relied upon by the person making it to show that the words in question were published by him innocently in relation to the party aggrieved; and for the pur-

poses of a defence under paragraph (b) of subsection (1) of this section no evidence, other than evidence of facts specified in the affidavit, shall be admissible on behalf of that person to prove that the words were so published.

(3) An offer of amends under this section shall be understood to mean an offer—

(a) in any case, to publish or join in the publication of a suitable correction of the words complained of, and a sufficient apology to the party aggrieved in respect of those words;

(b) where copies of a document or record containing the said words have been distributed by or with the knowledge of the person making the offer, to take such steps as are reasonably practicable on his part for notifying persons to whom copies have been so distributed that the words are alleged to be defamatory of the party aggrieved.

(4) Where an offer of amends under this section is accepted by the party aggrieved—

(a) any question as to the steps to be taken in fulfilment of the offer as so accepted shall in default of agreement between the parties be referred to and determined by the High Court, whose decision thereon shall be final;

(b) the power of the court to make orders as to costs in proceedings by the party aggrieved against the person making the offer in respect of the publication in question, or in proceedings in respect of the offer under paragraph (a) of this subsection, shall include power to order the payment by the person making the offer to the party aggrieved of costs on an indemnity basis and any expenses reasonably incurred or to be incurred by that party in consequence of the publication in question;

and if no such proceedings as aforesaid are taken, the High Court may, upon application made by the party aggrieved, make any such order for the payment of such costs and expenses as aforesaid as could be made in such proceedings.

(5) For the purposes of this section words shall be treated as published by one person (in this subsection referred to as the publisher) innocently in relation to another person if and only if the following conditions are satisfied, that is to say—

(a) that the publisher did not intend to publish them of and concerning that other person, and did not know of circumstances by virtue of which they might be understood to refer to him; or

(b) that the words were not defamatory on the face of them, and the publisher did not know of circumstances by virtue of which they might be understood to be defamatory of that other person.

and in either case that the publisher exercised all reasonable care in relation to the publication; and any reference in this subsection to the publisher shall be construed as including a reference to any servant or agent of his who was concerned with the contents of the publication.

(6) Paragraph (b) of subsection (1) of this section shall not apply in relation to the publication by any person of words of which he is not the author unless he proves that the words were written by the author without malice.

5. Justification

In an action for libel or slander in respect of words containing two or more distinct charges against the plaintiff, a defence of justification shall not fail by reason only that the truth of every charge is not proved if the words not proved to be true do not materially injure the plaintiff's reputation having regard to the truth of the remaining charges.

6. Fair comment

In an action for libel or slander in respect of words consisting partly of allegations of fact and partly of expression of opinion, a defence of fair comment shall not fail by reason only that the truth of every allegation of fact is not proved if the expression of opinion is fair comment having regard to such of the facts alleged or referred to in the words complained of as are proved.

7. Qualified privilege of newspapers

(1) Subject to the provisions of this section, the publication in a newspaper of any such report or other matter as is mentioned in the Schedule to this Act shall be privileged unless the publication is proved to be made with malice.

(2) In an action for libel in respect of the publication of any such report or matter as is mentioned in Part II of the Schedule to this Act, the provisions of this section shall not be a defence if it is proved that the defendant has been requested by the plaintiff to publish in the newspaper in which the original publication was made a reasonable letter or statement by way of explanation or contradiction, and has refused or neglected to do so, or has done so in a manner not adequate or not reasonable having regard to all the circumstances.

(3) Nothing in this section shall be construed as protecting the publication of any matter the publication of which is prohibited by law, or of any matter which is not of public concern and the publication of which is not for the public benefit.

(4) Nothing in this section shall be construed as limiting or abridging any privilege subsisting (otherwise than by virtue of section four of the Law of Libel Amendment Act 1888) immediately before the commencement of this Act.

(5) In this section the expression 'newspaper' means any paper containing public news or observations thereon, or consisting wholly or mainly of advertisements, which is printed for sale and is published in the United Kingdom either periodically or in parts or numbers at intervals not exceeding thirty-six days.

8. Extent of Law of Libel Amendment Act 1888, s 3

Section three of the Law of Libel Amendment Act 1888 (which relates to contemporary reports of proceedings before courts exercising judicial authority) shall apply and apply only to courts exercising judicial authority within the United Kingdom.

9. Extension of certain defences to broadcasting

(1) Section three of the Parliamentary Papers Act 1840 (which confers protection in respect of proceedings for printing extracts from or abstracts of parliamentary papers) shall have effect as if the reference to printing included a reference to broadcasting by means of wireless telegraphy.

(2) Section seven of this Act and section three of the Law of Libel Amendment Act 1888 as amended by this Act shall apply in relation to reports or matters broadcast by means of wireless telegraphy as part of any programme or service provided by means of a broadcasting station within the United Kingdom, and in relation to any broadcasting by means of wireless telegraphy of any such report or matter, as they apply in relation to reports and matters published in a newspaper and to publication in a newspaper; and subsection (2) of the said section seven shall have effect in relation to any such broadcasting, as if for the words 'in the news-paper in which' there were substituted the words 'in the manner in which.'

(3) In this section 'broadcasting station' means any station in respect of which a licence granted by the Postmaster General under the enactments relating to wire-less telegraphy is in force, being a licence which (by whatever form of words) authorises the use of the station for the purpose of providing broadcasting services for general reception.

10. Limitation on privilege at elections

A defamatory statement published by or on behalf of a candidate in any election to a local government authority or to Parliament shall not be deemed to be published on a privileged occasion on the ground that it is material to a question in issue in the election, whether or not the person by whom it is published is qualified to vote at the election.

11. Agreements for indemnity

An agreement for indemnifying any person against civil liability for libel in respect of the publication of any matter shall not be unlawful unless at the time of the publication that person knows that the matter is defamatory, and does not reason-ably believe there is a good defence to any action brought upon it.

12. Evidence of other damages recovered by plaintiff

In any action for libel or slander the defendant may give evidence in mitigation of damages that the plaintiff has recovered damages, or has brought actions for damages, for libel or slander in respect of the publication of words to the same effect as the words on which the action is founded, or has received or agreed to receive compensation in respect of any such publication.

13. Consolidation of actions for slander, &c

Section five of the Law of Libel Amendment Act 1888 (which provides for the consolidation, on the application of the defendants, of two or more actions for libel by the same plaintiff) shall apply to actions for slander and to actions for slander of title, slander of goods or other malicious falsehood as it applies to actions for libel; and references in that section to the same, or substantially the same, libel shall be construed accordingly.

14. *(Applies to Scotland.)*

15. *(Repealed by the Northern Ireland Constitution Act 1973, s 41(1), Sch 6, Part 1.)*

16. Interpretation

(1) Any reference in this Act to words shall be construed as including a reference to pictures, visual images, gestures and other methods of signifying meaning.

(2) The provisions of Part III of the Schedule to this Act shall have effect for the purposes of the interpretation of that Schedule.

(3) In this Act 'broadcasting by means of wireless telegraphy' means publication for general reception by means of wireless telegraphy within the meaning of the Wireless Telegraphy Act 1949, and 'broadcast by means of wireless telegraphy' shall be construed accordingly.

(4) Where words broadcast by means of wireless telegraphy are simultaneously transmitted by telegraph as defined by the Telegraph Act 1863, . . . the provisions of this Act shall apply as if the transmission were broadcasting by means of wireless telegraphy.

The words omitted from sub-s (4) were repealed by the Post Office Act 1969, s 76 and Sch 4, para 53.

17. Proceedings affected and saving

(1) This Act applies for the purposes of any proceedings begun after the commencement of this Act, whenever the cause of action arose, but does not affect any proceedings begun before the commencement of this Act.

(2) Nothing in this Act affects the law relating to criminal libel.

18. Short title, commencement, extent and repeals

(1) This Act may be cited as the Defamation Act 1952, and shall come into operation one month after the passing of this Act.

(2) This Act . . . shall not extend to Northern Ireland.

(3) *(Repealed by the SL(R) Act 1974.)*

The words omitted from sub-s (2) are repealed by the Northern Ireland Constitution Act 1973, s 41(1), Sch 6.

SCHEDULE   Sections 7, 16

NEWSPAPER STATEMENTS HAVING QUALIFIED PRIVILEGE

PART I

STATEMENTS PRIVILEGED WITHOUT EXPLANATION OR CONTRADICTION

1. A fair and accurate report of any proceedings in public of the legislature of any part of Her Majesty's dominions outside Great Britain.

2. A fair and accurate report of any proceedings in public of an international organisation of which the United Kingdom or Her Majesty's Government in the United Kingdom is a member, or of any international conference to which that government sends a representative.

3. A fair and accurate report of any proceedings in public of an international court.

4. A fair and accurate report of any proceedings before a court exercising jurisdiction throughout any part of Her Majesty's dominions outside the United Kingdom, or of any proceedings before a court-martial held outside the United Kingdom under the Naval Discipline Act, [the Army Act 1955 or the Air Force Act 1955].

5. A fair and accurate report of any proceedings in public of a body or person appointed to hold a public inquiry by the government or legislature of any part of Her Majesty's dominions outside the United Kingdom.

6. A fair and accurate copy of or extract from any register kept in pursuance of any Act of Parliament which is open to inspection by the public, or of any other document which is required by the law of any part of the United Kingdom to be open to inspection by the public.

7. A notice or advertisement published by or on the authority of any court within the United Kingdom or any judge or officer of such a court.

The words in square brackets were substituted by the Revision of the Army and Air Force Acts (Transitional Provisions) Act 1955, s 3 and Sch 2, para 16.
Naval Discipline Act: see now Naval Discipline Act 1957.

PART II

STATEMENTS PRIVILEGED SUBJECT TO EXPLANATION OR CONTRADICTION

8. A fair and accurate report of the findings or decision of any of the following associations, or of any committee or governing body thereof, that is to say—

(a) an association formed in the United Kingdom for the purpose of promoting or encouraging the exercise of or interest in any art, science, religion or learning, and empowered by its constitution to exercise control over or adjudicate upon matters of interest or concern to the association, or the actions or conduct of any persons subject to such control or adjudication;

(b) an association formed in the United Kingdom for the purpose of promoting or safeguarding the interests of any trade, business, industry or profession, or of the persons carrying on or engaged in any trade, business, industry or profession, and empowered by its constitution to exercise control over or adjudicate upon matters connected with the trade, business, industry or profession, or the actions or conduct of those persons;

(c) an association formed in the United Kingdom for the purpose of promoting or safeguarding the interests of any game, sport or pastime to the playing or exercise of which members of the public are invited or admitted, and empowered by its constitution to exercise control over or adjudicate upon persons connected with or taking part in the game, sport or pastime,

being a finding or decision relating to a person who is a member of or is subject by virtue of any contract to the control of the association.

9. A fair and accurate report of the proceedings at any public meeting held in the United Kingdom, that is to say, a meeting bona fide and lawfully held for a lawful purpose and for the furtherance or discussion of any matter of public concern, whether the admission to the meeting is general or restricted.

10. A fair and accurate report of the proceedings at any meeting or sitting in any part of the United Kingdom of—

(a) any local authority or committee of a local authority or local authorities;

(b) any justice or justices of the peace acting otherwise than as a court exercising judicial authority;

(c) any commission, tribunal, committee or person appointed for the purposes of any inquiry by Act of Parliament, by Her Majesty or by a Minister of the Crown;

(d) any person appointed by a local authority to hold a local inquiry in pursuance of any Act of Parliament;

(e) any other tribunal, board, committee or body constituted by or under, and exercising functions under, an Act of Parliament,

not being a meeting or sitting admission to which is denied to representatives of newspapers and other members of the public.

11. A fair and accurate report of the proceedings at a general meeting of any company or association constituted, registered or certified by or under any Act of Parliament or incorporated by Royal Charter, not being a private company within the meeting of the Companies Act 1948.

12. A copy or fair and accurate report or summary of any notice or other matter issued for the information of the public by or on behalf of any government department, officer of state, local authority or chief officer of police.

PART III

INTERPRETATION

13. In this Schedule the following expressions have the meanings hereby respectively assigned to them, that is to say:—

'Act of Parliament' includes an Act of the Parliament of Northern Ireland, and the reference to the Companies Act 1948 includes a reference to any corresponding enactment of the Parliament of Northern Ireland;

'government department' includes a department of the Government of Northern Ireland;

'international court' means the International Court of Justice and any other judicial or arbitral tribunal deciding matters in dispute between States;

'legislature', in relation to any territory comprised in Her Majesty's dominions which is subject to a central and a local legislature, means either of those legislatures;

'local authority' means any authority or body to which the [Public Bodies (Admission to Meetings) Act 1960,] or the Local Government (Ireland) Act 1902, as amended by any enactment of the Parliament of Northern Ireland, applies;

'part of Her Majesty's dominions' means the whole of any territory within those dominions which is subject to a separate legislature.

14. In relation to the following countries and territories, that is to say, India, the Republic of Ireland, any protectorate, protected state or trust territory within the meaning of the British Nationality Act 1948, any territory administered under the authority of a country mentioned in subsection (3) of section one of that Act, the Sudan and the New Hebrides, the provisions of this Schedule shall have effect as they have effect in relation to Her Majesty's dominions, and references therein to Her Majesty's dominions shall be construed accordingly.

The words in square brackets were substituted by the Public Bodies (Admission to Meetings) Act 1960, s 2(2).

Statutes (selected extracts)

This Appendix contains individual sections, etc of Acts, as follows—

WIRELESS TELEGRAPHY ACT 1949

19. Interpretation

(1) In this Act, except where the context otherwise requires, the expression 'wireless telegraphy' means the emitting or receiving, over paths which are not provided by any material substance constructed or arranged for that purpose, of electromagnetic energy of a frequency not exceeding three million megacycles a second, being energy which either—

   (a) serves for the conveying of messages, sound or visual images (whether the messages, sound or images are actually received by any person or not), or for the actuation or control of machinery or apparatus; or

   (b) is used in connection with the determination of position, bearing, or distance, or for the gaining of information as to the presence, absence, position or motion of any object or of any objects of any class,

and references to stations for wireless telegraphy and apparatus for wireless telegraphy or wireless telegraphy apparatus shall be construed as references to stations and apparatus for the emitting or receiving as aforesaid of such electromagnetic energy as aforesaid:

Provided that where—

   (i) a station or apparatus for wireless telegraphy cannot lawfully be used without a wireless telegraphy licence or could not lawfully be used without such a licence but for regulations under section one of this Act; and

(ii) any such electro-magnetic energy as aforesaid which is received by that station or apparatus serves for the conveying of messages, sound or visual images; and

(iii) any apparatus is electrically coupled with that station or apparatus for the purpose of enabling any person to receive any of the said messages, sound or visual images,

the apparatus so coupled shall itself be deemed for the purposes of this Act to be apparatus for wireless telegraphy.

(2) In this Act, the expression 'station for wireless telegraphy' includes the wireless telegraphy apparatus of a ship or aircraft, and the expression 'electric line' has the same meaning as in the Electric Lighting Act 1882.

(3) Any reference in this Act to the emission of electro-magnetic energy, or to emission (as opposed to reception), shall be construed as including a reference to the deliberate reflection of electro-magnetic energy by means of any apparatus designed or specially adapted for that purpose, whether the reflection is continuous or intermittent.

(4) In this Act, the expression 'interference' in relation to wireless telegraphy, means the prejudicing by any emission or reflection of electro-magnetic energy of the fulfilment of the purposes of the telegraphy (either generally or in part, and, without prejudice to the generality of the preceding words, as respects all, or as respects any, of the recipients or intended recipients of any message, sound or visual image intended to be conveyed by the telegraphy), and the expression 'interfere' shall be construed accordingly.

(5) In considering for any of the purposes of this Act, whether, in any particular case, any interference with any wireless telegraphy caused or likely to be caused by the use of any apparatus, is or is not undue interference, regard shall be had to all the known circumstances of the case and the interference shall not be regarded as undue interference if so to regard it would unreasonably cause hardship to the person using or desiring to use the apparatus.

(6) Any reference in this Act to the sending or the conveying of messages includes a reference to the making of any signal or the sending or conveying of any warning or information, and any reference to the reception of messages shall be construed accordingly.

(7) In this Act, the expressions 'ship' and 'vessel' have the meanings respectively assigned to them by section seven hundred and forty-two of the Merchant Shipping Act 1894.

(8) References in this Act to apparatus on board a ship or vessel include references to apparatus on a kite or captive balloon flown from a ship or vessel.

(9) Any notice required or authorised by any provision of this Act to be served on any person may be served by registered post.

(10) Any reference in this Act to any enactment shall, except so far as the context otherwise requires, be construed as a reference to that enactment as amended by or under any other enactment, including this Act.

PARLIAMENTARY COMMISSIONER ACT 1967

10. Reports by Commissioner

(1) In any case where the Commissioner conducts an investigation under this Act or decides not to conduct such an investigation, he shall send to the member of the House of Commons by whom the request for investigation was made (or if he is no longer a member of that House, to such member of that House as the Commissioner thinks appropriate) a report of the results of the investigation or, as the case may be, a statement of his reasons for not conducting an investigation.

(2) In any case where the Commissioner conducts an investigation under this Act, he shall also send a report of the results of the investigation to the principal officer of the department or authority concerned and to any other person who is alleged in the relevant complaint to have taken or authorised the action complained of.

(3) If, after conducting an investigation under this Act, it appears to the Commissioner that injustice has been caused to the person aggrieved in consequence of maladministration and that the injustice has not been, or will not be, remedied, he may, if he thinks fit, lay before each House of Parliament a special report upon the case.

(4) The Commissioner shall annually lay before each House of Parliament a general report on the performance of his functions under this Act and may from time to time lay before each House of Parliament such other reports with respect to those functions as he thinks fit.

(5) For the purposes of the law of defamation, any such publication as is hereinafter mentioned shall be absolutely privileged, that is to say—

    (a) the publication of any matter by the Commissioner in making a report to either House of Parliament for the purposes of this Act;

    (b) the publication of any matter by a member of the House of Commons in communicating with the Commissioner or his officers for those purposes or by the Commissioner or his officers in communicating with such a member for those purposes;

    (c) the publication by such a member to the person by whom a complaint was made under this Act of a report or statement sent to the member in respect of the complaint in pursuance of subsection (1) of this section;

    (d) the publication by the Commissioner to such a person as is mentioned in subsection (2) of this section of a report sent to that person in pursuance of that subsection.

THEATRES ACT 1968

4. Amendment of law of defamation

(1) For the purposes of the law of libel and slander (including the law of criminal libel so far as it relates to the publication of defamatory matter) the publication of

words in the course of a performance of a play shall, subject to section 7 of this Act, be treated as publication in permanent form.

(2) The foregoing subsection shall apply for the purposes of section 3 (slander of title, etc.) of the Defamation Act 1952 as it applies for the purposes of the law of libel and slander.

(3) In this section ''words'' includes pictures, visual images, gestures and other methods of signifying meaning.

(4) (*Applies to Scotland.*)

7. Exceptions for performances given in certain circumstances

(1) Nothing in sections 2 to 4 of this Act shall apply in relation to a performance of a play given on a domestic occasion in a private dwelling.

(2) Nothing in sections 2 to 6 of this Act shall apply in relation to a performance of a play given solely or primarily for one or more of the following purposes, that is to say—

    (a) rehearsal; or
    (b) to enable—
        (i) a record or cinematograph film to be made from or by means of the performance; or
        (ii) the performance to be broadcast; or
        (iii) the performance to be transmitted to subscribers to a diffusion service;

but in any proceedings for an offence under section 2, 5 or 6 of this Act alleged to have been committed in respect of a performance of a play or an offence at common law alleged to have been committed in England and Wales by the publication of defamatory matter in the course of a performance of a play, if it is proved that the performance was attended by persons, other than persons directly connected with the giving of the performance or the doing in relation thereto of any of the things mentioned in paragraph (b) above, the performance shall be taken not to have been given solely or primarily for one or more of the said purposes unless the contrary is shown.

(3) In this section—

    'broadcast' means broadcast by wireless telegraphy (within the meaning of the Wireless Telegraphy Act 1949), whether by way of sound broadcasting or television;
    'cinematograph film' means any print, negative, tape or other article on which a performance of a play or any part of such a performance is recorded for the purposes of visual reproduction;
    'record' means any record or similar contrivance for reproducing sound, including the sound-track of a cinematograph film;

and section 48(3) of the Copyright Act 1956 (which explains the meaning of references in that Act to the transmission of a work or other subject-matter to subscribers to a diffusion service) shall apply for the purposes of this section as it applies for the purposes of that Act.

18. Interpretation

(1) In this Act—
    'licensing authority' means—
        (a) as respects premises in Greater London, the Greater London Council;
        (b) as respects premises in a district in England and Wales, the council of that district;
        (c) *(applies to Scotland)*;
    'plays' means—
        (a) any dramatic piece, whether involving improvisation or not, which is given wholly or in part by one or more persons actually present and performing and in which the whole or a major proportion of what is done by the person or persons performing, whether by way of speech, singing or acting, involves the playing of a role; and
        (b) any ballet given wholly or in part by one or more persons actually present and performing, whether or not it falls within paragraph (a) of this definition;
    'police officer means a member, or in Scotland a constable, of a police force;
    'premises' includes any place;
    'public performance' includes any performance in a public place within the meaning of the Public Order Act 1936 and any performance which the public or any section thereof are permitted to attend, whether on payment or otherwise;
    'script' has the meaning assigned by section 9(2) of this Act.

(2) For the purposes of this Act—

    (a) a person shall not be treated as presenting a performance of a play by reason only of his taking part therein as a performer;
    (b) a person taking part as a performer in a performance of a play directed by another person shall be treated as a person who directed the performance if without reasonable excuse he performs otherwise than in accordance with that person's direction; and
    (c) a person shall be taken to have directed a performance of a play given under his direction notwithstanding that he was not present during the performance;

and a person shall not be treated as aiding or abetting the commission of an offence under section 2, 5 or 6 of this Act in respect of a performance of a play by reason only of his taking part in that performance as a performer.

The words in square brackets were substituted by the Local Government Act 1972, s 204(b).

CIVIL EVIDENCE ACT 1968

11. Convictions as evidence in civil proceedings

(1) In any civil proceedings the fact that a person has been convicted of an offence by or before any court in the United Kingdom or by a court-martial there or else-

where shall (subject to subsection (3) below) be admissible in evidence for the purpose of proving, where to do so is relevant to any issue in those proceedings, that he committed that offence, whether he was so convicted upon a plea of guilty or otherwise and whether or not he is a party to the civil proceedings; but no conviction other than a subsisting one shall be admissible in evidence by virtue of this section.

(2) In any civil proceedings in which by virtue of this section a person is proved to have been convicted of an offence by or before any court in the United Kingdom or by a court-martial there or elsewhere—

(a) he shall be taken to have committed that offence unless the contrary is proved; and

(b) without prejudice to the reception of any other admissible evidence for the purpose of identifying the facts on which the conviction was based, the contents of any document which is admissible as evidence of the conviction, and the contents of the information, complaint, indictment or charge-sheet on which the person in question was convicted, shall be admissible in evidence for that purpose.

(3) Nothing in this section shall prejudice the operation of section 13 of this Act or any other enactment whereby a conviction or a finding of fact in any criminal proceedings is for the purposes of any other proceedings made conclusive evidence of any fact.

(4) Where in any civil proceedings the contents of any document are admissible in evidence by virtue of subsection (2) above, a copy of that document, or of the material part thereof, purporting to be certified or otherwise authenticated by or on behalf of the court or authority having custody of that document shall be admissible in evidence and shall be taken to be a true copy of that document or part unless the contrary is shown.

(5) Nothing in any of the following enactments, that is to say—

(a) [section 13 of the Powers of Criminal Courts Act 1973] (under which a conviction leading to probation or discharge is to be disregarded except as therein mentioned);

(b) section 9 of the Criminal Justice (Scotland) Act 1949 (which makes similar provision in respect of convictions on indictment in Scotland); and

(c) section 8 of the Probation Act (Northern Ireland) 1950 (which corresponds to the said section 12) or any corresponding enactment of the Parliament of Northern Ireland for the time being in force,

shall affect the operation of this section; and for the purposes of this section any order made by a court of summary jurisdiction in Scotland under section 1 or section 2 of the said Act of 1949 shall be treated as a conviction.

(6) In this section 'court-martial' means a court-martial constituted under the Army Act 1955, the Air Force Act 1955 or the Naval Discipline Act 1957 or a disciplinary court constituted under section 50 of the said Act of 1957, and in relation to a court-martial 'conviction', as regards a court-martial constituted under

either of the said Acts of 1955, means a finding of guilty which is, or falls to be treated as, a finding of the court duly confirmed and, as regards a court-martial or disciplinary court constituted under the said Act of 1957, means a finding of guilty which is, or falls to be treated as, the finding of the court, and 'convicted' shall be construed accordingly.

Sub-s (5) amended by the Powers of Criminal Courts Act 1973, ss 56(1), 60(2) and Sch 5.

13. Conclusiveness of convictions for purposes of defamation actions

(1) In an action for libel or slander in which the question whether a person did or did not commit a criminal offence is relevant to an issue arising in the action, proof that at the time when that issue falls to be determined, that person stands con-victed of that offence shall be conclusive evidence that he committed that offence; and his conviction thereof shall be admissible in evidence accordingly.

(2) In any such action as aforesaid in which by virtue of this section a person is proved to have been convicted of an offence, the contents of any document which is admissible as evidence of the conviction, and the contents of the information, complaint, indictment or charge-sheet on which that person was convicted, shall, without prejudice to the reception of any other admissible evidence for the purpose of identifying the facts on which the conviction was based, be admissible in evidence for the purpose of identifying those facts.

(3) For the purposes of this section a person shall be taken to stand convicted of an offence if but only if there subsists against him a conviction of that offence by or before a court in the United Kingdom or by a court-martial there or elsewhere.

(4) Subsections (4) to (6) of section 11 of this Act shall apply for the purposes of this section as they apply for the purposes of that section, but as if in the said sub-section (4) the reference to subsection (2) were a reference to subsection (2) of this section.

(5) The foregoing provisions of this section shall apply for the purposes of any action begun after the passing of this Act, whenever the cause of action arose, but shall not apply for the purposes of any action begun before the passing of this Act or any appeal or other proceedings arising out of any such action.

REHABILITATION OF OFFENDERS ACT 1974

1. Rehabilitated persons and spent convictions

(1) Subject to subsection (2) below, where an individual has been convicted, whether before or after the commencement of this Act, of any offence or offences, and the following conditions are satisfied, that is to say—

   (a) he did not have imposed on him in respect of that conviction a sentence which is excluded from rehabilitation under this Act; and
   (b) he has not had imposed on him in respect of a subsequent conviction during the rehabilitation period applicable to the first-mentioned conviction in

accordance with section 6 below a sentence which is excluded from rehabilitation under this Act;

then, after the end of the rehabilitation period so applicable (including, where appropriate, any extension under section 6(4) below of the period originally applicable to the first-mentioned conviction) or, where that rehabilitation period ended before the commencement of this Act, after the commencement of this Act, that individual shall for the purposes of this Act be treated as a rehabilitated person in respect of the first-mentioned conviction and that conviction shall for those purposes be treated as spent.

(2) A person shall not become a rehabilitated person for the purposes of this Act in respect of a conviction unless he has served or otherwise undergone or complied with any sentence imposed on him in respect of that conviction; but the following shall not, by virtue of this subsection, prevent a person from becoming a rehabilitated person for those purposes—

(a) failure to pay a fine or other sum adjudged to be paid by or imposed on a conviction, or breach of a condition of a recognisance or of a bond of caution to keep the peace or be of good behaviour;

(b) breach of any condition or requirement applicable in relation to a sentence which renders the person to whom it applies liable to be dealt with for the offence for which the sentence was imposed, or, where the sentence was a suspended sentence of imprisonment, liable to be dealt with in respect of that sentence (whether or not, in any case, he is in fact so dealt with);

(c) failure to comply with any requirement of a suspended sentence supervision order.

(2A) Where in respect of a conviction a person has been sentenced to imprisonment with an order under section 47(1) of the Criminal Law Act 1977, he is to be treated for the purposes of subsection (2) above as having served the sentence as soon as he completes service of so much of the sentence as was by that order required to be served in prison.

(3) In this Act 'sentence' includes any order made by a court in dealing with a person in respect of his conviction of any offence or offences, other than—

(a) an order for committal or any other order made in default of payment of any fine or other sum adjudged to be paid by or imposed on a conviction, or for want of sufficient distress to satisfy any such fine or other sum;

(b) an order dealing with a person in respect of a suspended sentence of imprisonment.

(4) In this Act, references to a conviction, however expressed, include references—

(a) to a conviction by or before a court outside Great Britain; and

(b) to any finding (other than a finding linked with a finding of insanity) in any criminal proceedings or in care proceedings under section 1 of the Children and Young Persons Act 1969 that a person has committed an offence or done the act or made the omission charged;

and notwithstanding anything in section 9 of the Criminal Justice (Scotland) Act 1949 or section 13 of the Powers of Criminal Courts Act 1973 (conviction of a person put on probation or discharged to be deemed not to be a conviction) a conviction in respect of which an order is made placing the person convicted on probation or discharging him absolutely or conditionally shall be treated as a conviction for the purposes of this Act and the person in question may become a rehabilitated person in respect of that conviction and the conviction a spent conviction for those purposes accordingly.

The words in square brackets were added by the Criminal Law Act 1977, s 47, Sch 9, para 11.

4. Effect of rehabilitation

(1) Subject to sections 7 and 8 below, a person who has become a rehabilitated person for the purposes of this Act in respect of a conviction shall be treated for all purposes in law as a person who has not committed or been charged with or prosecuted for or convicted of or sentenced for the offence or offences which were the subject of that conviction; and, notwithstanding the provisions of any other enactment or rule of law to the contrary, but subject as aforesaid—

    (a) no evidence shall be admissible in any proceedings before a judicial authority exercising its jurisdiction or functions in Great Britain to prove that any such person has committed or been charged with or prosecuted for or convicted of or sentenced for any offence which was the subject of a spent conviction; and

    (b) a person shall not, in any such proceedings, be asked, and, if asked, shall not be required to answer, any question relating to his past which cannot be answered without acknowledging or referring to a spent conviction or spent convictions or any circumstances ancillary thereto.

5. Rehabilitation periods for particular sentences

(1) The sentences excluded from rehabilitation under this Act are—

    (a) a sentence of imprisonment for life;

    (b) a sentence of imprisonment [youth custody] or corrective training for a term exceeding thirty months;

    (c) a sentence of preventive detention;

    (d) a sentence of detention during Her Majesty's pleasure or for life, [or under section 205(2) or (3) of the Criminal Procedure (Scotland) Act 1975,] or for a term exceeding thirty months, passed under section 53 of the Children and Young Persons Act 1933 or under section 57 of the Children and Young Persons (Scotland) Act 1937 (Young offenders convicted of grave crimes) [(young offenders convicted of grave crimes) or under section 206 of the said Act of 1975 (detention of children convicted on indictment)] [or a corresponding court-martial punishment];

    [(e) a sentence of custody for life]

and any other sentence is a sentence subject to rehabilitation under this Act.

[(1A) In subsection (1)(d) above 'corresponding court-martial punishment' means a punishment awarded under section 71A(3) or (4) of the Army Act 1955, section 71A(3) or (4) of the Air Force Act 1955 or section 43A(3) or (4) of the Naval Discipline Act 1957.]

(2) For the purposes of this Act—

(a) the rehabilitation period applicable to a sentence specified in the first column of Table A below is the period specified in the second column of that Table in relation to that sentence, or, where the sentence was imposed on a person who was under seventeen years of age at the date of his conviction, half that period; and

(b) the rehabilitation period applicable to a sentence specified in the first column of Table B below is the period specified in the second column of that Table in relation to that sentence;

reckoned in either case from the date of the conviction in respect of which the sentence was imposed.

TABLE A

Rehabilitation periods subject to reduction by half for persons under 17

Sentence	Rehabilitation period
A sentence of imprisonment [or youth custody] or corrective training for a term exceeding six months but not exceeding thirty months.	Ten years.
A sentence of cashiering, discharge with ignominy or dismissal with disgrace from Her Majesty's service.	Ten years.
A sentence of imprisonment [or youth custody] for a term not exceeding six months.	Seven years.
A sentence of dismissal from Her Majesty's service.	Seven years.
Any sentence of detention in respect of a conviction in service disciplinary proceedings.	Five years.
A fine or any other sentence subject to rehabilitation under this Act, not being a sentence to which Table B below or any of subsections (3) to (8) below applies.	Five years.

TABLE B

Rehabilitation periods for certain sentences confined to young offenders

Sentence	Rehabilitation period
A sentence of Borstal training.	Seven years.
[A custodial order under Schedule 5A to the Army Act 1955 or the Air Force Act 1955, or under Schedule 4A to the Naval Discipline Act 1957,	Seven years.]

where the maximum period of detention specified in the order is more
than six months.

[A custodial order under section 71AA of the Army Act 1955 or the Air Force Act 1955, or under section 43AA of the Naval Discipline Act 1957, where the maximum period of detention specified in the order is more than six months.	Seven years.]
A sentence of detention for a term exceeding six months but not exceeding thirty months passed under section 53 of the said Act of 1933 or under section 57 of the said Act of 1937 [206 of the Criminal Procedure (Scotland) Act 1975.]	Five years.
A sentence of detention for a term not exceeding six months passed under either of those provisions.	Three years.
An order for detention in a detention centre made under [section 4 of the Criminal Justice Act 1982,] section 4 of the Criminal Justice Act 1961 or under section 7 of the Criminal Justice (Scotland) Act 1963.	Three years.
[A custodial order under any of the Schedules to the said Acts of 1955 and 1957 mentioned above, where the maximum period of detention specified in the order is six months or less.	Three years.]
[A custodial order under section 71AA of the said Acts of 1955, or section 43AA of the said Act of 1957, where the maximum period of detention specified in the order is six months or less.	Three years.]

(3) The rehabilitation period applicable—

  (a) to an order discharging a person absolutely for an offence; and
  (b) to the discharge by a children's hearing under section 43(2) of the Social Work (Scotland) Act 1968 of the referral of a child's case; shall be six months from the date of conviction.

(4) Where in respect of a conviction a person was conditionally discharged, bound over to keep the peace or be of good behaviour, or placed on probation, the rehabilitation period applicable to the sentence shall be one year from the date of conviction or a period beginning with that date and ending when the order for conditional discharge or probation order or (as the case may be) the recognisance or bond of caution to keep the peace or be of good behaviour ceases or ceased to have effect, whichever is the longer.

(5) Where in respect of a conviction any of the following sentences was imposed, that is to say—

  (a) an order under section 57 of the Children and Young Persons Act 1933 or section 61 of the Children and Young Persons (Scotland) Act 1937 committing the person convicted to the care of a fit person;
  (b) a supervision order under any provision of either of those Acts or of the Children and Young Persons Act 1963;
  (c) an order under section 413 of the Criminal Procedure (Scotland) Act 1975 committing a child for the purpose of his undergoing residential training;]
  (d) an approved school order under section 61 of the said Act of 1937;
  (e) a care order or a supervision order under any provision of the Children and Young Persons Act 1969; or

(f) a supervision requirement under any provision of the Social Work (Scotland) Act 1968;

[(g) a community supervision order under Schedule 5A to the Army Act 1955 or the Air Force Act 1955, or under Schedule 4A to the Naval Discipline Act 1957;

(h) a reception order under any on those Schedules;]

the rehabilitation period applicable to the sentence shall be one year from the date of conviction or a period beginning with that date and ending when the order or requirement ceases or ceased to have effect, whichever is the longer.

(6) Where in respect of a conviction any of the following orders was made, that is to say—

(a) an order under section 54 of the said Act of 1933 committing the person convicted to custody in a remand home;

(b) an approved school order under section 57 of the said Act of 1933; or

(c) an attendance centre order under section 19 of the Criminal Justice Act 1948;

the rehabilitation period applicable to the sentence shall be a period beginning with the date of conviction and ending one year after the date on which the order ceases or ceased to have effect.

(7) Where in respect of a conviction a hospital order under Part V of the Mental Health Act 1959 [Part III of the Mental Health Act 1983] or under Part V of the Mental Health (Scotland) Act 1960 (with or without an order restricting discharge [a restriction order] was made, the rehabilitation period applicable to the sentence shall be the period of five years from the date of conviction or a period beginning with that date and ending two years after the date on which the hospital order ceases or ceased to have effect, whichever is the longer.

(8) Where in respect of a conviction an order was made imposing on the person convicted any disqualification, disability, prohibition or other penalty, the rehabilitation period applicable to the sentence shall be a period beginning with the date of conviction and ending on the date on which the disqualification, disability, prohibition or penalty (as the case may be) ceases or ceased to have effect.

(9) For the purposes of this section—

(a) 'sentence of imprisonment' includes a sentence of detention in a young offenders institution in Scotland [under section 207 or 415 of the Criminal Procedure (Scotland) Act 1975] and a sentence of penal servitude, and "term of imprisonment" shall be construed accordingly;

(b) consecutive terms of imprisonment or of detention under section 53 of the said Act of 1933 or section 57 of the said Act of 1937 [section 206 of the said Act of 1975] and terms which are wholly or partly concurrent (being terms of imprisonment or detention imposed in respect of offences of which a person was convicted in the same proceedings) shall be treated as a single term;

(c) no account shall be taken of any subsequent variation, made by a court in dealing with a person in respect of a suspended sentence of imprisonment, of the term originally imposed; and

(d) a sentence imposed by a court outside Great Britain shall be treated as a sentence of that one of the descriptions mentioned in this section which most nearly corresponds to the sentence imposed.

(10) References in this section to the period during which a probation order, or a care order or supervision order under the Children and Young Persons Act 1969, or a supervision requirement under the Social Work (Scotland) Act 1968, is or was in force include references to any period during which any order or require-ment to which this subsection applies, being an order or requirement made or imposed directly or indirectly in substitution for the first-mentioned order or requirement, is or was in force.

This subsection applies—

(a) to any such order or requirement as is mentioned above in this subsection;

(b) to any order having effect under section 25(2) of the said Act of 1969 as if it were a training school order in Northern Ireland; and

(c) to any supervision order made under section 72(2) of the said Act of 1968 and having effect as a supervision order under the Children and Young Persons Act (Northern Ireland) 1950.

[(10A) The reference in subsection (5) above to the period during which a reception order has effect includes a reference to any subsequent period during which by virtue of the order having been made the Social Work (Scotland) Act 1968 or the Children and Young Persons Act (Northern Ireland) 1968 has effect in relation to the person in respect of whom the order was made and subsection (10) above shall accordingly have effect in relation to any such subsequent period.]

(11) The Secretary of State may by order—

(a) substitute different periods or terms for any of the periods or terms men-tioned in subsections (1) to (8) above; and

(b) substitute a different age for the age mentioned in subsection (2)(a).

Sub-s (1): in paras (b), (c), (e) amendments in square brackets made by the Criminal Justice Act 1982, ss 77, 78, Sch 14, para 36, Sch 16; in para (d), words underlined repealed and first and second amendments in square brackets made by the Criminal Justice (Scotland) Act 1980, s 83(2), Sch 7, para 24, as from a day to be appointed; final amendment in para (d) made by the Armed Forces Act 1976, s 22, Sch 9, para 20(4).
Sub-ss (1A), (10A): added by the Armed Forces Act 1976, s 22, Sch 9, paras 20(5), 21(3).
Sub-s (2): Table A amended by the Criminal Justice Act 1982, s 77, Sch 14, para 37; in Table B, words under-lined prospectively repealed and third amendment in square brackets prospectively made by the Criminal Justice (Scotland) Act 1980, s 83(2), Sch 7, para 24, as from a day to be appointed; first and fifth amendments in square brackets made by the Armed Forces Act 1976, s 22, Sch 9, para 21(1); second and sixth amendments in square brackets made by the Armed Forces Act 1981, s 28, Sch 4, para 2; fourth amendment in square brackets made by the Criminal Justice Act 1982, s 77, Sch 14, para 37.
Sub-s (5): para (c) substituted by the Criminal Justice (Scotland) Act 1980, s 83(2), Sch 7, para 24; paras (g), (h) added by the Armed Forces Act 1976, s 22, Sch 9, para 21(2).
Sub-s (7): first words underlined prospectively repealed and subsequent words in square brackets prospectively substituted by the Mental Health Act 1983, s 148, Sch 4, para 39, as from 30 September 1983; second words underlined prospectively repealed and subsequent words in square brackets prospectively substituted by the Mental Health (Amendment) Act 1982, s 65(1), Sch 3, para 49 as from 30 September 1983.
Sub-s (9): words underlined prospectively repealed and amendments in square brackets prospectively made by the Criminal Justice (Scotland) Act 1980, s 83(2), Sch 7, para 24, as from a day to be appointed.

7. Limitations on rehabilitation under this Act etc

(3) If at any stage in any proceedings before a judicial authority in Great Britain (not being proceedings to which, by virtue of any of paragraphs (a) to (e) of subsection (2) above or of any order for the time being in force under subsection (4) below, section 4(1) above has no application, or proceedings to which section 8 below applies) the authority is satisfied, in the light of any considerations which appear to it to be relevant (including any evidence which has been or may thereafter be put before it), that justice cannot be done in the case except by admitting or requiring evidence relating to a person's spent convictions or to circumstances ancillary thereto, that authority may admit or, as the case may be, require the evidence in question notwithstanding the provisions of subsection (1) of section 4 above, and may determine any issue to which the evidence relates in disregard, so far as necessary, of those provisions.

8. Defamation actions

(1) This section applies to any action for libel or slander begun after the commencement of this Act by a rehabilitated person and founded upon the publication of any matter imputing that the plaintiff has committed or been charged with or prosecuted for or convicted of or sentenced for an offence which was the subject of a spent conviction.

(2) Nothing in section 4(1) above shall affect an action to which this section applies where the publication complained of took place before the conviction in question became spent, and the following provisions of this section shall not apply in any such case.

(3) Subject to subsections (5) and (6) below, nothing in section 4(1) above shall prevent the defendant in an action to which this section applies from relying on any defence of justification or fair comment or of absolute or qualified privilege which is available to him, or restrict the matters he may establish in support of any such defence.

(4) Without prejudice to the generality of subsection (3) above, where in any such action malice is alleged against a defendant who is relying on a defence of qualified privilege, nothing in section 4(1) above shall restrict the matters he may establish in rebuttal of the allegation.

(5) A defendant in any such action shall not by virtue of subsection (3) above be entitled to rely upon the defence of justification if the publication is proved to have been made with malice.

(6) Subject to subsection (7) below a defendant in any such action shall not, by virtue of subsection (3) above, be entitled to rely on any matter or adduce or require any evidence for the purpose of establishing (whether under section 3 of the Law of Libel Amendment Act 1888 or otherwise) the defence that the matter published constituted a fair and accurate report of judicial proceedings if it is proved that the publication contained a reference to evidence which was ruled to be inadmissible in the proceedings by virtue of section 4(1) above.

(7) Subsection (3) above shall apply without the qualifications imposed by subsection (6) above in relation to—

 (a) any report of judicial proceedings contained in any bona fide series of law reports which does not form part of any other publication and consists solely of reports of proceedings in courts of law; and
 (b) any report or account of judicial proceedings published for bona fide educational, scientific or professional purposes, or given in the course of any lecture, class or discussion given or held for any of those purposes.

(8) (*Applies to Scotland*.)

LEGAL AID ACT 1974

SCHEDULE 1, PART II: EXCEPTED PROCEEDINGS

1. Proceedings wholly or partly in respect of defamation, but so that the making of a counterclaim for defamation in proceedings for which legal aid may be given shall not of itself affect any right of the defendant to the counterclaim to legal aid in the proceedings and so that legal aid may be granted to enable him to defend the counterclaim.

LIMITATION ACT 1980

2. Time limit for actions founded on tort

An action founded on tort shall not be brought after the expiration of six years from the date on which the cause of action accrued.

This section derived from the Limitation Act 1939, s 2(1)(a).

5. Time limit for actions founded on simple contract

An action founded on simple contract shall not be brought after the expiration of six years from the date on which the cause of action accrued.

This section derived from the Limitation Act 1939, s 2(1)(a).

7. Time limit for actions to enforce certain awards

An action to enforce an award, where the submission is not by an instrument under seal, shall not be brought after the expiration of six years from the date on which the cause of action accrued.

This section derived from the Limitation Act 1939, s 2(1)(c).

8. Time limit for actions on a specialty

(1) An action upon a specialty shall not be brought after the expiration of twelve years from the date on which the cause of action accrued.

(2) Subsection (1) above shall not affect any action for which a shorter period of limitation is prescribed by any other provision of this Act.

This section derived from the Limitation Act 1939, s 2(3).

9. Time limit for actions for sums recoverable by statute

(1) An action to recover any sum recoverable by virtue of any enactment shall not be brought after the expiration of six years from the date on which the cause of action accrued.

(2) Subsection (1) above shall not affect any action to which section 10 of this Act applies.

This section derived from the Limitation Act 1939, ss 2(1)(d), 32.

11. Special time limit for actions in respect of personal injuries

(1) This section applies to any action for damages for negligence, nuisance or breach of duty (whether the duty exists by virtue of a contract or of provision made by or under a statute or independently of any contract or any such provision) where the damages claimed by the plaintiff for the negligence, nuisance or breach of duty consist of or include damages in respect of personal injuries to the plaintiff or any other person.

(2) None of the time limits given in the preceding provisions of this Act shall apply to an action to which this section applies.

(3) An action to which this section applies shall not be brought after the expiration of the period applicable in accordance with subsection (4) or (5) below.

(4) Except where subsection (5) below applies, the period applicable is three years from—

    (a) the date on which the cause of action accrued; or
    (b) the date of knowledge (if later) of the person injured.

(5) If the person injured dies before the expiration of the period mentioned in subsection (4) above, the period applicable as respects the cause of action surviving for the benefit of his estate by virtue of section 1 of the Law Reform (Miscellaneous Provisions) Act 1934 shall be three years from—

    (a) the date of death; or
    (b) the date of the personal representative's knowledge; whichever is the later.

(6) For the purposes of this section 'personal representative' includes any person who is or has been a personal representative of the deceased, including an executor who has not proved the will (whether or not he has renounced probate) but not

anyone appointed only as a special personal representative in relation to settled land; and regard shall be had to any knowledge acquired by any such person while a personal representative or previously.

(7) If there is more than one personal representative, and their dates of knowledge are different, subsection (5)(b) above shall be read as referring to the earliest of those dates.

This section derived from the Limitation Act 1939, ss 2(8), 2A(1)–(5), (9), (10).

24. Time limit for actions to enforce judgments

(1) An action shall not be brought upon any judgment after the expiration of six years from the date on which the judgment became enforceable.

(2) No arrears of interest in respect of any judgment debt shall be recovered after the expiration of six years from the date on which the interest became due.

This section derived from the Limitation Act 1939, s 2(4).

36. Equitable jurisdiction and remedies

(1) The following time limits under this Act, that is to say—

(a) the time limit under section 2 for actions founded on tort;
(b) the time limit under section 5 for actions founded on simple contract;
(c) the time limit under section 7 for actions to enforce awards where the submission is not by an instrument under seal;
(d) the time limit under section 8 for actions on a specialty;
(e) the time limit under section 9 for actions to recover a sum recoverable by virtue of any enactment; and
(f) the time limit under section 24 for actions to enforce a judgment;

shall not apply to any claim for specific performance of a contract or for an injunction or for other equitable relief, except in so far as any such time limit may be applied by the court by analogy in like manner as the corresponding time limit under any enactment repealed by the Limitation Act 1939 was applied before 1st July 1940.

(2) Nothing in this Act shall affect any equitable jurisdiction to refuse relief on the ground of acquiescence or otherwise.

This section derived from the Limitation Act 1939, ss 2(7), 29.

MAGISTRATES' COURTS ACT 1980

8. Restrictions on reports of committal proceedings

(1) Except as provided by subsections (2), (3) and (8) below, it shall not be lawful to publish in Great Britain a written report, or to broadcast in Great Britain a

report, of any committal proceedings in England and Wales containing any matter other than that permitted by subsection (4) below.

(2) [Subject to subsection (2A) below] a magistrates' court shall, on an application for the purpose made with reference to any committal proceedings by the accused or one of the accused, as the case may be, order that subsection (1) above shall not apply to reports of those proceedings.

[(2A) Where in the case of two or more accused one of them objects to the making of an order under subsection (2) above, the court shall make the order if, and only if, it is satisfied after hearing the representations of the accused, that it is in the interests of justice to do so.

(2B) An order under subsection (2) above shall not apply to reports of proceedings under subsection (2A) above, but any decision of the court to make or not to make such an order may be contained in reports published or broadcast before the time authorised by subsection (3) below.]

(3) It shall not be unlawful under this section to publish or broadcast a report of committal proceedings containing any matter other than that permitted by subsection (4) below—

(a) where the magistrates' court determines not to commit the accused, or determines to commit none of the accused, for trial, after it so determines;

(b) where the court commits the accused or any of the accused for trial, after the conclusion of his trial or, as the case may be, the trial of the last to be tried;

and where at any time during the inquiry the court proceeds to try summarily the case of one or more of the accused under section 25(3) or (7) below, while committing the other accused or one or more of the other accused for trial, it shall not be unlawful under this section to publish or broadcast as part of a report of the summary trial, after the court determines to proceed as aforesaid, a report of so much of the committal proceedings containing any such matter as takes place before the determination.

(4) The following matters may be contained in a report of committal proceedings published or broadcast without an order under subsection (2) above before the time authorised by subsection (3) above, that is to say—

(a) the identity of the court and the names of the examining justices;

(b) the names, addresses and occupations of the parties and witnesses and the ages of the accused and witnesses;

(c) the offence or offences, or a summary of them, with which the accused is or are charged;

(d) the names of counsel and solicitors engaged in the proceedings;

(e) any decision of the court to commit the accused or any of the accused for trial, and any decision of the court on the disposal of the case of any accused not committed;

(f) where the court commits the accused or any of the accused for trial, the charge or charges, or a summary of them, on which he is committed and the court to which he is committed;

(g) where the committal proceedings are adjourned, the date and place to which they are adjourned;

(h) any arrangements as to bail on committal or adjournment;

(i) whether legal aid was granted to the accused or any of the accused.

(5) If a report is published or broadcast in contravention of this section, the following persons, that is to say—

(a) in the case of a publication of a written report as part of a newspaper or periodical, any proprietor, editor or publisher of the newspaper or periodical;

(b) in the case of a publication of a written report otherwise than as part of a newspaper or periodical, the person who publishes it;

(c) in the case of a broadcast of a report, any body corporate which transmits or provides the programme in which the report is broadcast and any person having functions in relation to the programme corresponding to those of the editor of a newspaper or periodical.

shall be liable on summary conviction to a fine not exceeding [level 5 on the standard scale.]

(6) Proceedings for an offence under this section shall not, in England and Wales, be instituted otherwise than by or with the consent of the Attorney-General.

(7) Subsection (1) above shall be in addition to, and not in derogation from, the provisions of any other enactment with respect to the publication of reports and proceedings of magistrates' and other courts.

(8) For the purposes of this section committal proceedings shall, in relation to an information charging an indictable offence, be deemed to include any proceedings in the magistrates' court before the court proceeds to inquire into the information as examining justices; but where a magistrates' court which has begun to try an information summarily discontinues the summary trial in pursuance of section 25(2) or (6) below and proceeds to inquire into the information as examining justices, that circumstance shall not make it unlawful under this section for a report of any proceedings on the information which was published or broadcast before the court determined to proceed as aforesaid to have been so published or broadcast.

(9) Any report in a newspaper, and any broadcast report, of committal proceedings in a case where publication is permitted by virtue only of subsection (3) above, published as soon as practicable after it is so permitted, shall be treated for the purposes of section 3 of the Law of Libel Amendment Act 1888 (privilege of contemporaneous newspaper reports of court proceedings) and section 9(2) of the Defamation Act 1952 (extension of the said section 3 to broadcasting) as having been published or broadcast contemporaneously with the committal proceedings.

(10) In this section—

'broadcast' means broadcast by wireless telegraphy sounds or visual images intended for general reception;

'publish', in relation to a report, means publish the report, either by itself or as part of a newspaper or periodical, for distribution to the public.

Commencement order: SI 1981/457.
This section derived from the Criminal Justice Act 1967, ss 3, 5, 36(1).
Sub-s (2): amended by the Criminal Justice (Amendment) Act 1981, s 1.
Sub-ss (2A), (2B): added by the Criminal Justice (Amendment) Act 1981, s 1.
Sub-s (5): maximum fine increased and converted to a level on the standard scale by the Criminal Justice Act 1982, ss 37, 38, 46.

REPRESENTATION OF THE PEOPLE ACT 1983

106. False statements as to candidates

(1) A person who, or any director of any body or association corporate which—

(a) before or during an election,

(b) for the purpose of affecting the return of any candidate at the election,

makes or publishes any false statement of fact in relation to the candidate's personal character or conduct shall be guilty of an illegal practice, unless he can show that he had reasonable grounds for believing, and did believe, the statement to be true.

(2) A candidate shall not be liable nor shall his election be avoided for any illegal practice under subsection (1) above committed by his agent other than his election agent unless—

(a) it can be shown that the candidate or his election agent has authorised or consented to the committing of the illegal practice by the other agent or has paid for the circulation of the false statement constituting the illegal practice; or

(b) an election court find and report that the election of the candidate was procured or materially assisted in consequence of the making or publishing of such false statements.

(3) A person making or publishing any false statement of fact as mentioned above may be restrained by interim or perpetual injunction by the High Court or the county court from any repetition of that false statement or of a false statement of a similar character in relation to the candidate and, for the purpose of granting an interim injunction, prima facie proof of the falsity of the statement shall be sufficient.

(4) The foregoing provisions of this section do not apply to or in relation to an election of councillors in Scotland.

(5) Any person who, before or during an election, knowingly publishes a false statement or a candidate's withdrawal at the election for the purpose of

promoting or procuring the election of another candidate shall be guilty of an illegal practice.

(6) A candidate shall not be liable, nor shall his election be avoided, for an illegal practice under subsection (5) above committed by his agent other than his election agent.

(7) In the application of this section to an election where a candidate is not required to have an election agent, references to an election agent shall be omitted and the reference in subsection (6) above to an illegal practice committed by an agent of the candidate shall be taken as a reference to an illegal practice committed without the candidate's knowledge and consent.

(8) Except in Scotland, the jurisdiction vested by subsection (3) above in the High Court in matters relating to parliamentary elections shall, subject to rules of court, be exercised by—

    (a) one of the judges for the time being on the rota for the trial of parliamentary election petitions,

    (b) in Northern Ireland, one of the judges of the High Court or the Court of Appeal for the time being selected under section 108 of the Judicature (Northern Ireland) Act 1978,

sitting either in court or at chambers, or by a master of the Supreme Court in manner directed by and subject to an appeal to those judges.

(9) The jurisdiction vested by subsection (3) in a county court may, except in Northern Ireland, be exercised otherwise than in open court, and, in Northern Ireland, shall be exercised in accordance with rules of court.

An appeal lies to the High Court from any order of a county court made by virtue of subsection (3).

Commencement order: SI 1983/153.
  This section derived from the Representation of the People Act 1949, s 91(1)–(7).

Practice Direction (Judge in Chambers: Procedure)

[Practice Note (Judge in Chambers: Procedure) [1983] 1 All ER 1119, [1983] 1 WLR 433; see para 20.13, ante, and appendix 1, ante.]

1983 March 30   Lord Lane CJ, Taylor
                                                      and McCowan JJ

Practice—Chambers applications—Queen's Bench Divison—Inter partes applications and appeals estimated to last more than 30 minutes—Special appointments—Ex parte applications—New procedure

LORD LANE CJ, at the sitting of the court, gave the following practice direction.

A. Queen's Bench judge in chambers: special appointments
1. A sharp increase in the volume of work listed to be heard by the Queen's Bench judge in chambers has led to unacceptable delays in the hearing of inter partes applications and appeals estimated to last more than 30 minutes. The following steps will be taken to reduce these delays.
2. All inter partes applications and appeals to the Queen's Bench judge in chambers will initially be entered in a general list. Whenever it appears or is agreed that any application or appeal is likely to last more than 30 minutes, it will in future be immediately and automatically transferred to a list of matters requiring special appointments. This will be a floating list and fixed dates will not be granted save on application to the judge when special circumstances will have to be shown. The unavailability of counsel will not, save exceptionally, amount to a special circumstance. Every effort will be made to give at least seven days' notice before cases in this list are listed for hearing.
3. Cases for which fixed dates have already been given will retain those dates unless earlier dates acceptable to both parties can be granted. Any outstanding applications and appeals (estimated to last more than 30 minutes) and not already entered in the special appointment list should be entered in it at once. *Counsel's clerks must take particular care to ensure that such outstanding applications and appeals do not remain in suspense.*
4. In order to ensure that a complete set of papers is available for perusal by the judge before hearing such applications and appeals, it shall hereafter be required that not less than five clear days before the date fixed for a special appointment (where a date has been fixed) and not later than 24 hours after a case in the floating

special appointment list has been warned for hearing, (*a*) each party shall bespeak the affidavits already filed which it proposes to use; (*b*) each party shall lodge in room 128, Royal Courts of Justice, the exhibits to the affidavits referred to in (*a*); (*c*) the appellant or application shall lodge in room 128 a bundle of the pleadings and previous court orders. Except with the leave of the judge, no document may be adduced in evidence or relied on unless it has been bespoken or lodged as required.

B. *Queen's Bench judge in chambers: ex parte applications*

A large increase in the number of applications made ex parte to the Queen's Bench judge in chambers makes it necessary to introduce a new and clearly understood procedure, which will be strictly followed.

1. The standard procedure, suitable for all ordinary ex parte applications, will be: (1) that the applicant shall lodge with the clerk to the judge in chambers by 3.00 p.m. on the day before the application is to be made, papers which should include (*a*) the writ (*b*) the affidavit in support and (*c*) a draft minute of the order sought; (2) that the judge in chambers will hear the application at 10.00 a.m. on the following morning before embarking on his published list.

2. There will be some cases where the 3.00 p.m. deadline specified in paragraph 1 (1) *cannot* be met and where the urgency is too great to permit up to 24 hours' delay. Such applications should be dealt with in one or another of the three following ways. (1) The applicant's advisers shall attend on the clerk to the judge in chambers at 9.50 a.m. and lodge with him the papers listed in paragraph 1 (1) and also a certificate signed by counsel (or solicitor if counsel is not instructed) that the application is of extreme urgency. The application will be heard by the judge in chambers at 10.00 a.m. (2) The applicant's advisers shall lodge the papers with the clerk to the judge in chambers by 12.30 p.m. (such papers to include all those specified in paragraph 1 (1)) and attend on the clerk at 1.50 p.m. The application will be heard at 2.00 p.m. (3) In the very rare case where the application is of such urgency as to preclude either of the foregoing procedures the applicant's advisers may give notice to the clerk to the judge in chambers and the judge in chambers will hear the application at once, interrupting his list if necessary. In such a case the applicant's counsel or solicitor must be prepared to justify taking this exceptional course.

3. (1) Attention is drawn to the provisions of RSC, Ord 29, r 1 which ordinarily requires the issue of a writ or originating summons and the swearing of an affidavit in support of an ex parte application for an injunction before it is made. (2) The affidavit in support should contain a clear and concise statement: (*a*) of the facts giving rise to the claim against the defendant in the proceedings; (*b*) of the facts giving rise to the claim for interlocutory relief; (*c*) of the facts relied on as justifying the application ex parte, including details of any notice given to the defendant or, if none has been given, the reasons for giving none; (*d*) of any answer asserted by the defendant (or which he is thought likely to assert) either to the claim in the action or to the claim for interlocutory relief; (*e*) of any facts known to the applicant which might lead the court not to grant relief ex parte; (*f*) of the precise relief sought. (3) Applicants for ex parte relief should prepare and lodge with the papers relating to the application a draft minute of the order

sought. Such minute should specify the precise relief which the court is asked to grant. While the undertakings required of an applicant will vary widely from case to case, he will usually be required: (*a*) to give an undertaking in damages; (*b*) to notify the defendant of the terms of the order forthwith, by cable or telex if he is abroad; (*c*) in an application of *Mareva* type, to pay the reasonable costs and expenses incurred in complying with the order by any third party to whom notice of the order is given; (*d*) in the exceptional case where proceedings have not been issued, to issue the same forthwith; (*e*) in the exceptional case where a draft affidavit has not been sworn, or where the facts have been placed before the court orally, to procure the swearing of the affidavit or the verification on affidavit of the facts outlined orally to the court.

The order should as a general rule contain provision for the defendant to apply on notice for discharge or variation of the order and for costs to be reserved.

History of distinction between libel and slander[1]

1. In early times, when few people were literate and printing had not been invented, proceedings for slander quite substantial in volume were entertained in local manorial and seignorial courts, and also in the ecclesiastical courts. Such proceedings resulted in fines or ecclesiastical pains. The King's courts took no cognizance of defamation except in cases where the statutes about *scandulum magnatum* applied. In the course of the 16th century, however, the common law courts began to develop an action on the case for defamation. They may have been concerned with the public order aspect, and no doubt they were, as ever, avid for jurisdiction. As the action was on the case, damages were the gist of it, and it was not generally recognised that defamation was an act wrongful per se. No distinction was observed between written and spoken defamation, but it is to be recalled that the first English printed book was published in 1474, and that printing required a licence until 1697. The origin of the common law exceptions to the rule that slander required proof of special damage is obscure. That relating to imputation of crime may well have started from the purpose of delimiting the respective jurisdictions of the common law and the ecclesiastical courts, but it is hard to see what the presence or absence of special damage had to do with this. It may well be that all three exceptional cases were thought so obviously likely to result in damage that no proof was necessary. At all events these exceptions were all well established by the middle of the 17th century. The common law jurisdiction proved extraordinarily popular, largely perhaps, because damages were found to be a more useful and attractive remedy than ecclesiastical pains, and during the reigns of Elizabeth I, James I and Charles I there was an extraordinary flood of litigation. In their attempt to stem this, the courts introduced the rule of *mitior sensus*, whereby no words alleged to be defamatory per se were held to be defamatory if a non-defamatory meaning could possibly be screwed out of them. The prime example of this is *Holt v Astgrigg*[2] in which Sir Thomas Holt failed in his action, although the defendant had said that he 'struck his cook on the head with a cleaver, and cleaved his head; the one part lay on the one shoulder and another part on the other', on the ground that the defendant had not said that Sir Thomas had killed the cook. The rule that in other cases ascertainable 'temporal' damage had to be proved was strictly insisted on, and repetition of a slander was not held to be actionable until early in the 19th century.

2. In the meantime, another and distinct line of legal development was opening up. This was connected with the establishment in 1488 of the Court of Star Chamber, which came to be very much concerned with the suppression of duelling and also with the control of printing, particularly in relation to seditious

libels. In that court any defamation was a crime, and truth was no defence, except in the case of non-seditious slanders. The remedies available there were thus more efficacious than under an action on the case. The Court of Star Chamber was abolished in 1641. After the Restoration the common law judges, who had been represented in the Court of Star Chamber, took over the rules which had there been formulated and applied and developed them so as to create a new tort of libel, for the constitution of which proof of actual damage was not required. Their purpose, no doubt, was to deal with the same social problems, in particular duelling, which had led the Court of Star Chamber to adopt the rules in the first place. At all events in *King v Lake*[3] it was held that libel evinced more malice than slander and was therefore actionable per se.

1 Report of the Faulks Committee (Cmnd 5909) Appendix VI.
2 (1608) Cro Jac 184.
3 (1670) Hard 470.

Singapore
Defamation Act, s 18

[See para 18.24, ante]

18. Separate assessment of damages in certain cases in actions for libel

Whenever in an action for libel the plaintiff sues more than one defendant, whether jointly, severally, or in the alternative, and evidence is given of malice in one defendant or of any other matter of aggravation which would not be admissible in evidence against any other defendant if he were sued alone, such other defendant may apply to the court to have the damages against himself and his co-defendants separately assessed, and if such application be made the court shall assess the damages separately against each defendant and no defendant shall be liable nor shall execution issue against him for any further or other damages than those so assessed against him.

Index

[All references are by paragraph number]